WORKING FOR A BETTER WORLD:
A GUIDE TO VOLUNTEERING IN GLOBAL DEVELOPMENT

Updated and Revised Edition
COMHLÁMH

GW00715494

Barry Cannon, Dervla King and Siobhan Sleeman

WORKING FOR A BETTER WORLD
First published
2007 by New Island
2 Brookside
Dundrum Road
Dublin 14
www.newisland.ie

ISBN 978-1-905494-80-4

Cover design by Inka Hagen
Cover images: Colourful display of spices at a grocery store in Sulemania in Northern Iraq.Photographer: Shehzad Noorani. Copyright: Majority World.
Multi-coloured threads used to produce cloth by the women who are part of the women's self help group in a village near Nagpur, Maharashtra, India. Photographer: Suchit Nanda. Copyright: Majority World.
Students of the Institute of Fine Arts paint alpona (color designs) on the road in front of Shahid Minar (Martyr's Monument), Dhaka, Bangladesh. Photographer: Md. Main Uddin. Copyright: Majority World.

The paper used in the production of this book is sourced from wood grown in sustainable forests.

Typeset by TypeIT, Dublin
Printed in Finland by WS Bookwell

CONTENTS

ACKNOWLEDGMENTS

Thanks to the following for their invaluable advice and expertise throughout the compilation of both this and the previous (2005) edition of the guide: Kate Boylan, Aidan Cahill, Jean-Marie Cullen, Christine Higgins, Isabelle Kidney, Emma Lane-Spollen, Alison Leahy, Sharon McDaid, Anne Molloy, Aidan Mulkeen, Conall O'Caoimh, Paul O'Mahony, John Ryan and Johnny Sheehan.

Dr Kate Simpson contributed the text for Chapter 4 ('What Have I got Myself Into?'), and we gratefully acknowledge this and her continual assistance throughout the compilation of the guide.

Special thanks to all the organisations that contributed information for the guide, and to the former volunteers who provided us with testimonials about their experiences. Many thanks are also due to the host organisations who contributed their time and expertise to the research for this resource.

Disclaimer

The aim of this guide is to promote informed decision-making by people who are interested in volunteering overseas in developing countries. The inclusion of information on any organisation does not signify that it has been recommended by Comhlámh. People who are using this guide are strongly advised to carry out their own research into any organisation with which they are considering undertaking a placement.

While every effort has been made to ensure that the information contained in this book is up to date and error-free at the time of going to press, Comhlámh does not accept any responsibility for inaccurate information. Potential volunteers should be aware that organisations can, at short notice, change their objectives, cease their activities, modify their contact details, relocate their projects, or carry out a host of other actions that may affect their volunteer-placing activities.

Due to space constraints, we have been able to discuss only briefly many important issues, such as trade, aid, HIV/AIDS and gender issues. Where possible, we have provided details of other resources that contain more detailed information on these topics. If you have information on an organisation or resource that you think might be of interest to future readers, we'd be happy to hear from you. You can email us at info@volunteeringoptions.org. For further updates and information about international volunteering, go to **www.volunteeringoptions.org**.

FOREWORD

In my work I have learned a great many lessons from travelling abroad and engaging in dialogue with people from developing countries. I firmly believe that the experiences of people in other situations of conflict have taught us a great many lessons in our own journey towards peace.

We have learned about many of these experiences from the countless Irish people who have contributed to this country's long history of volunteering overseas. Irish volunteers have travelled across the globe to take part in a broad range of projects and to share their skills with people in developing countries. This sharing of human and professional experiences has not only made an important contribution to other countries, but volunteers have also brought an unequalled richness of experience back home.

This dialogue between peoples is fundamental to promoting greater equity among nations. The experience of returned volunteers has enriched the dialogue about international development issues here in Ireland. And Comhlámh, for over thirty years, has offered support to many of the returned development workers who have raised awareness of these issues in Ireland. Furthermore, Comhlámh has been pioneering in addressing issues of inequality here at home and pointing out the links between those issues and international development.

This book is extremely timely, given the many people in Ireland that are now travelling to developing countries. It provides a very useful guide for Irish people who wish to inform themselves accurately on the issues involved in volunteering and how to navigate the increasing number of volunteering options available. It also offers an important critical perspective on development processes.

My work in the peace process in Ireland has taught me that communication, dialogue and co-operation are keys to finding a means for communities to co-exist peacefully. If Ireland is to contribute to the building of peace and the eradication of poverty in the world, it is important that future volunteers go out into the world well prepared and well informed. This guide is an important step in that direction.

John Hume

INTRODUCTION

Are you thinking about volunteering overseas in a developing country? Maybe you are considering it as an option for a gap year, as a career break, after your retirement, or for other reasons? Are you interested in using your time as an overseas volunteer to work towards a more just and sustainable world? Would you like to find out more about what it's like for people who volunteer in a completely different culture? If the answer to any of these questions is yes, read on!

Drawing on the experiences of people who have volunteered in developing countries, this book will assist you through all stages of the volunteer experience. Overseas volunteering can be seen as a continuum that encompasses deciding to go abroad, choosing a sending organisation, being in your placement overseas, and bringing your experiences back home to help educate others. This book will provide you with practical advice and information on planning each phase of your experience, including a directory with information about more than 110 organisations that arrange volunteer placements. Throughout, you will be encouraged to think about volunteering within the context of global development work.

About us: Comhlámh and the Volunteering Options Programme

This book has been developed as part of the Volunteering Options Programme, which was set up by Comhlámh in 2004. Funded by Irish Aid, the programme was established in response to the growing interest among the Irish public in volunteering overseas in developing countries for short periods of anything up to one year. Comhlámh has provided advice and orientation for people interested in overseas development work for over thirty years. In recent times, we have seen an increasing demand for our services from people who are interested in shorter-term volunteering. Some of the reasons why shorter term volunteering has become more popular are:

- the increasing professionalisation of development work, which has made it more difficult for people without particular skills or experience to find overseas placements;
- changes in the Irish economy, which mean that people may not be able to make a long-term commitment to overseas work;
- an increase in the number of organisations that offer short-term volunteer placements.

The Volunteering Options Programme aims to develop best practice in the growing sector of overseas volunteering, and to support volunteers in a longer-term commitment to development.

Volunteering and global development

Although short-term volunteering can be very different from long-term overseas assignments, the context in which they take place is similar. Both volunteers and professional development workers encounter the same issues of inequality, injustice and underdevelopment. As a result, both are encouraged to examine what they do within the framework of 'global development work'. This involves carrying a critical perspective of global issues in your work. What makes someone a 'global' worker is that they bring with them an awareness of the forces that influence and link development and underdevelopment throughout the world. They try to integrate this into their work, wherever they might be located. We therefore talk about a 'development worker continuum', in which people carry a global awareness in their action for change, whether they are working abroad as a short-term volunteer, as a community worker in an Irish inner-city area, or on an overseas assignment of several years.

There are three main stakeholders involved in any volunteer placement: you, the potential volunteer; the organisation that arranges your placement; and the host community and people you will be working with. We believe that it is in the best interests of all three, but most importantly in those of the host community, that you are informed and think critically about issues of global development before making any final decisions about volunteering. Doing so will help to ensure that not only you, but also the people in your host project, will gain the most from the volunteer experience.

For example, issues that potential volunteers are encouraged to consider are:

- Why does the programme that you are considering exist? Who asked that it be set up? Is it something that the host community requested and is directly involved with?
- If you are paying for your placement, how is the money being spent? Is the organisation arranging your placement accountable to anyone for its actions? Does the placement programme fit in with the local development agenda?
- Have you considered the impact your placement might have on the host community? Is it possible that your presence might displace a local person from employment? Or that you are being requested because, as a volunteer from a wealthy country, you can help an organisation to attract funding?

The book doesn't pretend to answer all of the many questions that you might come up with. It's up to you to provide those. What we do hope to do is to encourage you to critically consider the important issues, and to draw on the advice and expertise of former volunteers and volunteer placement organisations that will help you to arrive at your own answers.

How to get the most out of this guide

This book is divided into eight chapters, each of which deals with a different stage of volunteering. In Chapter 1, we place volunteering abroad in its wider context, providing a brief outline of development and how it has changed over the last fifty years. This includes an analysis of the main structure influencing our world today – globalisation – and its effects on poverty and democracy in the developing world. In Chapter 2, we examine how overseas volunteering has evolved and discuss some of the main issues that you might have to consider as a volunteer – namely, power relations, racism and gender – and how to respond to them. In Chapter 3, we look in more detail at the motivations behind making a decision to go overseas. The different types of organisations that arrange volunteer placements are also examined. Chapter 4 provides information and advice on being overseas, covering topics such as settling in to a host community, coping with culture shock, and suggestions on how to learn from your experiences. Chapter 5 considers the process of coming home, including the ways in which volunteering overseas may affect your life, and how to stay involved in the area of development on your return. Chapter 6 includes information on further resources for people who are considering volunteering, such as where to get medical information, where to look for country profiles, and where to find resource centres that will have useful information.

Throughout the book, we have included testimonials provided by former volunteers that provide first-hand insights into some of the many issues raised. In Chapter 3, the topics they discuss include their reasons for deciding to volunteer abroad, examples of the types of work they did while overseas, and recommendations on how best to prepare yourself for a placement. In Chapter 4, they share the high and low points of their experiences abroad. The testimonials also point to deeper issues, such as the impact that volunteering can have on development, and how that is affected by greater structures that are difficult to confront, including globalisation and modernisation.

The directory of volunteer placement organisations is set out in Chapter 7. This contains information and contact details for over 110 organisations which arrange a wide variety of volunteer placements in developing countries. For ease of use, it is divided between organisations that are based in Ireland and international organisations. The tables in Chapter 8 provide an easy-to-use guide that will help you select an organisation according to a number of different criteria, including the duration of placements and continents where placements are available. Finally, Comhlámh's *Code of Good Practice for Sending Organisations* and our *Volunteer Charter* are included in the appendix. These documents set out, respectively, what sort of services you can ideally expect from a sending organisation; and what a sending organisation, and your host project, can expect from you. The Code of Good Practice is a quality standard to which Irish-based organisations can sign up. By doing so, they are promising to provide a first-rate service to both volunteers and host projects.

We strongly advise first-time readers to look through the first six chapters of the book before looking at the list of organisations. These chapters will provide you with advice on how best to judge what organisations would be most suitable for you to get in touch with when arranging your placement. They will give you ideas for questions you could ask organisations that will help ensure that your placement is best suited to your requirements. Additionally, they will help you to come up with queries that will help you evaluate an organisation's ethos, and on ensuring that your own motivations for volunteering fit in with that ethos. All these are steps towards adopting the global development worker perspective mentioned above.

This book is not just a guide to help you in your initial search for a placement, but a companion for the whole process of volunteering – from the decision to go, to coming home, and beyond – in other words, the continuum mentioned above. You should therefore hold on to the guide and dip into it throughout the whole volunteering experience to help deal in a positive, enriching manner with each new part of that experience as it presents itself.

Some terms used

We use the following terms throughout the book to describe different components of the volunteer experience.

Short-term volunteering: For our purposes, short-term volunteering is defined as any period from one week to one year. While recognising that there can be big differences between the experiences of people who volunteer for a few weeks and people who volunteer for almost twelve months, there can be enough similarities between their experiences to warrant their being considered under the same heading.

Sending organisations: These are agencies, organisations or commercial companies that arrange volunteer placements in developing countries. All have offices outside the destination country through which they recruit volunteers.

Host communities: people with whom volunteers live and work while undertaking their overseas placements.

Host projects: organisations or community groups in the destination country that receive volunteers. In general, they do not have offices outside the countries in which they work.

Placement organisations: This is a general collective term used to describe both sending organisations and host projects.

What to call 'them'?

We have lots of different names to call those countries that are not as wealthy as ours, and all of them are problematic! Here's a brief description of some of these terms:

Third World: this term came about as a result of the Cold War. The First World was considered the richest part of the globe; the Second, the old Socialist bloc, was seen as having medium income; and the Third World was seen as the poorest. This term, however, implies that the First World is inherently superior to the Second and Third Worlds. In addition, since 1989, the Second World of the Soviet Union and the Eastern bloc no longer exists.

Underdeveloped and Less Developed countries: implies that development simply refers to economics. It does not take into account the highly-developed social, cultural and environmental attitudes and living arrangements in many communities overseas. It also suggests that many developed countries no longer need to develop, in spite of the fact that large segments of the populations in these countries experience poverty, hunger and homelessness.

Poor countries: ignores the fact that many of these countries are rich in resources and that many people within them have relatively high living standards, just as many people in rich countries are in fact poor.

Global South or *South:* are not generally recognised as terms. Furthermore, there are a number of high-income nations located in the South, such as Australia and New Zealand.

In this book, despite reservations, we frequently use the term *developing countries* because it is the most generally accepted term, and because we wish the reader to focus on issues of development when considering volunteering overseas. Some of the other terms are also used at times, in order to provide a fuller perspective.

(Adapted from Collins, J., DeZerega, S., and Zahara Heckscher
How to Live Your Dream of Volunteering Overseas; London: Penguin, 2002, p.27.)

TRINITY COLLEGE
The University of Dublin

Irish School of Ecumenics
Ireland's Centre for Reconciliation Studies
Full details on all programmes are available at www.tcd.ie/ise

Contributing to Irish Civil Society: The new inter-religious, multi-cultural Ireland – Are We Ready?

M.Phil. in Ecumenical Studies (Dublin)
Email: ecumsec@tcd.ie

From a perspective informed by Christian theology, Ecumenical Studies focuses on three key arenas of dialogue in order to promote a critical understanding of relationships within and between traditions – dialogue within Christianity, with other religions, and with others committed to a study of the ethical dimensions of political engagement.

M.Phil. in International Peace Studies (Dublin)
Email: peacesec@tcd.ie

International Peace Studies examines the sources of war and armed conflict and suggests methods of preventing and resolving them through processes of peacemaking and peacebuilding. The programme combines perspectives from international relations, ethics and conflict resolution to reflect critically on the wide range of social, political and economic issues associated with peace and political violence. Students can pursue either a broad-ranging programme in International Peace Studies or specialisations in Ethics in International Affairs or Peacebuilding and Development.

A week-long Mediation Summer School also provides an opportunity to develop practical skills in the area of conflict resolution and mediation.

M.Phil. in Reconciliation Studies: Learning to Transform Relationships - (Belfast)
Email: reconsec@tcd.ie

This Belfast-based M.Phil. in Reconciliation Studies is an innovative cross-border programme. It takes an inter-disciplinary approach to the challenges of social reconciliation in the aftermath of armed conflict. Courses allow specialisation in the fields of politics, social research, theology and religions. All courses on this programme are taught in Belfast apart from a one week Spring School in Dublin.

Postgraduate Diploma in Conflict & Dispute Resolution Studies (Dublin)
Email: cdrssec@tcd.ie

This course interests those in both the public and private sectors, who wish to study civil mediation and other non adversarial dispute and conflict resolution processes (ADRs) which are increasingly a part of legislative and management structures in the EU and internationally. Through an alliance with Mediation Forum Ireland those who complete the CDRS programme, will have the opportunity to have their names included in the relevant specialist panel of Accredited Mediators. This programme involves two evenings per week plus two Saturday workshops.

ISE is recognised world-wide for the unique manner in which it brings the fields of politics, sociology, theology and religion into a disciplined interaction. Each programme of study fosters critical, scholarly engagement with key themes, and, in addition to a core curriculum, students are encouraged to develop their specialist interests.

- A service-learning component is available to students on both the Ecumenical Studies and Reconciliation Studies programme who wish to deepen the experiential concerns of the programme.

- An optional field study visit to Belfast is offered to students on the Ecumenical and International Peace Studies programme.

- Students on each of the three degree programmes may also attend courses on each of the other programmes.

For further information about our programmes please visit our website: www.tcd.ie/ise or contact:

Bea House, Milltown Park, Dublin 6,
Tel. +353.1.2601144,
Fax. +353.1.2601158

683, Antrim Road, Belfast, BT15 4EG,
Tel. +44.28.9077.5010
Fax. +44.28.9037.3986

CHAPTER 1

ISSUES IN DEVELOPMENT

1.1 Overseas volunteering in context

Most of us who volunteer abroad do so for a variety of reasons (see Chapter 3). Among the chief reasons we hear from people who are interested in overseas volunteering are to 'give something back' and to 'help' others in the developing world. What we argue, however, is that in order to achieve this and maximise your impact, it's best to see your volunteering experience as part of a continuum in which you develop awareness within yourself, in the institution or organisation you're working in, and at home when you get back. Only by doing this, we argue, and by seeing your short-term volunteering experience in a long-term context, can you really effect change. Part of this process of raising awareness is placing your volunteering experience in the wider context of development and the structures that affect it, namely globalisation. Our main aim in this chapter is to place volunteering in these contexts by attempting to provide answers to the questions: What is development? What is globalisation? And what effect has globalisation had on development and democracy?

1.2 What is development?

The modern concept of development emerged out of the devastation of World War Two and the hope that the rebuilding process would provide a new world order of justice, welfare and democracy for all the peoples of the world. However, it is also said that 'development' is in fact a revision of the relationship between Europe and North America and parts of Africa, Asia, and Latin America, which has historically been based on imperialism, colonisation and repeated interference in local economies and societies. Development, in this view, is the latest, most 'enlightened' concept to emerge from a long history of 'western' ideas about the wider world.

From the age of exploration in the fifteenth century to the recent invasion of Iraq, Europeans and, latterly, North Americans have often justifed their actions in terms of 'helping' the peoples of Africa, Asia and Latin America. Invasions, occupations and colonisation were framed as bringing 'civilisation' to 'barbarians', or nowadays as bringing 'democracy' to the 'oppressed'. Development, too, can be seen in this way: it can be what *we* think is good for the people we are claiming to help, rather than their own self-identified needs and aspirations.

Keeping this in mind, we will look at development from three perspectives. A first and basic perspective equates economic growth with development. From this viewpoint, development means modernisation, and modernisation means pursuing industrialisation and economic development. Economic growth in turn, it is said, helps improve standards of living, which brings with it increased democracy. Modernisation is seen as being synonymous with westernisation, in that it takes as its model western industrialised democracies.

This modernisation perspective of development began to be questioned by some from the late 1960s onwards. Critics pointed out that no two countries start from the same position, and that even if they follow the modernisation model, it is not guaranteed that they will arrive at 'developed' country status. This may not even be the appropriate route for them to take. Furthermore, much so-called underdevelopment is in fact a direct result of exploitative policies by rich countries, such as the extraction of primary resources for low prices and unfair trading practices (see Box 1.3).

As a result of these criticisms, international development agencies began to adopt a second, wider perspective for measuring development. As the United Nations Development Programme (UNDP, 1990) puts it, development is 'to lead long and healthy lives, to be knowledgeable, to have access to the resources needed for a decent standard of living and to be able to participate in the life of the community'. The United Nations thus measures human development by surveying a wide range of statistics grouped around health, education, the economy and gender. The UNDP publishes annual Human Development Reports showing global progress in these indicators. In the year 2000, members of the United Nations synthesised much of this thinking into a set of eight Millennium Development Goals (MDGs) which are a further measure of global development based on achievable targets (see Box 1.1).

Box 1.1: The Millennium Development Goals

By 2015		The Reality
Goal 1	Eradicate extreme hunger and poverty.	The UN estimates that 824 million people in the developing world were affected by chronic hunger in 2004.
Goal 2	Achieve universal primary education.	Globally, more than one in five girls and one in six boys of primary school age are not in school.
Goal 3	Promote gender equality and empower women.	Ongoing factors that limit women's economic advancement include wage differentials, higher unemployment rates, and their disproportionately high representation in the informal and subsistence sectors.
Goal 4	Reduce child mortality.	Although children's survival prospects have increased worldwide, in 2004 10.5 million children died before their fifth birthday.

Box 1.1: The Millennium Development Goals (contd.)

By 2015		The Reality
Goal 5	Improve maternal health.	Worldwide, some 200 million women who wish to space or limit their childbearing lack access to contraception.
Goal 6	Combat HIV/AIDS, malaria and other diseases.	The number of people living with HIV rose from 36.2 million in 2003 to 38.6 million in 2005.
Goal 7	Ensure environmental sustainability.	Half of developing country populations continue to lack basic sanitation. CO_2 emissions continue to rise, despite efforts to combat global warming.
Goal 8	Develop a global partnership for development.	Although aid to developing countries has increased since 1997, much of this is accounted for by debt relief and emergency and disaster relief – these do not address long-term development needs.

Source: United Nations (2006), Millennium Development Goals Report

In a 2005 report, Trócaire found that MDGs were not being reached or were being manipulated by national governments. In response, Trócaire made four recommendations to make MDGs more feasible:

1. Stronger emphasis on human rights, national priorities and local participation in MDGs.
2. Reform of global governance organisations (the United Nations, International Monetary Fund and World Bank, as well as the World Trade Organization (see Box 1.2 below)) to make them more democratic and more responsive to local political realities, in particular, the needs of the poor.
3. Global trade to take account of people's rights to food, shelter, work and health.
4. Aid from Organisation for Economic Cooperation and Development (OECD) countries to be increased to 0.7% of gross national product (GNP) and the aid system reformed, including 100% debt cancellation for poorer countries, making aid less dependent on rich countries' priorities.

Source: Trócaire (2005), 'More than a Numbers Game? Ensuring that the MDGs address structural injustice' (**http://trocaire.org/pdfs/policy/mdg/morethananumbersgame.pdf**)

Achieving human development is intimately linked to a third perspective of development, which goes beyond these measurable indicators, but is seen as a way to achieve them. This perspective views development as freeing people from obstacles that hinder their ability to develop their own lives and their communities.

Development, in this perspective, is not simply about 'western' aid agencies, and 'westerners' building schools, roads, hospitals, and providing emergency relief. It is more fundamentally about shifting the balance of power in favour of ordinary people. Development, therefore, is empowerment. It is about local people taking control of their own lives, expressing their own demands and finding their own solutions to their problems.

> Development is an ever-moving target. It can never be finally achieved and the process should never be arrested. It will best be moved forward if all citizens contribute actively to decisions about it and there is a constant opportunity for individuals and groups to participate in all aspects of it.
> (Lalage Brown in *80:20: Development in an Unequal World.*)

However, this is of course easier said than done. People do not live in a vacuum but within particular social, economic and political structures, at the local, national and global level. These structures can limit the freedom of people in the developing world to decide on their own futures. While there is not enough space here to examine all these structures in detail, the next section will look at what is arguably the most important, one that affects us all but has particular implications for developing countries: globalisation.

1.3 Globalisation and development

Globalisation can have different meanings for different people. Some see globalisation as real and beneficial to everyone; others see it as politically and economically negative. Some talk of global citizens and global culture, while others say that the national and the local are still important. Some say that globalisation is simply domination by the rich, by capitalism, and others that it is beneficial to the poor. In reality, there is no one 'true' way to interpret globalisation. The various interpretations of globalisation are, however, made in a context of power. In this context it is the powerful institutions and groups associated with neoliberalism that monopolise the meaning of globalisation.

But what is 'neoliberalism'? It is a particular view of freedom, in which money and goods can move about the globe totally unhindered and mostly unregulated. This frees money and entrepreneurship from their social contexts and obligations. Neoliberalism is, in effect, the market being given greater freedom and influence than many national governments and states in the politics, economy and society of most of the countries of the globe.

Neoliberalism is an ideological belief system that stems from the work of the Austrian economist Friedrich Hayek and the American economist Milton Friedman. It was most famously put into practice in industrialised countries by Margaret Thatcher (UK Prime Minister 1979–92) and Ronald Reagan (US President 1981–89). It is implemented mostly through economic programmes that favour free trade, unregulated investment, the removal of the state from the economy (through privatisation, for example), an increased influence of business in the provision of goods and services – including in such areas as education, health, electricity and water – and in government decision-making. These economic programmes were initially in the form of Structural Adjustment Programmes (SAPs), and more recently Poverty Reduction Strategy Papers (PRSPs). The policies are usually implemented in developing countries at the insistence, and with the assistance, of international organisations such as the International Monetary Fund, the World Bank and the World Trade Organization. All these organisations are controlled by the principal economic powers of the Group of Eight (G8).

Box 1.2: Major international institutions

The World Bank (WB) was initially established to rebuild Europe after World War Two. Today, it provides long-term loans to developing countries. It has its headquarters in Washington and is usually led by a US appointee.

The International Monetary Fund (IMF) was also established after World War Two to ensure that international exchange rates were kept stable and to encourage free trade. It provides loans to countries experiencing short-term balance of payments problems (where imports exceed exports). Since 1982, when Mexico came close to defaulting on its debt, the IMF has been providing loans to countries on the brink of bankruptcy. It also has its headquarters in Washington and is usually led by a European appointee.

IFIs (international financial institutions) usually refers to the WB and the IMF.

The G8 ('Group of Eight') comprises the seven richest countries in the world (Italy, the USA, the UK, France, Germany, Japan, Canada) plus Russia. Together, they represent about 65% of the world economy. The members of the G8 are the most powerful members of both the IMF and the WB, and set the agenda for these bodies. Without Russia the group is known as the G7 ('Group of Seven').

Transnational corporations (TNCs, also known as multinational corporations, or MNCs) are large international companies with manufacturing bases throughout the world, but usually with headquarters in developed countries. Examples are Microsoft, Nike, Coca-Cola and General Motors. Some of these companies earn more per year than many countries and even groups of countries.

The World Trade Organization (WTO) is an international organisation that oversees a large number of agreements defining the 'rules of trade' between its member states. Its broad goal is the reduction or abolition of international trade barriers. Located in Geneva, Switzerland, it has 148 member states. It sometimes holds ministerial meetings, such as those in Seattle in 1999, Cancun in 2003, and Hong Kong in 2005, which were the focus of many protests.

Source: **www.wikipedia.org**

In some cases, these policies can have positive effects. For example, in the 1980s and 1990s some Latin American countries which implemented neoliberal policies increased their economic growth and expanded and diversified their exports, and so their foreign exchange earnings rose. Chile under the Pinochet dictatorship (1973–90) is often cited as a successful example of a country that implemented these policies in the right way, allowing it to expand its trade with the rest of the world and reduce its level of poverty dramatically. Many other countries in the region that implemented these policies achieved very low levels of inflation and high rates of economic growth, though few had the success of Chile.

Overall, however, economic growth in those developing countries that have followed neoliberal policies recommended by the IFIs has not been that great. Generally speaking, growth was much higher during the 1960s and 1970s, when governments invested heavily in industry, which was sheltered behind protective taxes against imports. Much recent economic growth has been in the export sector, but most income from exports goes out of the developing countries in payment for international debt (see Box 1.3) or as repatriated profits by TNCs. Furthermore, international trade is heavily weighted in favour of the rich countries, restricting the ability of developing countries to earn more for their products.

If we look at the fifty least developed countries (LDCs) in the world,* we see that there has been little improvement in terms of economic growth or reducing poverty levels. These countries were encouraged by IFIs to implement neoliberal policies, in the form of 'structural adjustment programmes'. However, in twenty of these countries, it was found that economic growth was minimal, and actually fell in the three years after the application of the programmes. Neither was there any great improvement after that; over the next three years of the programmes, growth rose only by an average of 1.4% annually. In addition, poverty increased in these countries following the implementation of the programmes. The proportion of the total population living below the $1-a-day poverty line rose from 51% to 53% in the six years after the programmes' introduction. During the same period, those living on less than $2 a day went up from 83% to 84%.

Exports did rise quite significantly as a result of the application of these programmes, but this in itself was not sufficient to encourage sustainable development. Furthermore, most exports were of unprocessed commodities and primary goods, which suffer particularly from low prices. Coffee farmers in developing countries now receive only 25% of the price they got in 1960, for example. Additionally, while exports of many LDCs have increased, the total share of these countries in total world trade remains tiny, accounting for only 0.9% in 2006 (see **www.centad.org**). In other words, the implementation of neoliberal policies led to a small increase in economic growth, but no improvement in the number of people living in poverty. On the contrary, the proportion of people living on less than $1 or $2 a day had increased six years after the introduction of

---

* These are countries recognised by the United Nations as being the poorest in the world. Some of the largest of these countries are: Afghanistan, Bangladesh, Ethiopia, Nepal and Sudan. Smaller ones are: Bhutan, Cape Verde, Lesotho, Maldives and Tuvalu. For a full list see: **www.un.org/special-rep/ohrlls/ldc/list.htm**.

neoliberal policies, despite the countries having increased their exports, which was one of the main aims of structural adjustment programmes.

> The past two decades of World Bank and IMF structural adjustment in Africa have led to greater social and economic deprivation, and an increased dependence of African countries on external loans. The failure of structural adjustment has been so dramatic that some critics of the World Bank and IMF argue that the policies imposed on African countries were never intended to promote development. On the contrary, they claim that their intention was to keep these countries economically weak and dependent.
>
> (Ann-Louise Colgan, 'Hazardous to health: the World Bank and IMF in Africa', *Africa Action*, 18 April 2002.)

To sum up, 'the main conclusion that can be drawn from this is that [...] adjustment programmes have not delivered sustainable growth sufficient to make a significant dent in poverty' (UNCTAD, 2002:174). IFIs often complain that this is because the programmes are not properly applied. Yet even among those countries deemed by the IFIs themselves as 'strong compliers' of structural adjustment, poverty has increased. Looking specifically at African LDCs, for example, 'strong compliers' experienced a poverty increase from 48% in the five years previous to application of the programmes to 53% in the five-year post-adjustment period (*ibid*:175). Neoliberal globalisation may have benefited some countries, but as a route out of poverty for the poorest, it is not working.

Nonetheless, IFIs insist on their continued implementation, and either refuse to contemplate or simply gloss over other possible models. In a speech given in 2002 by Hörst Kohler, then president of the IMF, he lauded the achievements of South Korea as a successful example of globalisation. Yet Kohler neglected to mention that South Korea achieved its success through a combination of a gradual and selective opening of their economy to world trade and selective protection of key industries, a strategy that is anathema to the IMF.

Box 1.3: The debt crisis and trade

Developing country debt arose from the oil crisis in the 1970s when oil producers increased the price of oil and deposited their increased profits in commercial banks in the west. These banks lent this money at low interest rates to developing countries eager to promote their own development. In the 1970s and 1980s, however, prices for raw materials – such as sugar, coffee, tin, fruits and other products – fell dramatically, so borrowing countries' incomes fell, despite their exporting more. Meanwhile, interest rates rose substantially and the vicious cycle of debt began.

Box 1.3: The debt crisis and trade (contd.)

In 1982, Mexico declared that it was unable to repay its debts and the IMF and WB stepped in and worked out a system whereby indebted countries could spread out or reschedule their debts rather than default. New loans were offered only if countries followed neoliberal policies. Encouraging exports was one of these policies, as exports earned these countries the foreign currency needed to pay back the interest on the debt. Nonetheless, trade rules trapped many countries into exporting raw materials without allowing the exporters to add value to them through processing and manufacturing. In Mozambique, for example, as a result of World Bank-fostered liberalisation, the country has seen the closure of twelve of its thirteen cashew nut processing factories, resulting in the loss of 11,000 jobs (see **www.globalpolicy.org**).

The trade system is heavily weighted against developing countries, preventing them from increasing their income from exports and so financing social programmes. Some of these barriers are:

- Dumping: the rich world tells the poor world to get rid of subsidies, but continues to spend $1 billion a day subsidising its own farming enterprises. Rich countries dump subsidised produce on developing countries, driving down the price of local produce – with devastating effects on the local economy.
- Market access: rich countries charge high taxes on imported manufactured and processed goods, preventing poorer countries from earning more, and restricting them to exporting only raw materials.
- Commodity prices: these are set in developed countries, and usually at very low rates. For example, coffee prices fell by 6.7% between 1997 and 2002, costing poor countries $8 billion.
- Patent protection: this costs developing countries $40 billion each year. The rules governing this area were designed by TNCs to increase their profits. Different rules apply when these TNCs use the indigenous knowledge and traditions of communities in developing countries to develop new products, such as new forms of basmati rice or herbal treatments.

It is estimated by aid agencies that if Africa, East Asia, South Asia and Latin America each increased their share of world exports by just one per cent, they could lift 128 million people out of poverty. Furthermore, for every dollar given to poor countries in aid, they lose two dollars to rich countries because of unfair trade barriers against their exports. Debt and unfair trade place a double burden on developing countries, perpetuating their poverty and preventing their development. In recent years much has been done to highlight the fact that many countries cannot pay back the debt they owe. As the slogan of Jubilee South campaigners puts it: 'Don't owe – won't pay'.

Adapted from: Debt and Development Coalition (**www.debtireland.org/debt-issues/index.htm**) and Oxfam's **www.maketradefair.com**.

Globalisation policies have also led to job insecurity and casualisation. Many jobs are less secure than they were during the 1960s and 1970s, leaving millions working in the informal sector with little or no job protection and very low wages. Social welfare and health, among other services, have been reduced or privatised in many countries, making it harder for the poor and those on low incomes to access them. Inflation has been controlled but prices are high, wages are low and the gap between the poor and the rich – income inequality – has increased. Furthermore, these negative effects of neoliberalism often hit the most vulnerable groups (women, children, ethnic minorities or indigenous groups) disproportionately hard.

Many of the neoliberal policies adopted by governments have been very unpopular with their peoples, which has led to political instability. In Latin America, for example, almost all countries in the region are now democracies, yet many of the elected governments have been very unstable. A number of presidents have been ousted as a result of their implementation of neoliberal policies, such as in Argentina (2001), Bolivia (2003) and Ecuador (2005). Others were extremely unpopular and therefore quite ineffective, such as Alejandro Toledo in Peru (2001–06).

Most of these governments are unable or unwilling to challenge the IFIs or the larger world powers, such as the US. In effect, democratic leaders have little power in these democracies. In a 2004 UN report into democracy in the region, local leaders and ex-leaders identified the main powers in Latin America as the IMF and the World Bank, US embassies, the media and private international business interests; not national parliaments, presidents, local business, or even the army. Most of the major decisions that affect these countries are therefore made by unelected foreign powers or international organisations. Indeed, countries that refuse to implement suggested policies can often be punished through the withdrawal of investment, the refusal of credit, the massive sale of national currencies (which causes devaluation), and the removal of large sums of money abroad (capital flight). Sometimes, a refusal can even result in attempts to overthrow elected governments (as happened in Venezuela in April 2002), often with the support of major powers, such as the United States. Democracy, therefore, is in a precarious position in the region. In the same report, it was found that about half of Latin Americans would support an authoritarian government if it solved their economic problems.

Neoliberal globalisation has therefore, in general, increased inequality, failed to reduce overall poverty levels and decreased states' sovereignty in decision-making. This is particularly the case for developing states, where it has caused instability in developing democracies. The freedom of manoeuvre of national governments to address the development needs of their populations has been greatly reduced. Developing countries cannot afford, nor are they permitted, to invest heavily in the education and health of their people, as much of their income is diverted to paying the international debt. This leaves the richer developed states in a much better position to provide the infrastructure for the knowledge-based economy needed by globalisation.

1.4 Conclusion

As can be seen, the idea of development is a very complex one that is affected by a wide range of issues. While many of these issues may appear abstract and theoretical, the impact that they have on people's everyday lives is very real. To bring a global development perspective to your work as a volunteer, it is vital to have some knowledge of these topics. They form the wider context within which your experience will take place. Having some insight into the bigger picture will help you to understand the forces that might shape events at the local level of your placement.

In such a complicated context, with so many powerful forces and interests shaping people's lives in developing countries, it would be reasonable to wonder if being an international volunteer can make any difference at all! Certainly, examining the context closely could easily put you off going overseas. Volunteering can make a difference, however, if it's done with the right spirit. The next chapter will look at the meaning of volunteering. It also examines in more detail three important themes that need to be considered while volunteering: power relations, gender and racism.

National University of Ireland Maynooth

DEPARTMENT OF ADULT AND COMMUNITY EDUCATION

Continuing Education 2007 – 2008

Undergraduate Courses

COURSE TITLE	CONTACT	COURSE TITLE	CONTACT
Foundation Courses		**Certificate Courses**	
ECONOMICS & FINANCE (NEW)	046 9248867	DISABILTY STUDIES	01 708 4500
RETURN TO LEARNING	01 708 4500	GROUP WORK, THEORY & PRACTISE	01 708 4500
Certificate Courses		HERITAGE MANAGEMENT	01 708 4500
		LOCAL HISTORY	01 708 4500
ADDICTION STUDIES	01 708 4500	PSYCHOLOGY	01 708 4500
ADULT & COMMUNITY EDUCATION	01 708 4500	RACE AND ETHNIC STUDIES	01 708 4500
COMMUNITY DEVELOPMENT AND LEADERSHIP	01 708 4500	SOCIAL AND HUMAN STUDIES	01 708 4500
COUNSELLING SKILLS	01 708 3784		
DIRECTING	056 7775910		

Professional Development Courses

COURSE TITLE	CONTACT	COURSE TITLE	CONTACT
ADDICTION STUDIES (NEW)	01 708 3683	TRAINING & CONTINUING EDUCATION	01 821 0016
ADULT GUIDANCE THEORY & PRACTICE	01 708 3752	DIPLOMA IN TRAINING & DEVELOPMENT (FOR SOCIALLY INCLUSIVE WORKPLACES)	01 708 3683
COMMUNICATION & GROUP SKILLS FOR MANAGERS	01 708 4500	DIPLOMA IN ARTS (LOCAL & COMMUNITY STUDIES)	01 708 4500
EQUALITY STUDIES IN TRAINING & DEVELOPMENT	087 66683762	DIPLOMA IN RURAL DEVELOPMENT BY DISTANCE LEARNING	01 708 3590
INTEGRATING LITERACY	01 708 4500		

Degree Programmes

COURSE TITLE	CONTACT	COURSE TITLE	CONTACT
BA in Local Studies	01 708 4587	BA in Community Studies	01 708 4587
BSc in Rural Development by Distance Learning	01 708 3590		

To request a brochure please contact
Department for Adult and Community Education
National University of Ireland, Maynooth, Co. Kildare
Tel : 01 708 4500   Fax 01 708 4687
Email:adcomed@nuim.ie
Website: http://adulteducation@nuim.ie

CHAPTER 2

ISSUES IN VOLUNTEERING OVERSEAS

While the previous chapter discussed the wider context of development, this chapter will look at the more specific situation in which a volunteer will find him or herself. International volunteering does not take place in a vacuum: it is informed by a long history of interactions between host communities and foreigners. In order to better understand this, it is necessary to know something about the historical development of international volunteering. It is common to see volunteering as a simple act of kindness, but it takes place in a much wider context, and the relationship between volunteers and host communities will therefore be affected by a number of different issues. Three issues that will have an impact on volunteers are power relations, racism and gender. The overall aim of the chapter is to signal the bigger issues that you should consider, both before and during your time volunteering, in order to help you feel more prepared for it.

2.1 What is overseas volunteering?

The English word 'volunteer' comes from the Latin 'voluntas', which is synonymous with free will, personal choice or option. The word was first used in the English language in the seventeenth century, in reference to enlisted soldiers. According to the *Oxford English Dictionary*, the term was used to refer to 'a person who enters military service, not through obligation or as a regular soldier, but of one's own free will'. This implies that a volunteer makes a choice to offer her or his time to a cause that she or he feels is worthwhile. The word has significant military roots: people volunteered to fight in many of the wars of independence in South America in the early nineteenth century; in the Boer War in South Africa near the end of that century; and in the Spanish Civil War in the 1930s. Many of these military volunteers were international: for example, many Irish people participated in the Boer War to fight against British imperialism and in the Spanish Civil War to battle against fascism. The international nature of volunteering is far from new, and indeed is part of an established entanglement of idealism, conquest and travel.

Volunteering's primary origins may be military, but it was continued during Victorian times in Britain by philanthropists, many of them women, who provided support to those 'in need' whom the state was seen to be failing. This 'social' influence can be seen today in the nature of volunteering both at home and abroad. In more recent times, volunteering has taken on a liberal and youth-centred image. It is increasingly seen as a means to learning, which can contribute towards diplomas and university degrees and can be important for getting certain jobs. In the United States, for example, volunteering is part of service-learning programmes in which students work on community programmes as part of their wider studies.

Volunteering is viewed by most people as a way of developing one's sense of citizenship and community responsibility.

International volunteering, particularly flowing from developed to developing countries, grew in the early 1960s, principally through the establishment of state-supported organisations: Voluntary Services Overseas (VSO) was established in Britain in 1958; the Peace Corps was founded in the USA in 1960 at the behest of President Kennedy; and in Canada, the Canadian Executive Service Organisation (CESO) came into being in 1967. APSO, the Agency for Personal Service Overseas, was founded in 1973 in Ireland, and sent skilled Irish volunteers to developing countries until the programme ended in the early 2000s. The focus of all these organisations has been on extended placements of around two years and on skills-transfer programmes.

More recently, these state-supported organisations have been supplemented by a rapidly-growing number of organisations that arrange shorter overseas volunteer placements. In Britain, many of these are aimed at the 'gap year' market, which includes people who have completed second-level education or are taking time off from third-level education. Such organisations, some of which are for-profit and some which are not-for-profit, primarily provide short-term volunteer programmes that last for between a week and several months. Unlike the state-supported organisations mentioned above, many of these organisations do not require that volunteers have specific skills in order to participate. Instead, skills can be developed 'on the job', and the focus is often on intercultural exchange. This approach varies a good deal from that of many NGOs and missionary orders, for whom the focus on skills transfer and capacity building is central.

International volunteering, therefore, has a long and varied history. What unites volunteers through all these periods is the way that volunteering has offered access to alternative opportunities, whether for travel or work. For military campaigners, volunteering enabled them to leave impoverished or threatened lifestyles, often with the promise of access to land or work in a newly-liberated state. For Victorian women, volunteering became a way to escape the home and enter a public arena from which they were otherwise excluded. For many modern volunteers, it offers opportunities to develop skills and to get to know a community at a level that is not permitted to the average tourist.

2.2 Issues arising from volunteering abroad

Despite the good intentions that have motivated international volunteering for much of its existence, it is important to consider its other, less positive, aspects. Historically, the context of international volunteering has been defined by invasions, conquests and colonialism. In the past, host populations suffered from the negative effects of volunteering, including the arrival of over-zealous missionaries. In many cases, host communities had very little say about the types of activities that volunteers should or should not get involved with. Today's volunteers will therefore rarely be entering into a situation that is not in some ways defined or affected by the past actions of people from developed countries.

When you arrive in another country, you will not be the first foreigner to set foot in that land. Soldiers who invaded and conquered or missionaries who persuaded and converted will have preceded you [...] You may follow in the footsteps of tourists who have come simply to wallow in the local fleshpots or you might arrive in the shadow of previous volunteers who enthusiastically implemented a project that raised expectations but failed unequivocally.

(Collins et al., *How to Live Your Dream of Volunteering Overseas*, p. 19.)

An international volunteer's relationship with the host community will be, to some extent, affected by the history of volunteering and also by the historical relationship between the North and the Global South. Some of the big issues informed by this history that need to be considered by any volunteer are power relations, racism, and gender discrimination. While overseas, volunteers are likely to encounter these issues, all of which can have complex effects on the host communities. In this section, we will explore these issues further and look at why it is important for volunteers to consider them.

Power relations in development work

While overseas, it is likely that you will encounter personal challenges and potential conflicts based on your position as an outsider from the 'technically advanced' North. Some volunteers can be given positions of power and responsibility simply because they come from Western countries. Dr John Makumbe of Transparency International Zimbabwe points out that NGOs based in developed countries are often reluctant to provide financial assistance for operating or running costs for their Southern counterparts. This is in an attempt to avoid the creation of personal employment for those who operate programmes. However, it is often very difficult for NGOs to find alternative sources of funding to cover these costs, which include salaries. This can have two consequences: first, local NGOs may doctor and falsify their accounts; second, they may be forced to accept volunteers to carry out work for which they cannot afford to pay a local, qualified worker. Yet, Makumbe notes, these foreign 'experts' are often likely to make wrong assumptions about the local situation, as they are not fully conversant with the local culture. As a result, volunteers may be given positions of responsibility because their labour is free, they can sometimes bring in funds, and they can be seen as being more 'honest' than locals.

Such opinions are often rooted in attitudes – on both the Northern and the Southern sides – emerging from long experience of colonisation. One such attitude, identified by Eilish Dillon of the Development Studies Centre at Kimmage, Dublin, is the way that we in the Global North 'other' those in the Global South; that is that we highlight the differences between us and the people of developing countries rather than what we have in common. By doing this we contrast our 'superior' knowledge and abilities with their supposed 'lack' of them. This notion leads us to believe that 'we' can 'help', 'contribute', 'empower', 'change', whereas 'the other' is 'poor', 'needy', 'lacking in skills'. Sometimes citizens in developing countries can be equally susceptible to such attitudes, due to the experience of colonisation, thus prompting some NGOs to give Northerners more responsibilities than they would local people. However, as Dr Makumbe points out, local experts 'are likely to do a better job in the assignments they are hired to undertake because they are aware that they will have to live with the decisions they make, unlike the foreign expert who will leave for home at the expiry of their contract'.

It is important to be aware that if you have this kind of powerful position, you will have to make personal judgements about the appropriate way to use your power and influence. In doing this, you have to consider all the issues of fairness and dignity that you would consider in an organisation here. You should also consider how an outsider in a position of power influences the confidence and perspectives of local workers. Try to avoid underestimating the contribution that the knowledge, skills and experiences of the 'other' – that is the citizens of developing countries – can make to our knowledge, skills and experiences. It is important to challenge these assumptions, and the status quo in our volunteering work, and instead encourage solidarity between the peoples of the developing and developed world in order to achieve justice, equality and human rights – in a word, development – for all.

Gender in development

Gender refers to the socially determined roles and responsibilities of women and men in any community. It is related to how we are perceived and expected to act as women and men because of the way society is organised. Women, particularly in developing countries, constitute the majority of the poor, the non-literate and the disenfranchised. One analyst points out, for example, that although women represent half of the world's population and one third of its workforce, they receive only one per cent of the world's income and own less than one per cent of world's property. In many countries, there are cultural practices that disadvantage women. In the most extreme examples, such as female circumcision and female dowry, these can threaten women's lives. Gender-based violence may also be an issue for women in particular cultures, this is violence that is directed against a person on the basis of their gender or sex. In many countries, women are equal in legal terms, but gender inequalities are often ignored in the name of preserving culture and tradition.

Projects can sometimes reinforce these tendencies and practices. One project in the Gambia, for example, intended to increase rice production and therefore rural incomes. However, only men were consulted in the planning process, yet women traditionally owned the land. The result of the project led to land ownership being transferred legally to the men of the community from the traditional owners, local women. While the project did increase incomes, it was at the price of women losing their land and the independence that tradition had guaranteed them. An example such as this underlines the importance of considering the gender and equality impact of every project. Even projects that appear on the surface to have no gender implications may in fact have important unexpected impacts.

Racism

There is an argument that 'aid and development work presume a superiority which is racist'. This argument has some strong grounds that show how the 'donor-recipient' relationship is loaded with many inequalities. As we noted earlier, behind any western volunteer going to a developing country are five hundred years of an exploitative and colonial history, including slavery. This relationship has changed in some ways, but still the cultural attitudes of the North are not without racism. Also, some Northern people who work with Southerners are carrying an 'infused inferiority' arising from the experience of slavery and colonisation, and reinforced today by the burden of debt.

A volunteer from a developed country can go abroad with the moral high ground of being a volunteer, who is 'giving' and 'helping'. The recipient can be seen to be in need, suffering from poverty and requiring salvation from this by an 'expert' Northerner, whom it is presumed has the power to provide that salvation. It is forgotten that in many situations it was with the intervention of earlier Northern 'experts' that a lot of today's problems arose.

The volunteer worker, no matter how good their intentions, operates in a culture that conveys superiority on the basis of education and training, control of resources, positions of authority and access to money. The volunteer will have all these, while the recipients can be seen as less educated and less skilled, and their opinions of less value. Invariably, the difference between the lifestyles of the volunteers and the local community will emphasise the gap.

You may agree or disagree with this argument. Some conclude that it would be best that no more Northerners go overseas naively aspiring to do good. Others respond that there are various ways in which the individual volunteer, the sending organisation and the host community can work to reduce the risk of racism in development. Here are some questions worth asking of any particular relationship between a funder and a recipient:

- Who makes the decisions – white or 'Northern' personnel, or local nationals? Are there Southern people on the board of the Northern organisation?
- Are the recipients portrayed fairly in the agency advertising?
- Where are the decisions made – outside the country or locally?
- Who controls the purse strings?
- In whose language is work conducted?
- What is the practice (not just the policy) of any organisation you may link up with?
- Does the agency consider racism in its recruitment and give appropriate anti-racism training to assignees?

You can refer to the next chapter and to the *Code of Good Practice* and *Volunteer Charter* in the appendix for further discussion and guidelines on this issue. You may also be interested in reading the research conducted by Comhlámh into the impact of international volunteering on host organisations in India and Tanzania. This provides information about the views of host projects on the ways in which volunteering programmes can be structured in order to ensure that all participants benefit as much as possible. Copies can be downloaded from **www.volunteeringoptions.org**, or ordered through the Comhlámh office.

> What I have found in East Timor is that development work has done a lot of damage to the country and in many ways has perpetuated the colonialism of Portugal and the occupation by Indonesia, in that foreigners – international NGOs and the UN – have come in and imposed western forms of governance and politics, telling the Timorese people how to run the country and how to do things, so there is this idea that the 'foreigners know best', which in turn reinforces the idea of a first world and third world.
>
> (Fionuala, volunteer in Timor Leste.)

2.3 International volunteering and development: over to you!

As you can see, there is a lot to think about when deciding to volunteer and to consider while volunteering. The degree to which you have to contemplate the issues discussed above, and adapt them into your work, will often depend on the type of work you do. Generally speaking, there are two ways you can choose to volunteer.

First, as an international volunteer, you can simply attempt to tackle the symptoms of underdevelopment. By volunteering in this way, you can participate in the building of schools, houses, roads or in the provision of medical or educational services. As one volunteer, Áine, told us, a high point for her in her volunteering experience was 'seeing the improvement in the health status of malnourished children'. In other words, it is possible to see the direct impact of your work by volunteering in this way. In order to take the issues outlined above into consideration, it's important that your project is planned with the full participation of the local community, so that it responds to their real needs, and doesn't just simply reflect the wishes and views of the organisations, funders, government bureaucrats – or yourself! This is also important in terms of the long-term sustainability of the project – that is, that the project can last over a period of years and eventually become redundant as the need for it disappears or local people take it over.

A second form of volunteering is attempting to work a little bit deeper by challenging the issues outlined above and the structures that perpetuate poverty, as described in the previous chapter. This is a much more difficult route to developement, and often more frustrating for the volunteer. Change here is very slow, or imperceptible, and will be fiercely resisted by those who benefit from the status quo. An advantage of this work is that you can begin it at home by joining solidarity organisations and taking part in campaigns such as those on international aid, debt and trade (see Chapter 3).

Volunteering overseas allows you to learn more about the actual structures and agents that help perpetuate poverty in that country. It can be hard to immediately identify the larger issues that may affect a community, such as the impact of international trade laws or debt repayments. You can start by educating yourself about the country's history, economy and society before you go abroad and while you're there. So while you're overseas you should talk to the people of the country: your workmates, people in your local community, and people working in other areas, such as human rights, medicine, and social justice. By being an international volunteer you have a unique opportunity to be a witness to the economic, social and political situation of that particular country.

You will be able to learn about the country and bring that knowledge back home with you to help educate others. And much of what you learn will be useful in understanding your own country and how it functions in its own context and in the wider world. In other words, you are in a position to compare both societies and so learn what structures and obstacles are common to both, and which perpetuate poverty and inequality and block change. In this way, you participate in the continuum of volunteering, using your learning and experiences to heighten awareness in yourself, the organisations you work with overseas and here at home, contributing to the push for change in the structures that create and perpetuate global poverty and inequality.

2.4 Conclusion

International volunteering has existed in a variety of forms for hundreds of years. As a result, the volunteer does not enter into a vacuum when he or she goes overseas, but into a context that has usually had a long history of contact with the 'North'. Much of this contact may well have been negative and racist. The volunteer is also entering into a social context with its own cultural mores around race and gender, some of them stemming from experiences of colonisation and some of them from local tradition. A successful volunteer needs to be aware of these impacts and contexts before they go abroad and to seek to learn more about them while abroad. Chapter 4 will explore this issue in more depth. Before that, Chapter 3 will provide you with advice and tools to help you decide whether being an international volunteer is the right thing for you, and, if you decide it is, to help you choose the most suitable organisation for your needs.

kimmage DSC
development studies centre

COURSES IN DEVELOPMENT STUDIES

Contact the **Kimmage Development Studies Centre** for more information on full time and part time options in the following programmes:
- **MA/Post Graduate Diploma in Development Studies**
- **BA Degree in Development Studies**
- **'Understanding Development' evening course**

Study areas include: Political Economy of Development; Sociology of Development; Planning for Development; Gender; Environment and Development; Cultural Anthropology; Adult Education; Leadership in Groups; Sustainable Livelihoods; Human Rights; Emergency Relief; Research Methods; Participatory Tools

MA/ PG/BA are accredited by the **Higher Education and Training Awards Council of Ireland** (www.hetac.ie) and lead to an internationally recognised qualification.

For a Course Prospectus and further information contact:
**The Kimmage Development Studies Centre,
Kimmage Manor, Whitehall Road, Dublin 12
Telephone: 01 4064386 / 4064380 Fax: 01 4064388
E-mail: info@kimmagedsc.ie   Web: www.kimmagedsc.ie**

CHAPTER 3:

MAKING A DECISION

3.1 Examining your motivations

Volunteers' individual motivations for making the decision to go overseas can be very mixed. They can range from seeing volunteering as a means to helping you make bigger decisions about your life, to wanting to work to achieve specific development aims. For anyone who is thinking about volunteering overseas, it is very important to examine motivations before making any final decisions. Being aware of your motivations will help you to develop realistic expectations for your involvement.

In the table below you will find a selection of reasons often given by volunteers for their decision to take up a placement overseas, set out for you to help you assess your motivations for wanting to volunteer abroad. Score yourself for each item on a scale of 0 to 10, with 0 meaning that the statement is in no way a reason for your going and 10 meaning that it is a very important reason. Be as honest as possible: no one but you will see your answers!

Motivating reason	Score
To see the world	
To get away from life/work at home	
Solidarity with the oppressed	
To gain a first-hand knowledge about political issues	
To help people	
To get away from an unhappy relationship	
To get something different on my CV	
To contribute something	
Last chance to explore the world before settling down	
To pass on my skills	
To change the world	
To gain relevant professional work experience	
To work for justice	
Everyone else is doing it	
To challenge myself	
To respond to a religious or spiritual motivation	
To try something different and to experience different cultures	
To broaden my mind	

Is going overseas the right option for me?

Were you surprised by any of your answers? When looking at your score, remember that there should ideally be a balance between meeting your needs and meeting the needs of others when making a decision to volunteer overseas. Examine the main reasons that have emerged from the list, and think about whether volunteering is the best option for you.

For example, if your reasons for volunteering overseas are mostly personal ones (e.g., 'To get away from life/work at home', 'To see the world', 'To get away from an unhappy relationship'), you would need to consider the wider context of volunteering and the effects that you might have on other people. Volunteers can have a huge impact on projects, and their preparedness on arrival, both for the work and for living in what may be a very different culture, can have a big impact on their contribution to the success of a programme. It's important to remember that you may be closely involved with day-to-day life in the host community and that your motivations need to stem from a real willingness to assist with achieving the project's aims.

> I saw cases where personal issues rather than a desire to volunteer were the main motivations in going away. Often once it was realised that it was not just an exercise to improve your self esteem and that everything wouldn't necessarily go the way you would want it, there were significant problems.
>
> (Jane, volunteer in Zambia)

According to the volunteer placement organisation Casa Guatemala, 'volunteers are a wonderful input in our organisation, very necessary to our existence, they are always very welcome, but sometimes, we get volunteers who are a pain in the neck, and we have a hard time dealing with the situation'. Among the problems they list are a lack of respect amongst some volunteers for local staff, and the fact that some volunteers do not realise that there are differences between the way of doing things in the host country and what they are accustomed to at home.

> Some volunteers refuse to eat our local food; we have had some volunteers demand more than what they signed up for; some volunteers try to go outside the agreed/chosen program, interfering with the hosts' activities; some volunteers refuse to adhere to the rules and regulations in the host family.
>
> (Jubilee Ventures, Ghana, on some of the difficulties that can arise for host organisations if volunteers are not properly prepared for placements.)

If, on the other hand, your motivations are mainly based on meeting the needs of others (eg, 'To contribute something', 'To pass on my skills', 'To work for justice'), it's very important to consider what you will be able to bring to the placement, and whether your presence will contribute to achieving the goals of the project you choose.

For instance, if wanting to change the world is important to you, it is essential to consider whether the people with whom you will be working have the same views and ideals as you. Also remember that many volunteers express frustration at how little they can achieve in the face of overwhelmingly large problems, and try to adjust your expectations accordingly. According to Jubilee Ventures, some of the characteristics of successful volunteers include open-mindedness, a willingness to learn, and friendliness to the community.

3.2 Motivations for volunteering overseas: testimonials

We asked a number of former volunteers what had motivated them to work overseas. The answers confirm that there can be a wide range of reasons for making the decision to pack up and go.

Some volunteers saw it as an opportunity to help them make bigger decisions about their lives: Natasja, who volunteered in Tanzania for three months, says that she decided to volunteer 'because I had always wanted to go to Africa. I was in between jobs and didn't know where I was going (maybe not the best reason in the world but it helped with my life making decisions)'. For Eleanor, a volunteer in Kenya, 'after I finished university I was unsure what direction to take regarding my future and so I took a year out. I felt it was a worthwhile thing to do during this time'. Max was specifically motivated by a desire to volunteer in India: 'I didn't decide to go overseas but to go to India; a country so culturally rich and interesting that you have to experience this culture once in your life.'

Some found that their interest in volunteering was prompted by their work or what they had studied. Anna, who volunteered in Nepal for a year, says that before she decided to volunteer, 'I was working with a fundraising company, fundraising for several well-known charities. From that work, I developed a keen interest in development work overseas. It seemed like a great opportunity to make a difference and experience a completely different side of the world at the same time.' According to Anne, who volunteered independently in Laos and Thailand, 'I have a degree in anthropology and have studied about development and learned how aid is often misdirected and ill-conceived. I knew I would only see a small part of the picture but felt that by doing some voluntary work I would at least experience some of the immediate issues.'

I think vital characteristics of an enjoyable, constructive, learning and working relationship between the volunteer and the organisation include the volunteer actively considering their motives for volunteering in the first place. If you know *why* you are taking on the challenge of volunteering and you know your own physical, psychological and emotional limits from the very outset, you have potential to be far more useful to the organisation and end up having a much more beneficial experience overall.

(Andrew, volunteer in India)

Generally speaking, however, while individuals may have one main reason for volunteering abroad, most of us go for a variety of reasons. For example, Gráinne, who volunteered in Tanzania, explains that she went for 'a couple of reasons, some idealistic, some selfish: I was interested in development as a career; I wanted to go to Africa; I was a teacher and felt I had something to offer; I didn't feel that I could watch the AIDS crisis unfold and not do anything about it; I wanted to challenge myself and see if I could manage with the isolation, the lack of electricity and running water and a new language or two.'

What is most important is to remember that your motivations can have a big impact on your expectations for what a volunteer placement will be like, and on what your experiences will be like when you go overseas.

Reasons why volunteers have made an impact are:

- long-term commitment that they are willing to give to the organisation;
- patience to understand and assimilate the development context and responses;
- openness and initiative in identifying areas of work and making positive contributions;
- and cultural adaptability.

(Gram Vikas, Rural Development Organisation, India)

3.3 Alternatives to volunteering overseas

This leads on to another issue which should be considered: the possibility of volunteering at home as an alternative to going overseas. Both poverty and underdevelopment exist in Ireland, despite its wealth relative to that of many other countries. Actions to end poverty and injustice can therefore come from both a local and a global base. If we only go overseas to help, but do not act to challenge the root causes of global injustice, including its manifestations at home, our actions will not help prevent the recurrence of present problems.

Increasingly, people are becoming aware that the economic structures of the global economy, generally dictated by rich countries, bear responsibility for the unequal development of poorer countries. Some of these issues were discussed in more detail in Chapter 1. Comhlámh and other organisations work through development education to raise awareness, promote critical thinking and reflection, and encourage campaigning and lobbying on these issues. This work aims to increase understanding about these topics and to empower people in Ireland to take action for change. Some issues that are not likely to be resolved without a significant shift in public awareness leading to increased political will in developed countries include:

- debt burdens
- unfair trade relations
- arms sales
- the unrepresentative nature of the UN and other international bodies
- gender inequality
- environmental destruction and global warming
- low levels of development aid by rich countries
- sweat shops, child labour and lack of union recognition
- the activities of transnational corporations (TNCs).

There are a large number of groups in Ireland that work for development with a global perspective without undertaking projects overseas or regularly sending Irish people there. Examples include solidarity groups, development education groups, campaigns, fundraising groups, minority ethnic community groups and human rights organisations. These groups can focus their work on the situation in a particular country, or else work on a general theme. Their activities include sustaining links with groups in developing countries, development education, expressions of solidarity, intercultural celebration, campaigning and lobbying. If you are interested in finding out more about these organisations, Comhlámh's contact list, which contains information about many of them, is available on the Comhlámh website (**www.comhlamh.org/resources-index-contacts-list.html**).

Solidarity work from home can have the following positive effects:

- Raising awareness among Irish and European people about an issue, its causes and effects, and their potential role in working for change.
- Building the political will for change, so that politicians realise it is in their best interest to bring about change.
- Bothering and embarrassing the power abusers, whether they are Northern governments or firms, international organisations, or Southern undemocratic regimes.
- For people in developing countries who are struggling against oppression in one form or another, our solidarity can be an encouragement to them.
- It has a moral and 'historical' value, in that we benefit morally from having sought to convey the voices of those who are oppressed. Historians will be able to say that there were people in the rich countries calling for injustice to stop. In the very long term, the structures of injustice will be eroded by popular opposition.

However, it is worth remembering that solidarity work in Ireland will not provide you with the same experiences as volunteering overseas. The experience of being directly involved with a project in a developing country will give you first-hand insights into the realities of life for people in the host community. It may also allow you to engage directly with the immediate symptoms that are brought on by the underlying causes of global injustice. Solidarity work can require a more long-term vision, as progress can happen very slowly. Both types of work can be very valuable in working to achieve global justice. It's important to remember that they are not mutually exclusive and that many groups would welcome your involvement in solidarity work from home without your having previous experience of living or working in a developing country.

3.4 What are the differences between volunteer placement organisations?

Now you have considered your motivations for volunteering and looked at the possible alternatives, it's a good idea to start thinking about the type of organisation that is most suited to you. There are a large number of organisations which arrange volunteer placements, and the variety can be slightly overwhelming for someone who is just beginning to consider the options. For this resource, we have divided volunteer placement organisations into five categories: short-term/intercultural; long-term development; conservation/environment; recruitment/placement; and relief/emergency. All the organisations in the directory have been classified according to these headings. Below is a brief explanation of some of the differences between the organisations, which will affect the types of placement that they organise.

Short-term/intercultural: Provides a service to a community that is often on a short-term basis, or that focuses on the cultural learning experience; can be for-profit or not-for-profit. For the purpose of this resource, the term is used to cover all organisations that:

- offer short-term volunteer positions (from one week to one year)
- do not require that volunteers have specific educational/professional qualifications
- are not primarily concerned with conservation/environmental work (a separate category is provided for these organisations).

Long-term development: The focus of this work is on empowering local people. It often involves some kind of skills transfer, and will require specific educational or professional qualifications. For the purposes of this resource, all organisations classified as belonging to this category will:

- be not-for-profit
- require that volunteers have specific educational/professional qualifications
- include capacity building as a volunteer activity. This involves the transfer of required skills and knowledge to individuals and groups.

Conservation/environmental: Primarily concerned with conservation/environmental work. These organisations have been classified separately, as there is an increasing number of them working in this area and whose emphasis is slightly different to the intercultural exchanges. Again, these organisations can be for-profit or not-for-profit. The term is used to cover all organisations that list their primary activity as relating to conservation/environmental work.

Recruitment/placement: This category is used to cover organisations that match volunteers with placements or programmes, but that are not themselves involved in organising or running volunteer programmes. Such organisations may be for-profit or not-for-profit, and may or may not charge a fee for their services.

Relief/emergency: The focus of this work is on emergency situations, which could arise as a result of conflicts or natural disasters. It concentrates on basic needs, such as the provision of food, water, sanitation, medicine and shelter. Examples of work include food distribution and emergency healthcare. For many of these placements, specific professional and educational qualifications will be required, as will relevant prior experience.

Depending on the type of work in which you are interested, these categories should help you narrow down your choice. There can be advantages and disadvantages to all the different types of work, and it may be helpful for you to make a list of what you think these could be before making any final decision. You can use the box below to get you started:

	Advantages	Disadvantages
Short-term/ intercultural	Chance to experience a country and work with local people.	May be 'gap filling' if there is no long-term plan.
Long-term development	Usually working very closely with local people, on long-term issues.	Can take a long time to see the results of the programme.
Conservation/ environmental	Projects are often results-orientated.	May experience tensions between the destruction of environmental resources and the need for economic development.
Recruitment/ placement	Can help to find the best theoretical match between your skills and the jobs available.	Do not run programmes directly, so may not have strong connections with projects.
Relief/ emergency	Results of work are very visible.	Can be very stressful on a personal level.

3.5 What kind of work can volunteers do?

The differences between the types of organisation can lead to volunteers having a wide variety of work to do when on assignment. This ranges from assisting with projects where no particular skills or qualifications are needed, to performing highly skilled work for which several years' work experience is required. The type of work that volunteers undertake very much depends on the organisation that arranges their placement. For example, some organisations focus on intercultural placements where interaction with the host community can be more important than the physical work that is carried out. Others focus on long-term development, and emphasise organisational and community capacity building and transferring skills to other staff.

Some volunteers described working on basic construction projects where no previous experience was required, and where much of the value of the work was seen as being in the interaction with other people. Natasja describes her work in Tanzania: 'We started to make cement bricks with the villagers so that we could build a school for the children of the village. We spent five or six days a week, most mornings and a little after lunch (if it was not too warm) carrying bricks, cementing and mainly enjoying the happiness it brought to everyone.'

Others talked of teaching English, which is a very common activity for Irish volunteers, and of their additional educational work. In Anna's placement in Nepal, she 'taught English in secondary school and worked with fellow volunteers, teachers and students to rebuild a library, run a workshop on smokeless stove building and keep the Green Club active (with the GC, we mostly ran environmental awareness days and performed educational dramas with younger members of the community)'.

Others talked about the changes that took place in their work throughout the course of their placement. Eleanor, who volunteered with an environmental conservation organisation, found that the work she began in Kenya had to be altered because of a lack of resources: 'I started out working on a mapping project for the entire Diani region but this project had to be dropped due to lack of human resources. I then worked on the Pest Management project the Colobus Trust was working on and oversaw the redesign of the Visitor Center at the Colobus Cottage.' Áine also found that her administrator's role changed over time, as she became more accustomed to the project: 'Initially I worked mainly in administration, writing reports for the funders, looking after the finances, etc. After a few months ... I began to organise the nutrition component of the programme, i.e. organising nutrition clinics and home visits in the various outlying areas.'

For others, their work has involved using their educational qualifications and previous experience to contribute to projects in a range of areas. According to Pete, a volunteer in South Africa, 'my anchor project has been the Home Vegetable Growing project for villagers. I established a "model" vegetable nursery where local conditions and a wide range of vegetables are tested. The young plants raised are then distributed to members of the project for planting in their own village gardens.' Grace used her legal background when volunteering in Nigeria: 'I worked for Women's Rights Advancement and Protection Alternative [WRAPA] which is an organisation which provides legal advice or counselling to women who have been victims of domestic violence, rape, sexual harassment, etc.'

These descriptions illustrate only a small aspect of the different types of volunteer work that are available. One essential characteristic emphasised by former volunteers is the need to be flexible when undertaking a volunteer placement. Many volunteers have found that the work they signed up to do can be very different to what they actually undertake when they arrive in the host community. There are a number of reasons for this, including responding to needs as they arise, filling in if there is no one else available for the job, adapting to changes caused by a lack of resources, or simply because a project's objectives have changed over time.

3.6 Why pay to volunteer overseas?

People who are considering volunteering overseas sometimes express surprise at being asked to pay a participation fee. However, it needs to be remembered that volunteering can be an expensive undertaking, with possible costs including transport, accommodation, food, administration, training, on-the-ground support and, potentially, medical and other insurance. Most organisations cannot cover these costs unless your volunteering will make a significant contribution to their work, or unless they are in receipt of substantial financial supports, for example, from regular public donations or support from governments or religious organisations.

Remember also that there is a distinction between organisations that are run on a for-profit basis and those that are not. For-profit organisations are commercial businesses that make money by filling a consumer demand or social need, in this case by arranging volunteer placements and providing host projects with volunteers. As discussed in Chapter 2, the recent growth in the popularity of gap years and career breaks has led to a rise in the number of these organisations. Not-for-profit organisations, as the term suggests, do not seek commercial gain, though they are, of course, interested in their own financial survival. Their principal objective is usually to achieve certain social aims or fulfil certain social needs without financial gain. These objectives are normally set out in the organisation's mission statement. Information about whether organisations are for-profit or not-for-profit is included in the directory.

Participation fees can vary a great deal: it is often the case that organisations that require volunteers with specific educational or professional skills will not charge fees, and will cover accommodation and food costs for people while they are overseas. Some will also provide a small living allowance. Other organisations will not charge a placement fee, but will require that volunteers meet all their own travel costs. Some charge programme fees that cover matching volunteers to programmes, in-country transport, accommodation and food. Others charge fees that include everything from flights and visas to food and accommodation in the host community. Before making a final decision about which organisation you would like to volunteer with, ask for a breakdown of how the fee will be spent. This will help you to get a more detailed picture of how the organisation is structured. If you are planning to fundraise to cover the costs of your placement, it will also provide you with information to pass on to potential donors.

3.7 Choosing the right position: guidelines on making a decision about volunteering

There are two main parts to making a decision about which type of agency to volunteer with. The first relates to assessing your requirements, skills, and the type of work you would be best suited to undertake. The second involves deciding on the type of organisation that would best match your needs and skills. When making a decision, it is important at all times to consider the host community, remembering that your presence will have an impact not only on you but also on them. Use the following points as a guide to help you identify what you have to offer as a volunteer.

1 What are my skills?
Make a list of all the skills you have that you think would be relevant to volunteering overseas. This could include educational qualifications, paid and voluntary work experience, knowledge of languages, previous experience of living abroad, and any other interests that you think would be of use to a project. This will assist you when you approach the list of organisations, and give you a better idea of where you might be able to make the most useful contribution.

> We see many short-term volunteers here in Tanzania as it is a popular country to be in with lots of tourist places to see and experience, but the amount of work they actually do is questionable, mainly due to lack of experience and language skills.
>
> (Host organisation, Tanzania)

2 What type of work would be best suited to me?
It is very important to think about the type of work that will be the best match between your skills and the needs of a project. Think carefully before taking up a voluntary work placement that involves activities of which you have no experience. Aside from the fact that the host organisation may have to spend time and money on training you, there is also a possibility that you could find yourself in a position where you could cause more harm than good. Ask yourself whether you would be given similar responsibilities in Ireland: if not, think about the reasons why. For example, if you have no teaching qualifications or experience, would you get a job in a school here? Why should it be different in another country? Is it because there is a huge shortage of locally qualified people to do the job, or would your volunteering displace someone from getting paid employment? Or is the main point of the placement to provide an intercultural experience, rather than for you to pass on particular skills?

Additionally, being away from home in a new country where you've made a commitment to stay for a certain period of time may not be the best setting in which to discover that you hate your work. Think about the different types of placement that are available, e.g. short-term/intercultural or long-term development, and the pros and cons that you have drawn up for each. This should help you to make a decision about the type of placement that would be most suitable for you.

3 Would I like to work directly with the host community, or would I prefer to volunteer alongside other expatriates?

Some volunteer programmes may involve volunteers working only with local people, some will involve working primarily alongside other expatriate volunteers, and some involve a mixture of both (for example, having a local counterpart with whom you carry out your assigned work). Many people find some comfort in working with other expatriates with whom they have a common cultural background, especially if it is their first time volunteering overseas. On the other hand, some people prefer to immerse themselves completely in the local culture and not to have contact with other expats. Once you have decided, be sure to clarify what the situation will be with any agencies that you contact.

> Working on an equal level with an in-country volunteer is the most effective way of reducing the sense of 'us' and 'them'. My Ugandan partner became such a close friend, and I think he had much more of an impact on our students than I did because they could relate to him and he acted as a role model for them.
>
> (Orla, volunteer in Uganda)

4 What kind of conditions would be best for me when volunteering?

The conditions in which volunteers live and work can vary enormously, depending on whether they are based in urban or rural areas. You should carefully consider which you would be happier with, bearing in mind that the answer could affect your access to clean water, food supply, medical support, electricity and telephone. Your access to social amenities will also be affected, depending on the location you choose. Remember that while a placement in a rural area may impact on your access to these, it may also offer you a more easy-going pace of life, in a community where everyone will know you. These issues can have much more of an effect on your day-to-day life as a volunteer than you might expect. For instance, would you find it problematic to share accommodation with others, whether they are locals or expatriates? Would it bother you to live in accommodation that was of a higher standard than that of your co-workers? Would you find it difficult if you did not have access to a vehicle? Would you be able to cope with the local climate? One former volunteer who worked in an isolated rural area did not realise that she would have to spend up to two hours every morning making breakfast, due to the lack of piped water and electricity. Depending on your viewpoint, this could either be an adventurous and enriching experience, or a huge irritation.

> One needs to be mentally prepared for the nature and pace of work which may be very different from 'back home': entertainment and social life are also areas needing much adjustment.
>
> (Gram Vikas, rural development organisation, India)

5 How long am I prepared to commit myself for?

Former volunteers repeatedly stress the importance of organising a 'time-appropriate' placement. There are several different aspects to this. Some projects may be very interesting and attractive to you, but may require a greater time commitment than you can give in order to see them through to their conclusion. For example, long-term development work often involves spending a prolonged period overseas. It may take months before you know the country and the issues well enough to become really effective. In some cases, if you are not prepared to commit a particular amount of time, it may limit your contribution. However, it is very important not to commit yourself to something that you know you will not be able to finish. Another issue to consider is whether you are comfortable with spending a relatively short amount of time working on a project where you can build up very close relationships with local people, then having to leave. Previous volunteers have said that this can, in particular, have a detrimental effect on children who become very close to volunteers they may never see again. Make sure that you consider these issues before making any final decisions.

> Some of these volunteers would come and be with us, but just as we start to get used to working with them, they are already very tired and bored and need a break in Zanzibar. So they tell us they will work for two weeks, but after three days they want to go on safari.
>
> (Host organization, Tanzania)

6 What are my personal health and emotional needs?

Ask yourself under what circumstances you might find these needs to be overstretched. Volunteering overseas can require a certain amount of emotional robustness and flexibility. For any project you are considering, take these needs into account when making your decision. You may decide that you would prefer to work on a project with other expatriate volunteers, who could provide emotional support. Or you might like to look for a project that has a full-time contact person you can talk to if you are having difficulties. If you have problems coping in very warm or very cold climates, bear this in mind when considering your destination. If you are considering volunteering for several months or more, think about the impact that this might have on relations and friends.

Also give consideration to your personal circumstances. For instance, if you have a partner or children, can they come with you? If you have a disability, can this be accommodated by the placement organisation? Do you have any outstanding financial commitments (e.g., rent, a loan, or a mortgage) that will be affected by your volunteering overseas? If you are asked to pay for your placement, will this be a problem? For example, will you have the time to fundraise for the organisation, if that is required before you go overseas?

Some of the things I saw and heard and experienced really broke my heart but I had too much of a workload to process the many emotions which I was feeling until I got home. This was extremely stressful and it took a long time for me to recover. I would recommend that people make sure they will be well supported emotionally on placement and on their return and to be certain they are not taking on more work than they can reasonably do.

(Gwen, volunteer in India)

3.8 Deciding on an organisation

Answering the above questions will help you get a clearer picture of the type of voluntary work that would best suit your skills and interests, as well as an idea of the conditions under which you would like to live and work while overseas. These answers, and your answers to the questions below, can help you choose the most suitable organisation for you to volunteer with. The following is a list of questions you might want to ask any organisation:

1 What are the organisation's main aims and goals?
These will be set out in the organisation's mission statement and will help to provide you with a quick overview of its ethos. The directory below contains a section on 'stated missions' that will assist you with getting some idea of what the organisation is aiming to achieve and the methods it is using to do so. Contact the organisation to ask any more specific questions you have, and read their other promotional literature carefully (leaflets, brochures, websites, etc.).

2 What selection criteria does the organisation have when choosing volunteers?
Does the organisation require that volunteers have specific educational or professional qualifications, and, if so, do you meet these requirements? Do they have other requirements, such as age limits, particular religious beliefs, previous work experience and so on? Some of these questions will be answered in the directory, in the 'educational/professional qualifications' and 'other requirements' sections. If the organisation does not require volunteers to have specific educational or professional experience that you think would be necessary for the job, ask them why this is. For example, will the training they provide equip you with the necessary skills?

3 What is the involvement of the host community in the project?
It is very important to establish the level of involvement of the host community in the project. Key questions to consider include:

* Why has the project been set up?
* Who requested that it be set up? For instance, was the organisation approached by the local community and asked for their assistance, or did they identify the need themselves?

- Who asked that foreign volunteers be involved in the project?
- How included are the communities or people that the project aims to help in making decisions about the aims and objectives of the programme?

Asking these questions will help you find out whether non-local volunteers are actually required for a project. Occasionally, as we discussed in Chapter 1, expatriate volunteers can be 'free labour'. Volunteers may therefore displace local labour, as a small organisation or poorly resourced public service might not be able to say no to 'free labour', even if it is not ideally suited to their needs. As mentioned previously, there can also be a danger that organisations will view foreign volunteers as 'funding bait', to help secure money from overseas organisations.

> Lately, most of the volunteers have been sent to the host countries more to cater for the demand from the public for volunteer placements, rather than actually sending volunteers to address the local needs for development of the host country. This is also giving an opportunity to the volunteers to make it a holiday trip rather than actually contributing to the host country. This has to be discouraged, and hence it should be the responsibility of both the sending organisation and the host organisation that the volunteers are placed and assigned to appropriate projects with realistic objectives.
>
> (Host organisation representative, Tanzania)

4 Is there a role description available?

Ask if you can get a role description that sets out the work you will be undertaking, the hours you will be working, who you will be working with and the expectations that the organisation has about what you should achieve in your role. This will help to give you a better idea of the exact aims of the work and of the amount of time each week that you will be expected to commit to the project. Former volunteers have highlighted the need for volunteers to treat their placements as they would any paid, professional job; going through the job description will help you to prepare for your role. The existence of a detailed job description may also help to ensure that your work has been properly planned by the organisation and that there is a need for your presence. This of course shouldn't stop you being flexible while on the job, but it does give you confidence that the organisation is serious and also gives you some idea of what you will be doing.

> I was left to my own devices in the country. Obviously I had some help but there were many days where I had no work at all and with a little more organisation by the in-country co-ordinators I could have spent many hours working with disadvantaged children. They did not have enough projects organised for all the volunteers.
>
> (Lynn, volunteer in Brazil)

5 What are the conditions in which volunteers live and work?
Using the previous list of questions, raise any important issues with the organisation at this stage. Ask questions in relation to accommodation, the facilities in the area where you will be based, the availability of transport, and any major health issues you might need to consider. Find out whether the organisation provides insurance for volunteers, or whether this is something you need to organise yourself, and if it is the latter ask their advice.

6 Can the organisation put you in touch with previous volunteers?
Ask if you can be put in contact with former volunteers who have worked on the project, or in the area, or even simply with the organisation. As our testimonials show, these people can provide useful advice on the work in which you may be involved, the ethos of the organisation, and what they found useful to bring with them when they went overseas.

7 Can the organisation give you precise contact details for your chosen programme?
Some organisations arrange placements and projects and then fill the vacancies, while others wait for participants to sign up and then find relevant placements. The former system tends to produce much better projects than the latter. A good organisation with well-run programmes should know, and therefore be able to let you know several months before you travel, where you will be going and what exactly you will be doing. If they cannot or will not give you these details, remember that hastily arranged programmes can be disorganised, leaving both volunteers and local hosts with unclear expectations. Ask for specific contact details and then, if possible, contact the placement yourself and see what they expect of you, whether you can bring anything particularly useful, whether there is anything specific you can do to prepare, and most of all, whether they know you are coming. Some organisations may claim not to want to give you contact details until you have paid a placement fee, worried that you will just organise the placement independently. However, if they have proper relationships with the host organisations, the host will not be prepared to cut them out. So be wary of organisations that make this excuse, as it may be because they do not set up their placements until after you have paid for the placement.

A simple yet crucial tip I would always give is to touch base with the in-country co-ordinator/organisation prior to departure via telephone. It may not seem like much, but hearing someone's voice/foreign accent from the comfort of your home in Ireland makes the whole experience far more 'real'.

(Andrew, volunteer in India)

8 Does the organisation provide pre-programme training and post-programme support for volunteers?
Find out what type of training the organisation provides volunteers with before they begin their work overseas. Some organisations will offer pre-departure training,

some hold in-country training, and some may even offer both. Ask about the topics that are covered: useful areas highlighted by former volunteers include language skills; an introduction to development issues; country and programme orientation; anti-racism training; guidelines on living and working in an intercultural environment; health and safety, and conflict resolution. See if the organisation offers supports such as project evaluations, post-programme debriefings, and workshops for returned volunteers. Some information about the training offered is contained in the directory: you can contact the organisations directly to get more in-depth information.

[My placement organisation] provided excellent backup and training in the months before departure in the areas of fundraising, the medical/ immunisations issues involved, language training, conflict resolution, etc. Once in Tanzania, there was a further week of training to help the volunteers adjust to life on a camp in rural Tanzania, language training, how to relate to the local population, health issues and so on. The summer finished off with a feedback weekend in the UK, where the successes and failures of the summer were analysed and noted for further improvement of the programme.

(Declan, volunteer in Tanzania)

Learn the local language, if at all possible, before departure or at least learn the official language, if it is another European language. I think that it is particularly important when the placement is a short-term one only, as being able to meaningfully communicate with people means that you make the most of your time there.

(Áine, volunteer in Rwanda)

9 Are there costs associated with the volunteer placement and, if so, can you get a breakdown of how they are spent?

As mentioned previously, many placements involve paying money, whether it is to cover transport costs to the destination country or a fee for the placement. If the organisation is not covering all your costs, be sure to get an accurate idea of what the total price will be. If you are paying a placement fee, ask the organisation for a breakdown of how it will be spent. For example, how much goes on overheads and administration costs? How much goes directly to the host project or community? How much is spent on training for volunteers and in-country staff? It is useful to get a clear figure and not an estimated percentage. Make sure that you are happy with the answers before making a final decision. If you are fundraising to cover the costs of the placements, it will be important to have these answers to give to people who are making donations.

Get to know the area you are visiting through the internet or books. In particular, try to get to understand the people, their traits and cultural differences. Know what you are going to be doing and why you are doing it. Ask others who have been in that particular country what to expect. Know the organisation that is arranging your placement. Make sure they are a reputable organisation and that your safety and welfare are catered for while you are in the foreign country; i.e. food, medical aid, insurance, etc.

(Ryan, part-time volunteer in Belarus)

3.9 Recommendations: advice from former volunteers

So what words of advice do former volunteers have for people who are considering their options? Their suggestions cover all aspects of planning a placement, from thinking about why you want to go, to the best kind of attitude to have when you arrive in your host community.

Before you go

Claire suggests that people thinking of volunteering should put some work into researching all aspects of their placement before leaving Ireland: 'Do research so you know what to expect in terms of what type of clothing you should wear, the type of food you will have to eat, injections you will need, etc. Go with an open heart and mind, you will learn much more than you could ever give.' Lynn recommends that volunteers should question their motives before undertaking a placement, as well as doing practical things such as learning the language: 'Ask yourself why you want to go; be sure you are going for the right reasons; learn as much of the language before you go; be prepared for any eventuality.' Anna says: 'It is important that you are doing it for the right reasons. It is not a holiday but, having said that, you can take time to enjoy the experience from a tourist perspective too. Be willing to adapt to a foreign culture and accept what may seem strange initially.'

Orla recommends examining both your motivations and the type of programme you're going to do: 'Think very carefully about the type of programme you want to do and why you want to do it. There is such a huge variety of programmes available, you will find one that suits you. Most importantly you must respect the culture you are going into. Never try to impose your culture (even in simple things like how you dress) and always try and learn as much as you can from the people who live there. They know more than you do about what they need!'

While you are there

Anne has advice for people on their arrival in the host community: 'Be humble, you are a guest in their land, live by their laws and their customs. If you cannot do that consider leaving and see leaving as a personal learning experience.' Pete gives a more general suggestion: 'Bring an open and positive attitude; be prepared to mix at all levels; read up in advance about the country and ask questions'. Eleanor emphasises the importance of being flexible in your ideas and beliefs: 'Be prepared to change your ideals; what we perceive to be true is not always right – no matter how prepared you think you are'.

> Expect the unexpected: things will go wrong and there will be bad days. You may even feel useless from time to time and stop to ask yourself what you are doing there. The important thing is not to get disheartened. The difference that volunteers can make to the lives of others may be subtle or invisible and easily overlooked, but it should not be underestimated. It is often the simplest act of kindness or friendship that has a profound impact on someone's life.
>
> (Suzie, volunteer in India and the Dominican Republic)

The main thing, as Gráinne suggests, is that volunteers be adaptable and realise that they are there to learn more than teach: 'Throw yourself into what you're doing ... it gets easier as you learn the culture and the language. The main thing to realise is that you're the one with the disadvantage knowledge-wise.' This is echoed by Anna: 'I ... learned so much from such an amazing group of people. It was an equal exchange of cultural knowledge and experience.' And she finishes by quoting a former student: 'As one pupil recently wrote to me: "simple live and high think".'

MILLTOWN INSTITUTE
A Recognised College of the National University of Ireland

Broaden your Horizons at Milltown Institute

Summer School: June 2008

This Summer School offers an opportunity to explore spirituality through the lenses of theology, philosophy, sacred texts, poetry and psychology, in a pleasant environment.

Also available at Milltown Instutute:

BA (Honours) Social Justice Studies (CAO PTO17)
BA (Honours) Liberal Arts (CAO PTO16)
Graduate Diploma Ethical Studies
MA Applied Ethics and Theology
MA Faith and Culture

And much more ...

Milltown Instutite,
Milltown Park, Sandford Road, Dublin 6, IRELAND.
Tel: +353 1 277 6300. Fax: + 353 1 269 2528.
Email: info@milltown-institute.ie
Web: www.milltown-institute.ie

CHAPTER 4:

WHAT HAVE I GOT MYSELF INTO?
THOUGHTS ON BEING A VOLUNTEER AND GETTING THE MOST OUT OF THE EXPERIENCE

So you have found a volunteer placement that excites you, packed your expectations and your bags, and now you are off. This chapter will help you make sense of the experience once you arrive on your overseas volunteer placement; it will explore the relationship between host and volunteers and will try to help you ask some questions, and maybe produce a few answers. The key to overseas volunteering is to open your mind well before you leave home and keep it open all the time you are away, and this chapter aims to help you do just that.

The chapter is divided into two sections. The first section deals with arrival in your placement and the community in which you are about to spend time. Most people travel to learn. That is, to learn about the places they go, the people they meet and as often as not about themselves. However, the depth of such learning is not guaranteed, and travel alone is often not enough. The second section explores volunteers' and host communities' views of one another. This chapter is based on field research by Dr Kate Simpson* among volunteers in Peru and Malawi and testimonials given to Comhlámh from former volunteers. It uses case studies, stories and research to offer alternative ways of understanding your volunteer experience. It aims to show that in trying to understand the complex relationship between host and volunteer, you can get so much more out of your experience than by assuming it is all a simple case of the helper and the helped, the needy and the giver, of us and them.

4.1 Where in the world am I?

> I kind of got it wrong, I got quite a culture shock when I came [to Ecuador]. I just kind of thought, 'Oh, they speak Spanish, it will be just like Spain' ... I hadn't thought about it at all and it is not like Spain, obviously it is just so different, I mean it is a third world continent and things like that, so you know, it is kind of different to how I had expected.
>
> (Clare, a volunteer in Ecuador)

---

* For further information about Dr Simpson's work on volunteering, visit **www.ethicalvolunteering.org**

Going to a different country is about, well, just that, a different country. Most people who volunteer overseas have as one of their principal motivations the wish to travel. People travel, as they volunteer, to have new experiences, to learn new things and to meet new people. However, there are a lot of assumptions about just what travellers learn about their hosts, and about the countries they visit – indeed, as often as not, travellers tend to experience what they expect to experience, rather than actually anything new. In this section we will examine why travellers do not always learn as much as they think they will about those they meet, and what you can do to get the most out of your time volunteering overseas.

The relationship between travel and knowledge, between seeing a place and knowing a place, is a historic one. With this relationship goes the desirability of being 'well-travelled'; the idea that the traveller has broad horizons, has experience of the world and therefore command over it. As the German geographer and military man Peneck said, 'Knowledge is power and world knowledge is world power.' It was with such sentiments that Columbus sailed from Spain to see what he could see, and how, by adding to the canon of European knowledge, he could make his own fortune. In the same tradition of travel and knowledge, British aristocrats funded their sons to take the 'Grand Tour'. So too do today's backpackers, volunteers and travellers set off to 'broaden their horizons'. Through travel we supposedly learn, and consequently travel gives us social status. So the protagonist in William Sutcliffe's novel about the gap year, *Are You Experienced?*, upon reflecting on his travel experiences, is able to give himself a whole new social persona:

'... I would be able to begin again as the new me, not Dave the mediocre North London School Boy [...] but as Dave the traveller.'

Travel is supposed to teach us things, but what it teaches and how it does this, many in the travel and volunteer industry would struggle to tell you. One theory, 'experiential learning', holds that people learn best through a cycle of 'action and reflection', that is, by doing something and then thinking about it. The action side of the cycle is actually the easy part; it is the thinking about it that is hard, and so often gets left out. To put this in the context of international volunteering, and to explain why the thinking part is the hard part we need to turn to another theory known as the 'contact hypothesis'.

This theory claims that by coming into contact with people who are different from oneself, one will come to understand them better and be less prejudiced about them. Despite the popularity of this idea research has repeatedly shown that such learning is very limited. Rather, the most important factor in how we understand the people we meet on our travels and in our volunteer work is what we thought of them before we left home, to the extent that our views and understanding of the cultures and peoples we meet while we are travelling tend to be very similar to those we had before we ever left home. For example, when Sarah, a volunteer, was asked how people's lives in the shanty town in Peru in which she had been volunteering differed from her own, she replied: 'The people here ... they don't have TVs but it doesn't bother them because they don't expect one.'

This statement is factually dubious. The vast majority of the population where she had worked for the last month did have TVs. Furthermore, it is unclear on what basis she asserts that not having a TV didn't 'bother' people. She spoke very poor Spanish and there was no evidence she had been out and asked people how they felt about having TVs. So the question is: where did she get this knowledge from? Quite simply, she has been able to experience and see what she expected to see, somehow erasing the very obvious and plentiful TV aerials in the area, and concluding that people's feelings were as she expected them to be. Sarah is not unusual in this. Experiencing and even 'seeing' the unexpected is not as simple as theories such as the contact hypothesis would have us believe.

The reason for the failure of contact alone to change how we view others, and even what we see, is over-reliance on the action part of the experiential learning cycle, to the exclusion of the reflection part. The contact hypothesis assumes that the complexities of people's lives, cultures, histories and social relations are simply 'observable'. That is, they can be seen by the interested, but not necessarily informed, volunteer. To use an analogy, the contact hypothesis is the equivalent of assuming that just because you drive a car you know how one works; from sitting in the driving seat you are able to see how the internal combustion engine works. However, rather in the same way that it is possible to drive a car without knowing how it works, so it is possible to visit a country without ever really understanding it. Just as the internal combustion engine will only reveal itself when you open the bonnet and start asking questions, so too social, political and historical realities will only become apparent when you start asking questions and looking beyond the surface for answers. When we travel without accessing the complexities of others' lives, we travel without understanding those lives, and therefore without any hope of making sense of the choices others make, the ways they live their lives, and why – not just how – their lives might be different from our own.

The reason the reflection part of the experiential learning cycle so often gets ignored is because it is hard. Reflection here is not just a matter of sitting down with a beer or a cup of tea at the end of the day and having a muse, but rather a process of critical reflection. That is, a process of questioning what you have seen and done from other perspectives, of relating your own observations and knowledge: things you have read in books, know about politics and have heard from other informed parties and so on. For example, if you were to travel to Mali, one of the poorest countries in Africa, would you expect to be able to see, without reading the papers, talking to activists, NGOs or cotton farmers, that cotton subsidies in North America are a major contributor to this poverty? Reflection in this context demands that one is able to relate daily observations and experiences to other knowledge, and therefore explain why one are experiencing and observing certain things; so that when you walk through the markets of Mali, a country famed for its cotton growing and weaving, you are able to reflect on, and perhaps understand, why you can only find cotton prints from China to take home as souvenirs.

So why is the thinking part so hard and what can you do as a traveller to complete the action-reflection cycle and actually learn something new about those you visit rather than just confirm what you already knew? The thinking part is hard because it requires effort, it requires you to seek out more information and information that is below surface level; information that goes beyond the good weather, the crazy music and the cheap beer. It requires that you ask questions; it requires you to open the car bonnet and be ready to learn from other people and from books about the complexities of the internal combustion engine. You will never be able to make sense of the poverty or the Chinese cotton in Mali if you do not stop to find out a bit about international trade relations, a bit of history and a bit of the complexity of international development.

As a volunteer, there is a lot that you can do to open up a world of learning from your experiences. The key to all the following suggestions is to remember that, just as in whatever country it is that you come from, there will be different opinions, thoughts and interpretations. People will disagree on which is the best football team, whether the president is doing a good or bad job and what the country needs to change. Just as you would expect different opinions and stories at home, you need to seek these differences out when you are overseas, because it is these differences that make up the real-life complexities in which we all live. If you end up thinking a country or a situation is simple, you have probably missed half the story somewhere along the way. Finally, like any learning, gaining knowledge from overseas volunteering takes some effort, some curiosity and the asking of a whole lot of questions.

Here are a few suggestions of practical things you can do to help you learn from your international volunteering experience:

1) Perhaps the first thing to do is find out as much as possible about where you are going before you get there. The internet, books, international newspapers and, if you are lucky, maybe someone you know, are potential sources of information. Just make sure you look at a few different sources and seek out contradictory information and stories.

2) Literature, especially by authors from your chosen country, can be a wonderful way to explore some of the cultural subtleties of where you are going. If books are not available in a local library, bookshop or resource centre, they can usually be ordered from a number of websites.

3) When you get to wherever you are going, don't just rely on what you can 'see'. Read the local papers; if they are not in a language you can read, look to the BBC World Service. Find out about the local political situation; It is amazing the number of travellers and volunteers who never even manage to find out who is the head of state or what party is running the country. Find out what people care about in culture, sport and so on and go to a local football game, or whatever it is people like to watch. Participate in local social activities.

4) Talk to local people, and not just to book a bus ticket or find out where the cheapest restaurant in town is. If you are a volunteer you have a wonderful opportunity to stay in one place, to get to know local people and to learn from them. Ask them how they understand what is going on in their local area, country and so on. Ask them to explain their cultural practices and traditions rather than just assuming you know all about them already from what you have read.

5) Expatriate communities can be interesting, but remember they often have particular relationships with local people and issues that will be shaped by their own reasons for being in the country.

6) Seek out local organisations. These might be local development groups, councils or other forms of social movements. This will help you understand how people are organising themselves and what changes they are seeking to make in their own lives. As a volunteer there will probably be a local organisation hosting you or organising the project you are working on. Find out about the beliefs, structures and other projects that this organisation has: this can be a rich source of learning that is often simply not available to those who just travel through a country.

7) As we so often hear, we now live in a globalised world. Every country everywhere is affected by the global economy, politics and decisions made in other countries, as was discussed in Chapter 1. If you want to understand why a country is poor, then you need to try to understand their relationship with other countries and with the global world economy.

Doing all these things, searching out all these different sources of information and opinion, will give you the perspectives and knowledge you need to reflect on your own experiences, and to begin to understand the complexities and the realities of the country in which you are volunteering and travelling.

4.2 Here to help or here to learn?

You know why you want to be a volunteer, but have you wondered about how your hosts perceive you? Why they think you are here in their community? Your placement organisation may have promised you an eager welcome from your hosts, but often the reality is a bit more bewildering. People may be confused or uncertain about why you are working in their community and just what it is you are trying to achieve. This section of the chapter offers some reflections on the ways volunteers and hosts perceive one another.

Imagine that a group of, say, Peruvian young people arrived in a deprived part of London or Dublin, and attempted to run a play scheme for local children. Or perhaps you can imagine a group of Senegalese volunteers coming to teach French in British and Irish schools, or Eastern Europeans volunteering on construction projects. What sort of reception are all these international volunteers likely to receive from the local communities? Maybe confusion, maybe curiosity, maybe nervousness and maybe even hostility. Now turn this scenario around to your own volunteer objectives, and maybe you begin to get a perspective on some of the ways you may be received. In becoming a volunteer, whether you're joining a project alongside other volunteers or being on a placement on your own, it is important not to assume that the local population automatically know why you are there and what you are doing, or that they even want you there. As mentioned in the first section of this chapter, working with an organisation that has a strong relationship with the local communities you will work with is vital to the quality of the project. However, beyond this, you as a volunteer need to make the time to answer people's questions, to hang out with them and build relationships based on understanding, not assumptions. For, just as you are excited to learn about those you have come to work with, they may be equally curious about you.

Why we become international volunteers is usually complex and probably personal, but the idea of helping others is often primary. As part of a piece of research in Malawi on the ways pupils and teachers perceived international volunteers, people were asked why they felt volunteers came to their schools and their country. Although many identified altruism as a motive, people also recognised volunteers' personal motivations. The desire to explore Africa, to learn about development, to understand Malawian culture and to get away from their own home and problems, were all identified by Malawian teachers and pupils as motivating volunteers. Indeed, there was a strong sense that Malawi had something to offer volunteers, with some feeling that volunteers must have bad family situations if they want to spend so much time away from home, and in at least one case a suggestion that volunteers came because they could not get jobs at home.

When asked why she felt volunteers came to Malawi to work in schools, one head teacher responded, 'they have a personal interest in culture, to aid development, they want to experience Africa; it is a personal experience [...] maybe they don't have jobs in their own countries'.

Few volunteers set off thinking they will have a terrible time, not wanting to go but feeling that altruism demands it of them. Rather, international volunteering is exciting; it offers opportunities for new adventures in new places and to learn new things, all while (hopefully) doing something worthwhile. Acknowledging to our hosts our personal motivations for volunteering is not only honest but also recognises what they have to give, and breaks out of the traditional and paternalistic relationship of the 'helper and helped'. Being honest with those who host volunteer programmes opens up possibilities for working together and learning from one another.

Working with the communities you go to help is vital. There are far too many volunteer and development projects all over the world that thought they knew what was best for a local community and simply got on with it without stopping to ask. This has produced some disastrous projects. For example, the group of volunteers who decided to build speed bumps on the road leading up to the local school. They built the bumps without stopping to ask local people and they built them through the summer holiday period. When school re-started it turned out the bumps were too steep for the school bus; it could not get over them and the children were left having to walk to school. Projects like this are worse than doing nothing. Making sure your project or placement is worthwhile before you travel is only part of the process; in the end you will be the one there, you will be the one doing things day to day. Communicating with, working with and learning from your host are all things you will need to manage yourself in your everyday interactions. Travelling with the open-minded attitude that you are 'here to learn' rather than the closed-minded 'here to help' will make you ask the questions from which you learn, and not allow you to assume you always know the answers.

Furthermore, not only can you learn from those you meet, work with and seek out. You can also learn from your experiences, both the good ones and the bad ones. The following section aims to provide you with an idea of the kind of things that may happen to you while volunteering overseas. It is made up of the responses we received from former volunteers about the highs and lows of their time volunteering overseas. When you read this, we hope that you put yourself in their positions and imagine how you would react. Hopefully, like many of the volunteers who took the trouble to write to us, you will learn from their experiences in a positive manner.

4.3 High and low points of international volunteering: testimonials

It is certain that while volunteering overseas you will experience both high points and low points. It is not uncommon for people's experiences abroad to encompass both ends of the spectrum. High points usually centre on group interaction, intercultural learning and a sense of personal and professional achievement. Low points generally include to the difficulties that can arise from getting used to a different culture and different ways of working, and doubts about the actual impact of the work being undertaken.

High points

For many people, the most enjoyable part of their placement comes from getting to know the local community, and learning from their way of life. A high point for Aoife was 'living and working close to and within a community and culture so different to your own and seeing the smiles on the children's and adults' faces just for being there'. For Pete, high points included 'participating in the group dynamics in the house we volunteers share; meeting local and overseas folk in the region – of all ages, colours and cultures – under many different circumstances'. Orla found that 'the high point was really feeling welcome in the village, and learning from my Ugandan partner. I loved just hanging out at the house with the local kids. Also, the relationships with the other overseas volunteers (which are still just as strong now) were a really important part of the experience'. And for Anne, 'bringing diverse ethnicities together was the ultimate aim of one project and it was really nice to see that happening and being able to play an active part in that'. High points for Anna were:

> The wonderful Nepalese; the satisfaction of teaching; working with fellow, motivated individuals; the food (I hated it at first and then I grew to love it); community spirit; the pleasure of learning about a new and diverse culture; forever smiling students.

According to Gráinne, 'high points were the people I met, the small victories, learning the language, the adventure of everyday life, being involved in village life – even things like sitting around a fire helping the mamas to peel potatoes'. Eleanor found that 'the high points were working with like-minded people for a cause I believed in and having the opportunity to work with the local staff and experience their culture. I also learned a lot about their work ethic'. Áine found that 'the high points were the many friends and insights into local customs and culture that I gained. Seeing an improvement in the health status of malnourished children was also very important'.

The personal benefits of volunteering were highlighted by Samantha, who volunteered in Afghanistan: 'On a personal level, leadership and management skills are greatly enhanced by the work in the field, as volunteers work with challenges relating to culture and language that are rarely found at home. I certainly improved my communication skills at all levels, from liaising with large donors to drinking chai [tea] with village elders.'

Low points

However, overseas volunteering is not always a completely positive experience. Volunteers often live in conditions very different to those that they are used to at home, can be faced with issues and problems that they would never usually be confronted with, and have to deal with the realisation that they may not be able to achieve everything that they would like. Pete found that it was difficult to deal with the 'frustrations experienced at the slow pace at which certain public and private sector individuals move to execute often simple decisions or tasks – these delays adversely impact on momentum – promises made in a friendly fashion with no follow-up performance!' 'Motivating other teachers could be a little tedious at times', according to Anna, who also found the language barrier frustrating. Gráinne had some difficulties as a result of one individual trying to profit from the work of volunteers: 'The low points were having to leave the first school I was working for, as the principal was only interested in making as much money from me as he could for himself and the frustration of finding out other volunteers had felt the same but didn't inform the agency.'

> I saw much sickness and it was frightening to notice the stark difference in my standard of living and the people I met's standards of living. During my time as a volunteer, the people of Kenya saw me as very wealthy and thought I could solve all their problems.
>
> (Ciara, a volunteer in Kenya)

Aoife discovered that her enthusiasm was not necessarily shared by everyone: 'Sometimes you feel you are making changes for the better but only you are enthusiastic about it and only you can see the potential opportunities and benefits. The people you are doing it for can often be very unenthusiastic which can be very disillusioning.' Eleanor had to come to terms with the fact that the work could not necessarily achieve everything she might have hoped: 'The low point was coming to the realisation that there is very little we can do in Diani that could help the Colobus monkey, as its greatest threat is development. The local community will continue to develop in similar ways to Europe hundreds of years ago. The same environmental mistakes of deforestation and pollution will continue, yet we have no authority to stop this development and deprive people of the opportunities we have enjoyed from development.' Orla doubted how effective her work was in bringing about change: 'The low point was the feeling of frustration that we couldn't really change anything, and that we mightn't be doing any good at all.'

Gráinne was concerned about the effectiveness of the project, as well as very mundane issues of health and security: '... the realisation that what we were doing was really too little too late, the arguing with people about life and death matters, rats, muggings'. For Áine, the low points were 'the shock, isolation and loneliness felt initially as well as missing family and friends at home. The trauma and history of the place where I worked [in Rwanda] could sometimes be very difficult to deal with. Living interculturally could sometimes be a source of tension, as could cultural differences between the local staff and me. Being ill when so far from home was also tough.'

Finally, some people questioned the idea that volunteering is always a positive thing. For example, Anne found that 'a lot of volunteering we observed seemed to be more about the Western charities looking good (and staying in existence) than really doing what was needed on the ground'. And for Lynn, there was not enough work available for her on her placement: 'The little work I did do was very rewarding but this made the days where I did nothing more frustrating.'

4.4 Conclusion

In conclusion, volunteering overseas is a wonderful way to learn more about other people and places, and about yourself; but you will have to work at it. Like any process of learning it takes effort. Too often volunteers assume just looking at a place, just concentrating on the surface, is enough to tell them all they need to know. But if you want to actually learn about, and not just take photographs of, those you work with, you need to ask a lot of questions. Question the organisation you are going with before you go. If they cannot provide you with the answers you need, then look for an organisation that can (see Chapter 3). Then, when you are on your placement, keep asking questions, be ready to look for answers that are based on more than your own observations, and realise that understanding others is about seeking out the complexities of people's lives. Finally, a large part of being a volunteer is about forging relationships with others. Appreciating how your hosts may perceive you, and that it won't necessarily be the easy welcome your placement organisation promised you, will help build those relationships. This can lead to your having both good and bad experiences. The important thing throughout all of these, however, is being ready to open your mind as well as your eyes, and to learn from, and be helped by, those you've come so far to visit. So, volunteer with an open mind and start your learning from the very day you decide you've got itchy feet and want to be off somewhere new.

MA in Public Advocacy and Activism

The Masters Degree in Public Advocacy is an advanced programme for those who intend to work in advocacy, internationally and locally, in areas including community organisation, development, labour, rights, health and environment.

Organised through the J.E. Cairnes Graduate School of Business and Public Policy and the Huston School of Film & Digital Media, in association with the Irish Centre for Human Rights and the Social Sciences Research Centre.

National University of Ireland, Galway. Ireland
Tel +353 91 495 076, info@filmschool.ie

www.filmschool.ie

The Huston School of Film & Digital Media is supported by Coca-Cola HBC.

CHAPTER 5:

COMING HOME

5.1 Introduction

So now you're back home. You might have been gone for anything from a few weeks to over a year. You'll probably have mixed emotions about coming home – you'll be looking forward to seeing family and friends, you might even be relieved at leaving your host country, but you may also be sad at leaving new friends, not to mention the experiences, sights and sounds of what had become your temporary home.

You might ask yourself: is that it? Do you just get on with your life and leave your overseas experiences behind you – a distant memory that occasionally emerges when you hear a certain sound or smell a distinct (hopefully pleasant) odour? How will your friends and family react to your experiences? How, indeed, will you react to those experiences? Perhaps, rather than filing them away in your mind, you might want to actively recall them. Perhaps you might be spurred on to further action, so impressed (or depressed) were you with what you saw, experienced and learned. You might even wish to capitalise on and delve deeper into the new knowledge that you've gained through your experiences volunteering overseas.

This chapter has two main objectives. First, we aim to provide you with some pointers to how to adjust to coming home after an experience overseas. Second, we aim to furnish you with ideas and suggestions as to how to use your experiences to your own benefit, to the benefit of those you left behind and maybe even to the world itself.

5.2 Coming home

Each individual's reactions to their experiences volunteering overseas can vary. They will depend greatly on what kind of person you are, what you did while abroad, where you lived, how long you spent overseas, and what sort of experiences you had. Nonetheless, it is guaranteed that you will return changed to some extent by your experiences. Even if you were overseas for only a week, you may have witnessed a way of life and a level of poverty that you would never have seen before. Having witnessed poverty, you might find the affluence found at home and the waste of modern life difficult to comprehend, if only for a while. You might feel alienated by the increasing materialism and consumer culture found in Ireland. You may decide to try to change your life: from your eating habits to your interests and hobbies to your career; and perhaps even some of your friends and acquaintances. You may experience what is termed 'reverse culture shock' or 're-entry shock'. It is quite expected that when people arrive in a different country, with different customs and cultures, it will take a while for them to get used to being there. In other words, they may experience 'culture shock'. In that situation, foreigners are tacitly given a grace period to behave differently from the customs of the country while they adjust to the new culture. When you get back home, however, no such honeymoon is allowed. Friends and family expect you to be the same as you were before you went away. They didn't experience what you experienced and are often unable to grasp the impact it can have on you. They don't realise that the readjustment may be difficult for you and just expect you to 'get on with it'. 'Getting on with it' can entail a number of actions that, if you want to adjust well and capitalise on your experience overseas, you may want to carry out when you get back. In the following two sections, we will look at strategies to make settling in easier, and at how you can make the most of your overseas experiences at home.

5.3 Coping with re-entry

Health

When you get home, there are a number of things you should prioritise to ensure that you are mentally and physically fit after your experience overseas. First, you need to get yourself checked out medically to ensure that your health has not been affected by the different living conditions you may have experienced while abroad. With the excitement of returning home and the pressures of getting back to college, work or searching for a job, a medical check-up may be low on your list of priorities. However, getting used to being back home will be easier if you are in good physical health. It's important to get a check-up as soon as possible after you return.

A visit to your family doctor is not usually adequate: you need to visit a clinic that has specialist experience as well as the facilities needed for lab tests. (See Chapter 6 for further information.) A medical examination usually provides reassuring confirmation that you are in good health. However, it may occasionally reveal an unsuspected problem that might otherwise lie dormant for quite a while. Some people may be carrying unusual conditions like unerupted infectious diarrhoea, amoebiasis, giardiasis or intestinal worms. Remember that hepatitis A takes three to five weeks to appear, and hepatitis B as long as six to twenty-five weeks. You may also be deficient in micro-nutrients (e.g. calcium, iron or a vitamin). If you have returned from a malarial area, you should normally be taking your pills for some weeks after departing the country, or in accordance with the manufacturer's or doctor's instructions.

HIV/AIDS

AIDS knows no social or geographical boundaries, so it's important to be aware that you might have been exposed to HIV while overseas. Modes of transmission are through practising unsafe sex, by receiving untested blood into your bloodstream, or by being injected with an unsterilised needle. Although no cure has yet been found for AIDS, treatment can help to stall the onset of the disease and people with HIV can now live healthy lives for years. If you feel you may have been exposed to HIV, you may want to have your blood tested for the presence of HIV antibodies. There are numerous centres that provide a fully confidential service, offering blood testing facilities, information and advice. Don't allow yourself to be tested before considering the implications of the result with your doctor or a trained HIV counsellor. If you do test positive, be assured that treatment and support are on hand.

Mental and emotional health

Not only must you look out for your physical health, you also need to care for your mental and emotional well-being. Firstly, you should receive some form of debriefing from your sending organisation, preferably in-country and on return home. Debriefing gives you the opportunity to provide feedback on the project, and allows the agency to hear constructive comments and acknowledge the individual's role. Items that should be covered in debriefing are: project feedback; local conditions; suggestions for improving the project; dealing with or handing over unfinished business; and, last but not least, saying goodbye.

Processing your experiences: On returning, you may need time to process your experiences and to readjust to life at home. If you've only been overseas for a few weeks, you may find it relatively easy to readjust. However, if you were abroad for a longer term, were working in a rural community, a particularly deprived shanty town, or perhaps in a disaster zone, or on sensitive human rights issues, you might need more time to settle back into life in Ireland. Also, people who are sensitive to poverty and injustice might need to think through the effect volunteering overseas has had on them. For some, getting stuck into a job or studies immediately is an effective way to achieve this. However, for others it might be best to talk things through. Contact Comhlámh's Project Officer for Returning Development Workers to arrange meeting up with other returnees. Comhlámh facilitates 'Coming Home' weekends where longer-term returned volunteers and development workers can meet to talk through their time overseas and think about their plans for the future. If you've volunteered for less than three months, you might like to consider participating in Comhlámh's one-day 'Moving Forward' course. Think about having counselling if necessary. Comhlámh can put you in touch with trained counsellors accustomed to dealing with returnees, and can help out with costs if you've volunteered overseas for longer than three months.

Creating a supportive environment: It's also important that you create a supportive environment for yourself. Maintain or initiate friendships with other returnees, especially people who have been to the country or region where you lived. Participate in classes related to the culture of that region: the language, the dances, the food. Ireland is becoming increasingly multicultural, giving you many more choices in terms of ethnic restaurants where you can eat out with friends and shops where you can buy produce to prepare at home. Keep in touch with friends back in your placement country – by email, letter or phone. If you stay involved with the organisation that sent you abroad, as well as meeting other returnees, you can also meet future volunteers who can bring letters and photos to deliver to your friends overseas. Additionally, you could use your experience to help train others before they go abroad. Make friends with people living in your area who come from the region or country where you volunteered. Volunteer locally, either with organisations that deal with the issues and the region you worked in or with those that support people living in Ireland who come from that area (see below). Furthermore, you may notice that many of the problems and issues you learnt about overseas (including poverty, marginalisation, and discrimination) are also present at home. As we discussed in Chapter 3, volunteering locally is an opportunity to contribute to development in the local sense of the word as well.

Sharing your experiences: Share your stories with others to help you reflect on, and continue to learn from, your experiences. However, be prepared for the fact that family and friends might not be endlessly interested in hearing about your overseas experiences! Keep your eyes open for lectures, seminars or conferences that focus on the region or issue most prevalent in your volunteer experience, or those that examine development, inequality and interculturalism. Comhlámh is frequently looking for people to give talks about their overseas experiences; you can contact info@volunteeringoptions.org for further details about this. It may give you a taste for more extensive education in order to start a career in international development. You may also wish to take more direct action against global poverty and inequality. These issues are dealt with in the next section.

5.4 Making the most of your volunteering experience

Comhlámh's *'What Next?'* booklet is a step-by-step, practical guide for returning volunteers and development workers on involvement in global development from Ireland. It illustrates some of the various options available for remaining engaged in global development on your return, and sets out a range of useful resources. Contact the Comhlámh office or see our website for copies of the booklet.

Education

For reasons of career change or self-development, further study on return may be the thing for you. Postgraduate, degree, diploma, certificate and non-formal courses are all available; and there are full-time, part-time, distance, evening, and on-line courses to suit everybody. Many returnees report a desire to deepen their understanding of development or to specialise further in their work sector. If you've been gone for a long period, some time spent studying after your return to Ireland can also allow for a gentle re-introduction to the rapidly changing society you left behind, without the pressure to throw yourself immediately into the jobs market or the feeling that you are completely losing your connection to your time overseas. It can also be the gateway to a career in development work or a related area. You may be entitled to have your fees paid and to receive a local authority grant – check with your local authority for details. You might also be eligible for a Back to Education Allowance, so it's worth enquiring about that at your local Social Welfare office.

Development-related study

If you want to pursue a course of studies in this area, there are many possibilities: courses in development studies, development education, community and adult education, equality and intercultural studies, community and youth work, humanitarian aid and sustainable development are just some of the options available. As well as those available in Ireland there are a vast number of courses in Britain and elsewhere. The Comhlámh leaflet *'Careers and Courses Information: Third Level and Postgraduate Studies in Development Related Areas'* provides suggestions on a range of study options and contact details for a host of institutions in both Ireland and the UK. Contact Comhlámh for a free copy, or view the leaflet on the Comhlámh website, in the *'Support for Development Workers'* section.

Comhlámh and education

Comhlámh organises forums, workshops, weekend and night courses on a variety of development-related topics, depending on members' interests and demands. Courses cover areas such as:

- development education issues/skills;
- options and issues in global development work (for those considering getting involved in overseas development work and volunteering);
- anti-racism training;
- trade and globalisation;
- lobby skills;
- media skills;
- evaluation and planning.

In addition to holding forums and conferences throughout Ireland, Comhlámh is also involved in the organisation of in-service courses in development education for primary teachers. Additionally, in conjunction with DCU, Comhlámh has recently launched a Graduate Certificate in Development Education, which is a one-year distance-learning programme that aims to provide a professional pathway for people working in development education. Look at **www.dcu.ie** for more information on registering for this course. For further details on upcoming events and training, or to book a place on a particular course or workshop, contact the Comhlámh office in Dublin, keep an eye on the website, or sign up to receive e-Link (Comhlámh's email newsletter).

Employment in Development

Having returned home, you may decide you'd like to work with an international development organisation. You should ask yourself the following questions before you begin to search for work in this sector.

- Is my goal to work overseas or to do international work while based at home?
- Do I prefer working in an office or in the field?
- What type of work do I want to do – direct service, advocacy, economic development, policy/electoral, or community organising?
- Do I want to work for a small organisation where I may have more hands-on work, or a larger organisation that may be more stable?

If you wish to work more formally in the development sector, it's important that you learn about the area and its requirements. A good way to do this is by making contacts and networking. Let as many people as possible know that you are searching for work. Making contact with prospective employers face-to-face is recommended and more productive than sending CVs in the post or by email. Don't be afraid to telephone or call into the organisations you think you might like to work for and let them know that you are available. Try and get the name of an appropriate contact person, for instance a manager or personnel officer – someone who has the power to hire you. They will usually prefer you to make an appointment with them in advance of a meeting.

The development sector, however, is not an easy area to enter. While obviously volunteering overseas will help, and educational qualifications in the area would further boost your chances, even then it might be necessary to get involved with organisations on a voluntary or internship basis, if possible. This can give you a valuable insight into the sector if you're new to it; it can get you up to speed if you're returning; it fills what might otherwise look like a gap on your CV and when paid vacancies do arise you are much better placed if people know your work and you know the organisation.

One of Comhlámh's services to returned volunteers is one-to-one career advice. If you've been working in a voluntary capacity in a developing country for more than three months, Comhlámh will subsidise nearly all the costs of the session. The career coaches, who have a good understanding of development work and the Irish jobs market, will assist you in whatever area of the job search you most require support with. Contact the Project Officer for Returning Development Workers in Comhlámh's office for details. Comhlámh also has a jobs page on its website (**www.comhlamh.org/jobs-noticeboard.html**), which is a good place to start with your job hunt. Don't be disheartened if you are not offered the first job you apply for. Looking for work is hard work in itself and takes time. Don't give up; try to keep motivated, energetic, committed and positive. For more information on job hunting and relevant websites, see Comhlámh's 'Coming Home' booklet.

5.5 Keeping yourself involved

As we discussed in Chapter 3, working at home to effect change can often be just as effective as volunteering overseas. The worldwide anti-apartheid movement was a clear example of successful campaigning for changes in South Africa. While volunteering can give you direct experience and knowledge of the situation in developing countries, you can use that experience and knowledge to make your case much more effective at home as a solidarity worker. To be an effective campaigner, the first thing you should do is join a network so that you don't have to go it alone. These networks usually organise campaigning events that you can join, as well as courses, talks and publications that can help educate you more and to which you may be able to contribute. Comhlámh is one such network (see Box 5.1).

Box 5.1 Comhlámh's Activism

In addition to supporting returned development workers through offering services such as 'Coming Home' weekends, counselling and career tutoring, Comhlámh also supports its members at home in their work as educators and campaigners for a fair and equitable world, for aid relationships based on solidarity, for an anti-racist and intercultural Ireland, for rights for refugees and asylum seekers, and for the integration of development education into mainstream primary education, among other goals. At present, groups of active members exist around the country. Comhlámh also has access to other networks such as Integrating Ireland, a network of 100 countrywide asylum seeker and refugee support groups, and Compass, a coalition of development education organisations working to promote the integration of development education into the primary school system.

All Comhlámh projects are sustained by small groups of volunteers and are always open to new members. New groups emerge according to the interest and energies of current volunteers. For a complete list of groups and for dates of meetings and events, you can receive the latest e-Link (Comhlámh's email newsletter), visit the website, or contact your nearest Comhlámh office. If you are interested in joining Comhlámh, you can fill out the membership form from the Comhlámh website at **www.comhlamh.org/get-involved-join-us.html**.

If you have spent more than two months as a volunteer in a developing country, you are automatically entitled to membership of Comhlámh for your first year home, and will receive free all of the benefits of membership (including invitations to events, and Comhlámh publications) once we have accurate contact details for you. To register as a development worker, visit **www.comhlamh.org/get-involved-join-us.html** and fill in the online form.

A combination of acting locally and acting globally provides the satisfaction of helping people directly and of knowing that you are participating in long-term change that addresses the root causes of inequality and injustice.

Other solidarity and campaign groups throughout Ireland maintain contacts between Ireland and particular regions (country-specific groups) or campaign on particular issues (issue-specific groups). For example, check out **www.debtireland.org/campaigns/** for information on a number of debt-related issues and how to get involved with campaigning and raising awareness about them. There are also local One World centres around the country that promote development education and campaigns and that you can join. See Comhlámh's Index list on our website (**www.comhlamh.org/resources-index-contacts-list.html**). Working with solidarity and activist groups can help you hone specific skills. They often run courses on public speaking and you might then have an opportunity to be a public spokesperson for an organisation.

Increasingly, there are a number of online volunteering opportunities available that allow people to be involved with projects in developing countries. For example, the UNV Online Volunteering Service (**www.onlinevolunteering.org**) helps individuals to find online volunteering opportunities that match their personal profiles and interests. Some of the areas to which volunteers can contribute through the site include 'expert advice on a variety of topics, article research and editing, website development ... skills in project management, proposal writing, or information technology; knowledge about financial, legal or environmental issues; ideas for brochure design or a feature story'. Nabuur.com (**www.nabuur.com**) is another site that offers volunteers the opportunity to get involved online, and to offer their services and skills directly to people in other countries who are requesting them.

There are some more personal decisions you can take to help improve conditions in developing countries. First, you can buy fair trade products, thus ensuring that communities receive a fair price for their produce. If you buy ethical products you are guaranteeing fair prices, good working conditions and pro-environment production methods. You can also participate in organisations devoted to making 'regular' trade fairer, by helping monitor companies that exploit labour or damage the environment. Investigate whether any money you invest is invested ethically by asking your bank, financial advisors, etc. about where the funds are being invested. Other ways of making your life simpler include reducing the amount of possessions you have, eating more simply, and travelling more ecologically – by bike, on foot or on public transport. Check out sites such as **www.myfootprint.org** to find out more about the size of your ecological footprint, and to get information on how to reduce it.

Many people may have fundraised to help you pay for your time spent volunteering overseas. Don't forget that you have a duty to those who helped fund you. Many of the activities mentioned above, such as giving public talks and talking to the local media are ways of giving back to the community that helped you. However, you can also make a direct impact by becoming a volunteer fundraiser for international development organisations, your sending organisation, or for projects of the organisation/project you worked with in your host country.

Be good ambassadors for host communities. Be objective, even in presentation of the things that seem to be negative about the host communities. Share their experiences in a positive way. There is always a brighter side of everything.

(Host organisation, Tanzania)

5.6 Conclusion

Whatever you decide to do, remember that what you choose to do when you get home may be even more valuable than what you did while overseas. Volunteering overseas, as we mentioned in the Introduction to this book, is part of a continuum that encompasses the whole process, from when you first decide to go to a developing country to your activism when you get home. Former overseas volunteers have summed up one aspect of the coming home process by saying that 'commitment doesn't end at the airport'. Volunteering overseas, therefore, can be seen not so much as an end in itself but the beginning of a new way of looking at the world and a new means to interact with it in order to bring about change.

CHAPTER 6

FURTHER INFORMATION AND RESOURCES

In this chapter, we provide information about some resources that will be useful for people who are planning to volunteer overseas. This includes contact details for the Department of Foreign Affairs and the British Foreign and Commonwealth Office; information about different internet bulletin boards where you can post specific queries to help you plan your trip; some medical information; where to access specific country information; and other resources and services for volunteers.

6.1 General travel resources

Department of Foreign Affairs

The Department of Foreign Affairs' website offers a range of information that will be of use to people who are travelling overseas, including information on passports, visas and insurance. See www.dfa.ie for further general information about the Department. Specific travel advice is available at **www.dfa.ie/home/index.aspx?id-275.** You can also contact the Department at 80 St Stephen's Green, Dublin 2 (Tel: (01) 478 0822). Specific information on Irish embassies and consulates abroad, and on foreign embassies and consulates in Ireland, is also available on the Department's website.

According to the Department, 'You are strongly advised to take out travel insurance to cover medical treatment, accidents and unexpected losses such as cancelled flights, or stolen cash, cards, passports or luggage. Include enough cover to allow for the extra cost of travelling home (which might require an air ambulance) in an emergency. If you already have private medical cover, check with your insurer whether you are covered for foreign travel and, if so, find out how to avail of this cover.'

The Foreign and Commonwealth Office

This is the British government's foreign office. It offers travel advice for UK citizens, much of which is also applicable and useful for Irish citizens. This includes the 'Know Before You Go' campaign, which was set up in 2001, and which 'encourages British nationals to be better prepared for their overseas trips with a view to avoiding common travelling traumas, risks and dangers'. This includes travel advice by country, travel checklists to assist with planning trips, and advice on travel insurance and health. To access it, go to **www.fco.gov.uk/travel**.

Post your query: useful bulletin boards

Use the following bulletin boards to post any questions you might have and get answers from groups that include experienced aid workers, travellers and website moderators.

Aid Workers Forum (**www.aidworkers.net**): post a query here on any aspect of aid work. There is also a section on volunteering in developing countries. See the 'Living in the Field' section for suggestions on what to bring with you when you go to work overseas.

Thorn Tree (**http://thorntree.lonelyplanet.com/**). This site has a frequently used bulletin board where people can post any type of query relating to travelling in different regions of the world, e.g. information on visas, accommodation, getting around.

Travellerspoint (**www.travellerspoint.com**) is another site where anyone can post a travel-related query. The site also has blogs, a photo gallery, and information on accommodation.

6.2 Medical resources

Tropical Medical Bureau (TMB) Their website includes a section on vaccinations that are recommended for a variety of destinations. Further information is available at www.tmb.ie. The TMB has offices throughout Ireland; the central Dublin office can be reached on (01) 671 9200. To make an appointment with any of the clinics, go to **www.tmb.ie/makeappointment.asp**.

World Health Organisation (WHO) Its publication, *International Travel and Health*, is available online at www.who.int/ith/. This includes a section on health risks and precautions to take when travelling, and regularly updated disease maps. You can access the WHO's Weekly Epidemiological Record at **www.who.int/wer/en/**.

International Association for Assistance for Travellers (**www.iamat.org**) provides information about health risks for travellers and contact details for English-speaking doctors in various countries who are willing to see travellers. Access to the latter service is available for members only.

Fit for Travel (**www.fitfortravel.scot.nhs.uk/**) is a website provided by the NHS in Scotland that contains information for travellers on everything from accidents to yellow fever infected areas.

Mobility International (**www.miusa.org**). 'Empowering people with disabilities through international exchange and international development to achieve their human rights.' Useful contact lists and links.

HIV/AIDS A complete directory of countrywide support groups, organisations and clinics is available from Dublin Aids Alliance at the Eriu Centre, 53 Parnell Square West, Dublin 1. For more information, phone (01) 873 3799, email info@dublinaidsalliance.com, or see **www.dublinaidsalliance.com**. Freephone 1800 459 459 for more information about AIDS helplines nationwide.

6.3 Country information

OneWorld (**www.oneworld.net**). The OneWorld website offers news and views from over 1600 organisations that promote human rights awareness and fight poverty worldwide. The site has a large amount of information, including guides to selected countries.

Human Rights Watch (**http://hrw.org/**) has links to frequently updated articles about the human rights situation in countries worldwide.

AlertNet the Reuters Foundation's site (**www.alertnet.org**), includes a 'country profile' section, with basic information on countries and links to recent news articles about them.

ReliefWeb which is administered by the UN Office for the Coordination of Humanitarian Affairs, aims to assist the international humanitarian community in the effective delivery of emergency assistance. It provides country updates from around the globe, in addition to a dedicated map centre. To access the site, visit **www.reliefweb.int**.

Maps

Three sites that provide maps of many regions of the world:
- Google Earth (**http://earth.google.com/**)
- Multimap.com (**www.multimap.com**)
- National Geographic Map Machine
  (**http://plasma.nationalgeographic.com/mapmachine/**)

6.4 Resources and services for volunteers

Comhlámh (**www.comhlamh.org**), the Irish Association of Development Workers, offers a wide range of services for people who are interested in volunteering and working overseas or have returned from volunteering or working overseas. This includes providing one-to-one advice, pre-departure training, careers advice and a range of other post-return services. For further information, contact Comhlámh at 10 Upper Camden Street, Dublin 2; tel: (01) 478 3490; fax: (01) 478 3738; web: www.comhlamh.org; email: info@comhlamh.org.

Irish Missionary Union represents 75 Catholic congregations of sisters, brothers, priests and lay people currently working in the developing world. It includes a Returned Missionaries Office, the purpose of which is to be available for people home from mission on long- or short-term stay. Amongst the topics explored in the workshops offered by the IMU are the transition back to life in Ireland, the effects that trauma can have, and how to apply the skills, values and talents acquired overseas to the home environment. Address: St Paul's Retreat, Mount Argus, Lower Kimmage Road, Dublin 6W; tel: (01) 492 3326; fax: (01) 492 3316; web: **www.imu.ie**; email: failte@imu.ie.

Irish Aid (**www.irishaid.gov.ie**) is the Irish government's programme of assistance to developing countries. Information about its activities, and about a wide range of development issues, is available on their website. It can be contacted on (01) 408 2811.

Irish Aid and Volunteering

Ireland has had an official development assistance programme since 1974. It has grown steadily over the years, from modest beginnings to its current size (total ODA allocation in 2007 is €813m).

Irish Aid has funded overseas volunteering activities for over thirty years and has recently established a Volunteering Unit to facilitate and support Irish involvement in overseas development volunteering. At present, Irish Aid provides funding, through the Civil Society funding schemes, for more than 1,300 volunteers and development workers, lay and missionary, each year. To help promote best practice in overseas volunteering, Irish Aid supports Comhlámh's Volunteering Options programme, including the Volunteers Charter and Code of Good Practice.

A central element in this initiative is the establishment of an Irish Aid Centre in Dublin City Centre, where members of the public can access information on Irish Aid funding and activities, and on volunteering opportunities. This Centre, which will be located in Upper O'Connell Street in Dublin, is due to open officially in late 2007.

Irish Aid also supports multilateral volunteering through the United Nations Volunteer (UNV) programme. In 2007, Irish Aid is fully funding fifteen UNV volunteers and fifteen UNV intern placements. Irish Aid periodically facilitates recruitment for these and other short-term volunteer positions on behalf of UNV. For further information, please see the Irish Aid website: **www.irishaid.gov.ie**. All volunteering queries may be referred to the Volunteer Corps Unit at: Irish Aid, Bishops Square, Dublin 2; tel: (01) 408 2811; email: volunteercorps@dfa.ie.

Development Studies Centre, Kimmage Manor (**www.dsckim.ie**) offers a range of development-related courses and seminars, some of which are open to the public.

Dtalk (Development Training and Learning @ Kimmage) (**www.dtalk.ie**) was launched in 2005 and 'aims to promote a culture of learning and knowledge sharing within the Irish international development sector'. It offers training for people about to undertake work in the developing world, prepares people for overseas election monitoring, and provides professional development opportunities for head office and field-based staff. A schedule of training courses and topics, along with additional information about the programme, is available at **www.dtalk.ie/courses/scheduled/** or by phoning (01) 406 4386 or (01) 406 4307.

DCU's Centre for International Studies has an online resource centre with comprehensive links to sites that cover topics including general resources in international relations and resources in development education. For further information, see **www.dcu.ie/~cis/online_resources.htm**.

UCD's Development Studies Library is 'the major source of research materials in Ireland on development issues such as aid, agriculture, rural development, economics, environment, human rights, history, politics, refugees, urban development and women'. This service is open to members of the development community and the public. Non-UCD staff or students who wish to use the library should email the Development Studies Library for details. Further information is

available by phoning (01) 716 7560 or online at: **www.ucd.ie/library/services_&_
facilities/library_collections/dev_studies_library/index.html**.

Galway One World Centre (**www.galwayowc.org**) has a resource centre that is
open to members of the public. This includes materials on development education.
For more information, contact the centre on (091) 530590 or visit them at Bridge
Mills, Dominick Street, Galway.

Kerry Action for Development Education (**www.kade.ie**) has a resource room
development education lending library service that is open to members of the
public. 11 Denny Street, Tralee, Co. Kerry; tel: (066) 718 1358.

Centre for Global Education, Belfast (**www.centreforglobaleducation.com/**) aims to
'provide education services that will enhance awareness of international
development issues. Its central remit is to challenge dominant stereotypes and
commonly held perceptions of developing countries which are prevalent in our
society.'. Further information is available from the Centre at 9 University Street,
Belfast, BT7 1FY, Northern Ireland; tel:(028) 90241879; fax: (028) 9024 4120;
email: info@cge.uk.com.

Waterford One World Centre (**www.waterfordoneworldcentre.com**) is a
development education centre that works with a range of local groups to 'educate
and empower people to take action on global issues of social justice and human
dignity'. Further information is available at **www.waterfordoneworldcentre.com** or
from the Centre, 18 Parnell Street, Waterford; tel: (051) 873064; email:
info@waterfordoneworldcentre.com.

6.5 General information

Publications

Working for a Better World: Options for Working in Global Development (Comhlámh,
2004) is available free of charge from Comhlámh. It is aimed at people who are
thinking of working for global development, and discusses many of the issues raised
in this book.

The Coming Home Book (Comhlámh, 2007) is available free of charge from
Comhlámh. It is aimed at people who have returned from working overseas in global
development, and discusses many of the issues raised in Chapter 5 of this book.

Comhlámh's *What Next?* booklet (2007) is a step-by-step, practical guide for
returning volunteers and development workers on involvement in global
development from Ireland. Copies are available free of charge from Comhlámh.

How to Live Your Dream of Volunteering Overseas (Joseph Collins, Stefano
DeZerega, Zahara Hecksher: Penguin, 2002) is an excellent, extremely
comprehensive print resource that provides information and advice on all aspects of
overseas volunteering. It includes in-depth profiles of a wide range of volunteer-
placing organisations, many of which are based in North America.

*World Volunteers: The World Guide to Humanitarian and Development
Volunteering* (Fabio Ausende, Erin McCloskey, 2nd ed: We Care Guides, 2004)
includes an extensive list of organisations that arrange humanitarian and
development volunteering positions.

80:20 – Development in an Unequal World (80:20, 2006) is a comprehensive resource, now in its fifth edition, providing an introductory overview of the key issues, debates and challenges in development, human rights and related areas. It has an accompanying CD that provides additional information for use in a range of educational settings.

The Rough Guide to a Better World has been produced by Rough Guides and the UK Department for International Development. It is available free online (www.roughguide-betterworld.com) or you can order a copy to be posted to you.

Understanding Globalization (T. Schirato and J. Webb: Sage, 2003).

Other sources of information

International Lesbian and Gay Association (**www.ilga.org**) 'A world-wide network of national and local groups dedicated to achieving equal rights for lesbian, gay, bisexual and transgendered (LGBT) people everywhere. It is the only international non-profit and non-governmental community-based federation focused on presenting discrimination on grounds of sexual orientation as a global issue.'

Millennium Development Goals (MDGs) Further information about the MDGs, which were discussed in Chapter 2, is available at **www.un.org/millenniumgoals/**. Information about the Irish government's position on the MDGs can be found at **www.dci.gov.ie/challenges.asp**.

Dóchas (**www.dochas.ie**) The umbrella organisation of Irish NGOs involved in development and relief overseas and/or in the provision of development education. Its website contains many useful resources and links on a range of international development issues. This includes the Code of Conduct on Images and Messages, which sets out guidelines relating to communications about the developing world.

UNIFEM (**www.unifem.org**) This is the women's fund of the United Nations. The site contains comprehensive information on a variety of issues that affect women worldwide, including gender-based violence, HIV/AIDS, and poverty.

World Volunteer Web (**www.worldvolunteerweb.org**) This website supports the volunteer community by providing a global one-stop shop for information, resources and organisations linked to volunteerism.

Volunteering in Ireland

Volunteer Centres Ireland (**www.volunteer.ie**) 'The national organisation with responsibility for developing volunteering in Ireland, both nationally and locally.' Its website includes links to volunteer centres throughout the country, as well as a database of volunteer opportunities available nationwide.

Volunteering Ireland (**www.volunteeringireland.ie**) 'Volunteering Ireland promotes high quality voluntary activity, by encouraging organisations which involve volunteers to adopt good policy and practice, and by acting as a link between such organisations and individuals who wish to undertake meaningful voluntary work.' Their website contains details of a large number of voluntary work positions, ranging from time-limited commitments to longer-term opportunities. The website is updated regularly, and further information is also available from their office at Coleraine House, Coleraine Street, Dublin 7; tel: (01) 872 2622; email: info@volunteeringireland.com.

Comhlámh's INDEX Contact List The contact list (**www.comhlamh.org/resources-index-contacts-list.html**) contains further information on development education and solidarity groups working in Ireland, many of which would welcome the involvement of volunteers. Copies are also available on request from the Comhlámh office.

Community Exchange This website (**www.activelink.ie**) has a frequently updated section dedicated to volunteer positions. Other sections include information on upcoming courses, workshops, new publications and campaigns.

How You Can Help (**www.howyoucanhelp.ie**) This website is hosted by Dóchas, the Irish umbrella group of development NGOs. It 'provides suggestions on how you can help aid agencies to continue to give the right kind of aid. It has been developed in order to inform everyone – from staff working in aid agencies to members of the public – about how best to lend support in a time of emergency.'

6.6 Jobs noticeboards

The following websites contain useful information on paid positions, voluntary work and internships in developing countries:

- AlertNet (**www.alertnet.org/thepeople/jobs/index.htm**)
- DevNetJobs (**www.devnetjobs.org/**)
- Eldis (**www.eldis.org/news/jobs.htm**)
- Idealist (**www.idealist.org**)
- OneWorld (**www.oneworld.net/job/list/professional/**)
- Reliefweb (**www.reliefweb.int/rw/res.nsf/doc212?OpenForm**)

Comhlámh's website also has a jobs noticeboard, with information on jobs in Ireland and overseas (**www.comhlamh.org/jobs-noticeboard.html**).

Development Training and Learning @ Kimmage

www.dtalk.ie

Dtalk offers a range of short international development courses and seminars. Over 35 courses are offered and are categorized under 5 main clusters:

- Cross-cutting/Priority Thematic Issues
- Facilitation, Communication & Orientation Processes
- Institutional & Organizational Dynamics
- Programme Management Cycle
- Humanitarian Contexts

An outline of each course and dates of courses are available at www.dtalk.ie or by contacting the Dtalk office at the Kimmage Development Studies Centre (www.kimmagedsc.ie). The contact details are: patricia.wall@kimmagedsc.ie or telephone Kathleen Cox, Dtalk Administrator at 00 353 1 4064307.

A course outline for each course may also be found in the Dtalk Course Guide. A copy of the Dtalk Course Guide is available on the Dtalk website or a postal copy may be requested.

There is an online application facility on the website.

Dtalk is supported by Irish Aid

DIRECTORY OF VOLUNTEER PLACEMENT ORGANISATIONS

7.1 How to use this directory

We have attempted to include as much information as possible about the organisations with entries in this directory. As noted earlier, organisations can, at short notice, change their objectives, cease their activities, modify their contact details, relocate their projects, or carry out a host of other actions that may affect their volunteer placements. **We therefore recommend that you contact any organisation directly to confirm all details of placements.**

For ease of use, we have divided the directory into Irish-based and international organisations. This will help readers in Ireland to identify organisations with whom they can potentially make direct contact before making a decision about volunteering. Information about whether the organisations have signed up to Comhlámh's Code of Good Practice and support its Volunteer Charter is also set out in the Irish section (see the appendix for more details about the Code and Charter). The second section covers a wide range of other placement organisations that arrange volunteering opportunities, and that are based throughout both the global North and the global South.

Contact details: The contact details set out the organisations' addresses, their phone and fax numbers, their website address and the best email address to use if you want to contact them with a volunteer query. Updates to these details will be made available on Comhlámh's Volunteering Options website.

Organisational details: This sets out information on when the organisation was established, whether it is for-profit or not-for-profit, and the type of organisation it is (as discussed in Chapter 3). The 'Stated Mission' provides a very brief overview of the aims and ethos of the organisation; contact them directly if you have any further requests for information about this.

Volunteer placement details: This information covers the countries in which the organisations arrange volunteer placements, the activities volunteers can undertake, the duration of the placements, and age requirements, if any.

Activities: In general, most volunteer placing organisations cover a wide range of activities. In order to classify these, we have used the following sixteen headings. The definition of these categories is very broad, in order to accommodate the range of possible activities within them.

• *Administration/management*: Covers organisations where volunteers may participate in programme/project administration and management. Examples include assisting with the day-to-day running of a programme, financial/strategic planning and overall project management.

- *Agriculture*: Includes organisations where volunteers can be involved in agricultural activities ranging from assistance with planting/harvesting crops, to working with livestock, to working as an agronomist or vet.
- *Business*: Covers all aspects of developing, running and expanding businesses. This includes a large range of ventures, such as micro-finance initiatives, fair trade, eco-tourism, and sustainable income generating activities.
- *Capacity building*: Involves the transfer of required skills and knowledge to individuals and/or groups. Qualified/experienced personnel in general.
- *Children/young people*: Covers organisations that mention children/young people as a specific target group of their activities. Activities can include assisting with educational programmes, sport and arts activities, working in orphanages, etc.
- *Community development*: Organisations whose activities are targeted at strengthening and enhancing supports for the local community. Activities range from assisting with the construction of community facilities to working on human rights-based projects.
- *Conservation/environment*: Ranges from non-skilled help with environmental conservation projects to undertaking specialised research.
- *Construction*: Ranges from provision of non-skilled labour to provision of highly skilled input into building projects.
- *Disability/special needs*: Working in a variety of areas with people with disabilities and/or special needs.
- *Education*: Covers the informal and formal sectors; all areas from teaching English to training trainers.
- *Health/medical*: Covers all activities involving doctors, nurses, nutritionists and dentists. Also includes health education and awareness-raising programmes.
- *Human rights*: Any placements with a specific human rights dimension.
- *Internships*: Organisations that provide internships in developing countries.
- *Technical support*: Provision of skilled support to projects, ranging from IT to accounting to assisting with funding applications.
- *Women*: Covers organisations that mention women as a specific target group of their activities. Examples include working with women's micro-finance groups, working on activities to promote women's rights, women's educational projects.
- *Other*: For organisations involved in activities not outlined above. See the organisation's website for further details.

Other details include: whether the organisation has placements with disability access (in general, this tends to depend on the facilities available for the placement, so contact organisations to receive further details); 'Language requirements' specifies whether volunteers are required to have specific language skills for participation in a project; under the 'Educational/professional qualifications' heading, information is provided about the particular educational and/or professional qualifications that may be a prerequisite for participation. 'Other requirements' sets out whether there are any other requirements for participation – having particular religious beliefs, for example. The 'Application procedure' heading describes how to go about applying to an organisation if you are interested in volunteering with them, including whether references and an interview are required.

'Costs' includes details of any costs associated with the placement. Only programmes that have absolutely no costs, including travel expenses, will have 'no' as a response to this heading. Otherwise, we have attempted to give an idea of the figure at which costs can start. 'Benefits' means everything that is provided for volunteers as part of the programme. This can cover a wide range of things, such as all travel costs and medical costs, visas, accommodation, food, in-country training, donations to host community, insurance, and, in some cases, a small stipend for volunteers. It is important to note that both these categories will be subject to change, and that the most up-to-date information will be available directly from the organisation. The 'Work individually/in teams' heading will give you some more information about the type of situation in which you will work in-country.

The final headings are 'In-country support for volunteers', 'Pre-programme training', 'Post-programme debriefing' and 'Contact with returned volunteers'. The information contained under these aims to give potential volunteers more insight into the structures of the organisation and the supports it offers throughout the volunteering programme.

7.2 Volunteer placement organisations: Irish-based

AIESEC

Address: 63 Lower Gardiner Street, 3rd floor, Dublin 1
Telephone number: +353 (0)1 855 0091
Fax number: +353 (0)1 855 0089
Email: national@aiesec.ie
Website: www.aiesec.ie

Established in 1948, AIESEC is a not-for-profit organisation.

Type: Recruitment/placement.
Stated mission: 'AIESEC facilitates international internship exchanges and supporting activities that provide practical learning experiences for our interns and that facilitate the learning of our members and other stakeholders. Our vision: peace and fulfilment of humankind's potential.'
Countries: Africa, Asia, Latin America, Europe (various)
Activities: Administration/management, business, capacity building, children/young people, community development, education, health/medical, internships.
Duration: 2–18 months.
Age requirements: Minimum 18 years, maximum 30 years.
Disability access: Depends on placement; contact organisation for further details.
Language requirements: Depends on placement. Language requirements can range from basic knowledge to native knowledge of any given language.
Educational/professional qualifications: Yes; at least one year's third level education.
Other requirements: After joining and understanding AIESEC, applicants can enter a review process to assess their experiences and motivation for doing an AIESEC exchange.
Application procedure: AIESEC operates an online application procedure for its traineeships and placements abroad (see www.aiesec.net/snci). During this procedure applicants must state their academic and working experience, personal and professional skills as well as any language skills which must be backed up with the correct certificates.
Costs: Yes, €500.
Benefits: Pre-placement training; support in preparation for living and working abroad, including in-country support with accessing accommodation and local orientation; access to online database of internships; post-placement reintegration support.
Work individually/in teams: Both.

Code of Practice	Volunteer Charter	In-country support for volunteers	Pre-programme training	Post-programme debriefing	Contact with returned volunteers
Not available for public reference.	Not available for public reference.	Yes; available part-time.	Training covers topics including dealing with culture shock and using internship search systems.	Includes a written report and interactions with people preparing to go abroad.	Yes.

Billy Riordan Memorial Trust

Address: Kilfountain, Dingle, Co Kerry
Telephone number: +353 (0)87 283 5615
Email: mags@billysmalawiproject.org
Website: www.billysmalawiproject.org

Established in 2002, the Billy Riordan Memorial Trust is a not-for-profit organisation.

Type: Short-term/intercultural.
Stated mission: 'To provide for the benefit of the people of Cape Maclear (Malawi) a Medical Clinic; to provide education and support for the community of Cape Maclear; to provide for the relief of suffering and deprivation caused by the poor infrastructural amenities.'
Countries: Africa (Malawi).
Activities: Administration/management, construction, education, health/medical.
Duration: 3 months +.
Age requirements: Minimum 25 years.
Disability access: No.
Language requirements: Fluent English.
Educational/professional qualifications: Depends on placement. Professional medical qualifications are required for medical volunteers; administrative staff do not always require professional qualifications.
Other requirements: No.
Application procedure: Submit an application form, references from previous employers etc., followed by an interview.
Costs: Yes. Volunteers cover travel expenses and personal costs.
Benefits: Accommodation.
Work individually/in teams: In teams.

Code of Practice	Volunteer Charter	In-country support for volunteers	Pre-programme training	Post-programme debriefing	Contact with returned volunteers
Code of Practice operates within clinic.	No.	Yes; available full-time.	No, but applicants can be put in touch with previous volunteers.	Through written report and meeting with project director.	Yes.

Camara

Address: 15 Castleforbes Road, North Wall Quay, Dublin 1
Telephone number: +353 (0)1 681 1111
Fax number: +353 (0)1 681 1111
Email: kirsty@camara.ie
Website: www.camara.ie

Established in 2005, Camara is a not-for-profit organisation.

Type: Short-term/intercultural.
Stated mission: 'Camara has three main activities:
1 We take in second-hand computers that have been discarded by Irish organisations, refurbish them and send them to schools and colleges in Africa.
2 We send out groups of volunteers to train African teachers in basic computer literacy and more specialised technology areas.
3 We produce computer training materials, and educational multimedia content in areas such as HIV/AIDS.'
Countries: Africa (Ethiopia, Kenya, Uganda and Zambia).
Activities: Capacity building, education, technical support.
Duration: 4 weeks (in Africa), plus 50 hours' volunteering in Dublin.
Age requirements: Minimum 18 years.
Disability access: No.
Language requirements: Basic English is required, additional languages welcomed.
Educational/professional qualifications: No. All training required will be given at Camara, although if an applicant has some basic knowledge in computing or teaching experience it is a great bonus.
Other requirements: No.
Application process: Contact the organisation; two references are required; volunteer in Dublin for 50 hours; fundraise €1,500; attend the pre-trip training course.
Costs: Yes; volunteers must fundraise €1,500.
Benefits: Flights, accommodation, internal transport, insurance.
Work individually/in teams: In teams.

Code of Practice	Volunteer Charter	In-country support for volunteers	Pre-programme training	Post-programme debriefing	Contact with returned volunteers
Signatory to Comhlámh Code of Good Practice for Sending Organisations.	Supporters of the Comhlámh Volunteer Charter.	Yes, staff from the Dublin office accompany volunteers.	Yes, a two-day pre-departure training course is provided by Dtalk/Comhlámh.	Yes.	Yes, many returned volunteers are frequently in the workshop.

Chernobyl Children's Project International (CCPI)

Address: Ballycurreen Industrial Estate, Kinsale Road, Cork.
Telephone number: +353 (0)21 431 2999
Fax number: +353 (0)21 431 3170
Email: info@chernobyl-ireland.com
Website: www.chernobyl-ireland.com

Established in 1991, CCPI is a not-for-profit organisation.

Type: Short-term/intercultural.
Stated mission: 'The Chernobyl Children's Project International wishes to effect real change in the Chernobyl-affected areas harnessing the unique spirit of volunteerism that permeates every level of the organisation. We wish to develop, facilitate and effect long-term sustainable community-based solutions, providing effective principled humanitarian assistance while advocating for the rights of the victims and survivors of the Chernobyl Nuclear Disaster.'
Countries: Europe (Belarus, Russia)
Activities: Administration/management, children/young people, community development, construction, disability/special needs, health/medical, technical support, other.
Duration: 10 days to 3 months.
Age requirements: No.
Disability access: Depends on placement; contact organisation for further details.
Language requirements: No.
Educational/professional qualifications: Depends on placement. Areas in which qualifications and experience are welcomed include nursing, dentistry and construction.
Other requirements: Applicants are subject to character checks and clearance. Additionally, volunteers must be pro-active in meeting the needs of the beneficiaries and adapting flexibility in their own comforts/expectations.
Application procedure: References are required from all volunteers; applicants are also required to adhere to the CCPI's Contract and Code of Conduct for Volunteers.
Costs: Yes. Volunteers are requested to cover the costs of their trip. Assistance with fundraising may be available.
Benefits: Accommodation, food and travel costs
Work individually/in teams: Both.

Code of Practice	Volunteer Charter	In-country support for volunteers	Pre-programme training	Post-programme debriefing	Contact with returned volunteers
Signatory to Comhlámh Code of Good Practice for Sending Organisations.	Supporters of the Comhlámh Volunteer Charter.	Yes, available full-time.	Some pre-programme briefing is provided.	Project reports and feedback welcomed and encouraged.	Yes.

Columban Lay Missionaries

Address: St Columban's, Dalgan Park, Navan, Co. Meath
Telephone number: +353 (0)46 902 1525
Fax number: +353 (0)46 902 2799
Email: clmireland@yahoo.ie and columbanlm@oceanfree.net
Website: www.columban.com

Established in the late 1980s, the Columban Lay Mission Programme is a not-for-profit organisation.

Type: Long-term development
Stated mission: 'We are people of faith. An inter-cultural group of women and men, single, married and families, called to respond to God's mission by crossing boundaries of culture, gender, creed and race. We are sent as disciples of Jesus. With joy we witness to a new way of being church by finding and celebrating God's loving presence as we seek to live a simple way of life and journey with the poor and marginalized. In partnership with one another, with the ordained Columbans, and with local and home countries, and through mutual support and challenge, we strive to be catalysts of transformation in building God's reign.'
Countries: Asia (Fiji, Korea, Pakistan, Peru, Philippines, Taiwan), Latin America (Chile).
Activities: Agriculture, children/young people, community development, conservation/environment, disability/special needs, education, health/medical, human rights, women, others.
Duration: 3 years plus.
Age requirements: Minimum 23 years, maximum 40 years.
Disability access: No.
Language requirements: No. Volunteers spend the first 5–6 months overseas studying the local language.
Educational/professional qualifications: Yes. Secondary-level examinations and work experience.
Other requirements: Catholic, single or married couples, in good physical and psychological health, some experience or involvement in pastoral/social/community work. Willingness to live a simple way of life and work as a team and an openness to engage with other cultural and religious traditions.
Application procedure: Applicants need to be in contact with the Lay Mission Coordinator. Application to join the 6-month live-in Training Programme. In order to join the Training Programme the applicant is required to produce two references. They must also undergo a medical and psychological assessment and a formal interview.
Costs: No. However, applicants are encouraged to fundraise.
Benefits: Flights and travel costs, accommodation, food, small personal allowance.
Work individually/in teams: Both.

Code of Practice	Volunteer Charter	In-country support for volunteers	Pre-programme training	Post-programme debriefing	Contact with returned volunteers
Has Programme Policy Handbook.	No.	Yes, available full-time.	Includes 6-month live-in training programme.	Has post-return debriefing.	Yes.

EIL Intercultural Learning (Ireland)

Address: 1 Empress Place, Summerhill North, Cork
Telephone number: +353 (0)21 455 1535
Fax number: +353 (0)21 455 1587
Email: info@eilireland.org
Website: www.volunteerabroad.ie

Established in 1960, EIL Intercultural Learning in Ireland is a not-for-profit organisation.

Type: Short-term/intercultural.

Stated mission: EIL is a not for profit intercultural learning organisation dedicated to increasing equality and understanding between peoples and cultures across the world. EIL volunteers work and live alongside local people who are actively engaged in the fight against poverty, injustice and discrimination.

On their return to Ireland EIL asks volunteers to be the voice for the stories of the people they worked with and to highlight their experience of poverty and inequality through campaigning or by joining the EIL Development Education Network.

Countries: Africa (Morocco, Nigeria, South Africa), Asia (India, Nepal, Thailand), Latin America (Argentina, Bolivia, Brazil, Chile, Costa Rica, Ecuador, Guatemala, Mexico)

Activities: Community development, conservation/environment, education, health/medical, human rights, other. EIL also runs a Global Awareness Programme – a training, volunteering and awareness raising project focusing on HIV/AIDS.

Duration: 5 weeks to 11 months.

Age requirements: Minimum 18 years.

Disability access: Depends on project; further details available from organisation.

Language requirements: No. Programmes in Spanish-, Portuguese- and French-speaking countries include a language course in preparation for the volunteer placement.

Educational/professional qualifications: No, except for some health projects.

Other requirements: Volunteers should be independent-minded travellers, with the flexibility, initiative and maturity needed to volunteer in a developing country.

Application procedure: Completed application form with two referees, CV, two passport-sized photos and deposit of €250. This is followed by a telephone or face-to-face interview. Application forms available from the EIL office or website. Police checks may be necessary in certain cases.

Costs: Yes. Programme fees start from €1,195. Volunteers also cover travel costs. EIL also offer a number of fully and partially funded travel awards on an annual basis. Please see website for updates.

Benefits: Programmes include pre-departure workshop, information and support; airport pick-up and transfer; accommodation and food; language courses in Spanish-, Portuguese- or French-speaking countries; cultural orientation in-country; home stay element with local family; transportation to project; volunteer service placement; on-going support from local co-ordinator; medical, liability and travel insurance; support of the development education officer and the opportunity to join the EIL network on return to Ireland; debrief workshop and other volunteer network events.

Code of Practice	Volunteer Charter	In-country support for volunteers	Pre-programme training	Post-programme debriefing	Contact with returned volunteers
Signatory to Comhlámh Code of Good Practice for Sending Organisations.	Supporters of the Comhlámh Volunteer Charter.	Yes, 24-hour 7 days per week local support separate from host project.	Provides pre-departure workshops; country-specific pre-departure orientation materials; in-country cultural and language orientation.	EIL returned volunteers' network, debrief workshops and other informal events for returned volunteer.	EIL development network.

Friends of Africa

Address: 96 Glen Road, Newry, Co. Down, N. Ireland, BT34 1RH
Telephone numbers: +44 (0)48 3082 1224 and +44 (0)79 2336 1232
Email: info@friendsofafrica.org; info.friendsofafrica@gmail.com
Website: www.friendsofafrica.org

Established in 1998, Friends of Africa is a not-for-profit organisation.

Type: Short-term/intercultural.
Stated mission: 'Friends of Africa is an organisation whose mission is to manifest the goodwill and concern of its members and supporters into practical aid for Africa and its people. Through our shared history with the SMA, we benefit from over 150 years experience of working in Africa with those most in need. The main aims and objectives of the charity are:
• To be a voice for the people of Africa in our home countries.
• To fundraise for designated projects in Africa.
• To send volunteers to work in specific projects in Africa.'
Countries: Africa (South Africa, Zambia)
Activities: Children/young people, construction, education, health/medical.
Duration: Short-term programmes last 6 weeks; long-term projects are over 1 year.
Age requirements: Minimum 18 years.
Disability access: Not at present.
Language requirements: No. However, volunteers are expected to try to learn some of the local language.
Educational/professional qualifications: No, but it is preferable for long-term volunteers to have a trade or a degree behind them to suit the specific needs of the host country.
Other requirements: Volunteers must meet the training specifications that they are required to attend by Friends of Africa, before leaving Ireland for their placement.
Application procedure: Following the initial application form that the potential volunteer fills in, there are two interview sessions that take place during the year. There are interviews in October for both short- and long-term volunteering and at Easter for long-term volunteering. For both short- and long-term volunteering, the charity asks for two references.
Costs: Yes. Volunteers have to pay for travelling to their training. Short-term volunteers pay £750 to cover flights, accommodation and insurance.
Benefits: Accommodation, food, ongoing support.
Work individually/in teams: Both, depending on project.

Code of Practice	Volunteer Charter	In-country support for volunteers	Pre-programme training	Post-programme debriefing	Contact with returned volunteers
Signatory to Comhlámh's Code of Good Practice for Sending Organisations.	Supporters of Comhlámh's Volunteer Charter	Yes, a contact person is available full-time.	Yes, long-term volunteers do Dtalk training; short-term volunteers have training covering topics including health, stress management and intercultural issues.	Yes.	Yes, strongly supports returned volunteers being available for discussion with new volunteers.

Friends of Londiani, Ireland

Address: 9 Cois Cuain, Mosestown, Whitegate, Co. Cork
Telephone number: +353 (0)21 466 2730
Email: info@friendsoflondiani.com
Website: www.friendsoflondiani.com

Established in 2002, Friends of Londiani, Ireland is a not-for-profit organisation.

Type: Short-term/intercultural.
Stated mission: 'The mission of Friends of Londiani is to work in partnership with the people of Londiani and its surrounding villages to develop and complete sustainable community projects to enable and empower the people to achieve an improved quality of life based on their values and become the authors of their own development. The Friends of Londiani will endeavour to achieve these goals in a spirit of co-operation and mutual respect with one another and with the people of the area. This partnership will enable members of Friends of Londiani to further develop skills and a deeper cultural understanding.'
Countries: Africa (Kenya)
Activities: Community development, construction, education, health/medical, other.
Duration: 3–9 weeks.
Age requirements: Minimum 18 years.
Disability access: Depends on placement; contact organisation for further details.
Language requirements: English.
Educational/professional qualifications: No.
Other requirements: Volunteers must be willing to work on a team, attend the training weekends and debriefing/evaluation weekend.
Application procedure: Contact organisation for an application form; two references are requested with the form. There is a non-refundable deposit to be paid, and all applicants are interviewed.
Costs: Yes; from €1,650.
Benefits: Flights, food, accommodation, training, project support
Work individually/in teams: In teams.

Code of Practice	Volunteer Charter	In-country support for volunteers	Pre-programme training	Post-programme debriefing	Contact with returned volunteers
Signatory to Comhlámh Code of Good Practice for Sending Organisations.	Supporters of the Comhlámh Volunteer Charter.	Yes, available full-time.	Training on projects is provided pre-departure.	Has evaluation and debriefing weekend.	Yes.

GOAL

Address: PO Box 19, Dun Laoghaire, Co. Dublin
Telephone number: +353 (0)1 280 9779
Fax number: +353 (0)1 280 9215
Email: applications@goal.ie
Website: www.goal.ie

Established in 1977, GOAL is a not-for-profit organisation.

Type: Relief/emergency; long-term development.
Stated mission: 'To work towards ensuring that those poorest and most vulnerable in our world and/or affected by humanitarian crisis have access to the fundamental needs and rights of life, for example, food, water, shelter, medical attention and literacy. GOAL is an international humanitarian organisation dedicated to the alleviation of suffering amongst the poorest of the poor. It is non-governmental, non-denominational and non-political'
Countries: Africa (DR Congo, Ethiopia, Kenya, Malawi, Sierra Leone, Sudan, Uganda, Zimbabwe), Asia (India, Sri Lanka), Latin America (Honduras).
Activities: Administration/management, capacity building, children/young people, construction, education, health/medical, technical support, other.
Duration: Minimum of 1 year. May be shorter for emergency situations.
Age requirements: Minimum 23 years, no maximum.
Disability access: Depends on placement; contact office for further information.
Language requirements: Depends on placement, e.g. a working knowledge of French is required for the DR Congo.
Educational/professional qualifications: Yes. Volunteers must have two years' relevant post-qualification experience for overseas work. Areas of expertise include: doctors, midwives, nurses, social workers, engineers, accountants, project managers, logisticians, administrators, and mechanics (not an exhaustive list).
Other requirements: No.
Application procedure: Interested candidates should contact the organisation by phone or send their CV by email to applications@goal.ie.
Costs: No.
Benefits: Pre-departure medicals; dental check-up; annual return flight to field location; food and accommodation; annual holiday allowance; local 'live' allowance; post-exposure medicals; accident, illness and medical insurance and insurance for medical evacuation; and a re-settlement grant.
Work individually/in teams: Both.

Code of Practice	Volunteer Charter	In-country support for volunteers	Pre-programme training	Post-programme debriefing	Contact with returned volunteers
Signatory to Comhlámh Code of Good Practice for Sending Organisations.	Supporters of the Comhlámh Volunteer Charter.	Yes, available full-time.	In the areas of orientation, programme management, security, logistics and finance.	Yes, at the end of contract.	Yes.

Habitat for Humanity Ireland

Address: Quadrant House, Chapelizod, Dublin 20
Telephone numbers: +353 (0)1 629 9650; (0)1 629 9611
Fax number: +353 (0)1 629 9648
Email: globalvillage@habitatireland.ie
Website: www.habitatireland.ie

A not-for-profit organisation, Habitat for Humanity International was established in 1976; Habitat for Humanity Ireland was launched in 2002.

Type: Short-term/intercultural.
Stated mission: 'Habitat for Humanity seeks to eliminate poverty housing and homelessness from the world, and to make decent shelter a matter of conscience and action by building simple, decent, affordable homes in partnership with people in need. Through Habitat for Humanity's Global Village programme, teams of volunteers become active partners with host communities worldwide, helping to build a "global village" of homes, communities and hope.'
Countries: Africa (Ghana, Madagascar, Malawi, Uganda, Zambia), Asia (India, Philippines), Latin America (Chile, Costa Rica, Ecuador, Mexico, El Salvador).
Activities: Construction.
Duration: 1–3 weeks; longer individual placements may be available through other branches of the organisation.
Age requirements: Minimum 18 years; students who are part of a sponsoring school/organisation may be 16 years.
Disability access: Depends on placement; contact organisation for further details.
Language requirements: No. Language skills are an advantage, but not a requirement.
Educational/professional qualifications: No.
Other requirements: No. Habitat for Humanity is a faith-based organisation (Christian, not identified with any particular denomination), although volunteers and homeowners are from all and no faith backgrounds. Volunteers travel in teams of ten to thirty people from Ireland.
Application procedure: Open registration teams are announced in November/December for the following year. Interested people should submit an application form available from the office, and team members will be interviewed and selected at the discretion of the Team Leader. Any organisation (school, church, community group, company) wishing to organise a team should contact the office.
Costs: Yes. From €1,700. Volunteers are encouraged to do fundraising for their experience, and give a donation to the project they are visiting.
Benefits: Travel, accommodation, meals, in-country transport, cultural activities and R&R activities.
Work individually/in teams: In teams.

Code of Practice	Volunteer Charter	In-country support for volunteers	Pre-programme training	Post-programme debriefing	Contact with returned volunteers
Signatory to Comhlámh Code of Good Practice for Sending Organisations; also has 'Minimum Standards for Work Teams' documents.	Supporters of the Comhlámh Volunteer Charter.	Yes, available full-time.	Team leaders complete training on topics including leadership, cross-cultural relations, and debriefing.	Provided by team leaders.	Yes.

Health Action Overseas (HAO)

Address: Carmichael House, North Brunswick Street, Dublin 7
Telephone number: +353 (0)1 873 3173
Fax number: +353 (0)1 873 3006
Email: hao@iol.ie
Website: www.hao.ie

Established in 1991, HAO is a not-for-profit organisation

Type: Long-term development
Stated mission: 'The mission of HAO is to facilitate community service development for people with disabilities. HAO believes in working in partnership with authorities in host countries and the community and supports a rights-based approach to disability service provision. We are committed to the social model of disability, which places a person's disability in the context of disabling barriers to their participation in society.'
Countries: Asia (China), Europe (Macedonia, Romania)
Activities: Administration/management, capacity building, community development, disability/special needs, education and technical support.
Duration: 3 weeks to 1 year.
Age requirements: No.
Disability access: Varies depending on the host country.
Language requirements: No.
Educational/professional qualifications: Yes. Trained social workers; therapists (occupational/physio/speech and language); special needs teachers; managers in the disability sector.
Other requirements: No.
Application procedure: CV, interview, references, medical, Garda clearance.
Costs: No.
Benefits: Vaccinations before departure, airfares, settling-in allowance, monthly living allowance, contribution to utility bills, living allowance, insurance, medical check at end of assignment, resettlement allowance.
Work individually/ in teams: Both.

Code of Practice	Volunteer Charter	In-country support for volunteers	Pre-programme training	Post-programme debriefing	Contact with returned volunteers
Signatory to Comhlámh Code of Good Practice for Sending Organisations; also to the People in Aid Code of Good Practice.	Supporters of the Comhlámh Volunteer Charter and Volunteering Ireland Volunteers' Charter.	Varies depending on the placement.	Pre-departure training through Irish Aid.	Discussion covering the project, sending organisation and personal experiences.	Yes.

The Hope Foundation

Address: 3 Clover Lawn, Skehard Road, Cork
Telephone number: +353 (0)21 429 2990
Fax number: +353 (0)21 429 3432
Email: office@hopefoundation.ie
Website: www.hopefoundation.ie

Established in 1999, the Hope Foundation is a not-for-profit organisation.

Type: Long-term development.
Stated mission: 'The holistic care and development of severely underprivileged children/persons in India.'
Countries: Asia (India)
Activities: Administration/management, children/young people, community development, education, health/medical, women.
Duration: 3 months to 2 years.
Age requirements: Over 21 years.
Disability access: Contact organisation for further details.
Language requirements: Willingness to learn some Bengali.
Educational/professional qualifications: Yes, depending on post. For healthcare positions, qualified nurses and doctors are required. Primary level teaching qualifications and TEFL are required for educational positions, people with accountancy experience are required for administrative positions, etc. Other skills required include: counselling through art and drama, drug rehab, vocational training skills.
Other requirements: Volunteers are asked to do some fundraising to cover expenses and donate to HOPE's projects.
Application procedure: Submission of CV and cover letter outlining potential role. Completion of volunteer application form, followed by an interview with the directors. If accepted, volunteers are asked to attend a preparatory training course (1 week, Dtalk, Dublin).
Costs: Yes. Volunteers cover own travel arrangements, vaccinations, insurance.
Benefits: Bed and board, small living allowance for longer term volunteers.
Work individually/in teams: In teams, with HOPE staff, Indian partners and other volunteers.

Code of Practice	Volunteer Charter	In-country support for volunteers	Pre-programme training	Post-programme debriefing	Contact with returned volunteers
Signatory to Comhlámh Code of Good Practice for Sending Organisations.	Supporters of the Comhlámh Volunteer Charter.	Yes, available full-time.	Volunteers are sent on a Dtalk Initial Preparation training course for 1 week.	Volunteers are asked to provide a report on their findings and experiences and to meet with HOPE staff in Ireland to discuss same after their return.	Yes.

hopeXchange

Address (Ireland): 8 The Drive, Millbrook Lawns, Tallaght, Dublin 24
International Headquarters: Via Della Stazione Aurelia 95, 00165 Roma, Italy.
Telephone numbers: +353 (0)85 733 0191; +39 (0)66 651 2891
Fax number: +39 (0)66 651 2894
Email: info@hopeXchange.net
Website: www.hopeXchange.net

Established in 1985, hopeXchange is a not-for-profit organisation.

Type: Short-term/intercultural.

Stated mission: 'hopeXchange is an international Catholic humanitarian aid organisation dedicated to the integral development of people, and the fostering of charity and justice in the world. The means we use to achieve our goals are primarily those of education, healthcare and sustainable development, so that our efforts can contribute towards reducing poverty in a world of great need, while at the same time empowering the weak and oppressed to become agents of change. The inspiration for our work is drawn from the love of God and the social teaching of the Church which promotes the values of human dignity, stewardship and the integrity of creation. Throughout the year hopeXchange trains and mobilises teams for long and short-term missions worldwide. Our short-term projects are called Mission:Possible programmes.'

Countries: Africa (Ghana), Asia (India, Philippines), Europe (Albania).

Activities: Children/young people, construction, disability/special needs, education, health/medical, technical support.

Duration: 1–4 months, with the possibility of extension.

Age requirements: 18–75 years (and in good health).

Disability access: No

Language requirements: Basic spoken level of English is needed for all projects.

Educational/professional qualifications: No. However, hopeXchange aims to incorporate any skill or professional qualification a volunteer may have in the pre-project planning process.

Other requirements: hopeXchange is a Christian organisation, with a spiritual dimension to its work.

Application procedure: Applicants must complete an application form; and submit a copy of the main page of their passport, two references of professional or similar status, and a letter from a doctor giving a clean bill of health. Volunteers may need vaccinations depending on the country they volunteer for.

Costs: Yes; charge of €300 to cover board and lodging. Volunteers also cover travel expenses, necessary insurance cover and immunisation costs.

Benefits: Board and lodging.

Work individually/in teams: In teams; all volunteers work alongside professional staff.

Code of Practice	Volunteer Charter	In-country support for volunteers	Pre-programme training	Post-programme debriefing	Contact with returned volunteers
Signatory to Comhlámh Code of Good Practice for Sending Organisations.	Supporters of the Comhlámh Volunteer Charter.	Yes, full-time support.	Takes place in host country and includes orientation, intercultural learning, detailed planning of activities and information.	Ongoing debriefing throughout project; debriefing workshop in placement country.	Yes, provides unmediated access to former volunteers before their departure.

International Service Ireland (ISI)

Address: Office 16, Carmichael Centre, North Brunswick Street, Dublin 7
Telephone numbers: +353 (0)86 173 2347; (0)1 874 6007
Email: internationalserviceireland@eircom.net
Website: www.is-ireland.ie

International Service was established in 1953; International Service Ireland was set up in 2003. It is a not-for-profit organisation.

Type: Long-term development
Stated mission: 'Vision: We envisage a world where poverty and oppression are history. Mission: Our basic tenet is "Partners Against Poverty" and we see our role as combating poverty and oppression by strengthening the organisational development of the poorest groups in our countries of operation. Our mission is also to increase global understanding of development issues. Thematic priorities include sustainable livelihoods, disability and development, human rights, reproductive and sexual health. Target groups are women, disabled people, children and adolescents.'
Countries: Africa (Burkina Faso, Mali), Asia (Palestine), Latin America (Bolivia, Brazil).
Activities: Administration/management, capacity building, children/young people, community development, disability/special needs, education, health/medical, human rights, technical support, women, other.

International Service Ireland (ISI)

Ready for a new life-changing experience?
Willing to spend up to 2 years abroad?
Have you skills to help local organizations in developing countries?

If you have experience and skills in community development, capacity building, or working children/young people and those with special needs then give us a call! IS Ireland currently works in Latin America, West Africa and Palestine. For more information contact:

International Service Ireland (ISI)
Carmichael Centre, North Brunswick Street, Dublin 7.
Tel: 00353-1-8746007
E-mail: internationalserviceireland@eircom.net
Web: www.is-ireland.ie

Duration: 2 years, with some shorter-term placements also available.

Age requirements: 24–65 years.

Disability access: Depends on placement; contact organisation for further details.

Language requirements: No; language training is provided as necessary.

Educational/professional qualifications: Yes, relevant professional qualification and 2–3 years post-qualification experience.

Other requirements: No.

Application procedure: Jobs are posted on website or advertised on relevant jobsites/papers; applicants apply electronically or by post for a particular post on an application form (downloadable from website or posted on request). If pre-selected, applicants are invited to a two-day selection meeting (travel costs and accommodation paid) comprising a series of individual and group activities. Applicants are asked for two reference contacts on application and if appropriate, references will be requested from these contacts at this point. Depending on the result of selection meeting, candidates may be offered the post, kept on file for more suitable post, or rejected.

Costs: No.

Benefits: Travel costs to and from placements, a small settling in grant, accommodation, training, a living allowance, and a resettlement grant.

Work individually/in teams: In teams, with colleagues from the local organisation.

Code of Practice	Volunteer Charter	In-country support for volunteers	Pre-programme training	Post-programme debriefing	Contact with returned volunteers
Signatory to Comhlámh Code of Good Practice for Sending Organisations; has achieved 'Investors in People' accreditation and has internal staff policies.	Supporters of the Comhlámh Volunteer Charter; policies for development workers are outlined in handbook.	Yes, available full-time from field offices.	A one-week preparation course in the UK or Ireland; up to one-month in-country introductory programme.	Through face-to-face debriefing interview, and/or phone, postal contact.	Yes, when possible.

i-to-i International Voluntary Work and TEFL Training

Address: Exploration House, Grattan Square, Dungarvan, Co. Waterford
Telephone number: +353 (0)5 840050
Fax number: +353 (0)5 840059
Email: ireland@i-to-i.com
Website: www.i-to-i.com

Established in 1993, i-to-i is a for-profit organisation.

Type: Short-term/intercultural.
Stated mission: 'Since 1994, i-to-i has been driven by the inspiration of making worthwhile travel experiences widely available through opportunities to volunteer and work abroad. This began with a Teaching English as a Foreign Language (TEFL) course designed to give English-speaking travellers certification to help them find work teaching English overseas, and training to teach the language well to people who can gain by it. Since then, i-to-i has grown into a leading specialist in international volunteer projects which have two key aims: (a) to allow people of all ages and from all backgrounds to give something back by contributing to worthwhile projects during their travels; (b) to provide local projects around the world with a consistent supply of trained and committed volunteer workers who work towards their own goals.'
Countries: Africa (Ghana, Kenya, South Africa, Tanzania), Asia (China, India, Indonesia, Nepal, South Korea, Sri Lanka, Thailand, Vietnam), Latin America (Bolivia, Brazil, Costa Rica, Dominican Republic, Ecuador, Guatemala, Honduras, Mexico, Peru).
Activities: Business, children/young people, community development, conservation/environment, construction, education, health/medical, other.
Duration: 1 week to 1 year.
Age requirements: Minimum 17 years, maximum 70 years.
Disability access: Depends on placement; contact the organisation for further details.
Language requirements: Depends on the project. For example, it is better for volunteers in Latin American countries to have Spanish. For teaching/community development projects it is necessary for volunteers to have fluent English.
Educational/professional qualifications: No, except for work experience placements, where these will help the volunteer to get more responsibility.
Other requirements: No children, due to age restrictions.
Application procedure: Volunteers apply by filling out an application form with contact details, after which they receive a telephone interview and a 'welcome call'. They receive an information pack and a second application form (referees, education, qualifications, work experience, volunteering experience, letter of reference, medical history). They fill out another application form with flight details, and are given information on the country, project, inoculations, etc. They get a final 'Bon Voyage' call.

Costs: Yes; depends on country, demand and length of time. Volunteers also cover travel costs; i-to-i provides fundraising support and advice.

Benefits: Organisation of entire programme from Ireland, food, accommodation, insurance, orientation, airport pick-up, safety network in country.

Code of Practice	Volunteer Charter	In-country support for volunteers	Pre-programme training	Post-programme debriefing	Contact with returned volunteers
Signatory to Comhlámh Code of Good Practice for Sending Organisations; founder member of Year Out Group.	Supporters of the Comhlámh Volunteer Charter.	Yes, 1–3 full-time contact people in each country; 24-hour emergency contact in home country.	Safety advice, cultural training, country briefing CD, information on the project. TEFL teaching courses for some projects.	Feedback from project co-ordinators; volunteers complete questionnaires.	Yes.

Léargas – Youth Work Service

Address: 189/193 Parnell Street, Dublin 1
Telephone number: +353 (0)1 873 1411
Fax number: +353 (0)1 873 1316
Email: cdarcy@leargas.ie
Website: www.leargas.ie/youth and
http://ec.europa.eu/youth/program/sos/hei/hei_en.cfm
(search database to identify approved hosting organisations)

Established in the early 1990s, Léargas is a not-for-profit organisation.

Type: Short-term/intercultural.
Stated mission: 'To make an ongoing contribution to Ireland's capacity to provide innovative responses to the developing needs of our citizens in an increasingly interdependent world by: (a) educating, developing and broadening the perspectives of Irish young people and those that work with them by exposing them to international and bilateral cooperation programmes; (b) contributing to innovation in formal and informal education and vocational training policy and systems through involvement in these programmes.'
Countries: Africa (Algeria, Egypt, Morocco, Tunisia), Asia (Israel, Jordan, Lebanon, Morocco, Syria, Turkey, West Bank/Gaza Strip) and Europe (Albania, Armenia, Azerbaijan, Belarus, Bosnia Herzegovina, Bulgaria, Croatia, all EU countries, Georgia, Macedonia (FYROM), Moldova, Russia, Ukraine, former Yugoslavia,

Romania, Serbia and Montenegro). It is also possible to apply for volunteering projects in most other countries of the world but there is a separate application process that applies in these cases. Please contact Léargas for more information about this.

Activities: Children/young people, community development, conservation/ environment, disability/special needs, education, other.

Duration: 2–12 months (shorter periods (2 weeks–2 months) are also possible for group volunteering opportunities and for young people with fewer opportunities).

Age requirements: Minimum 18 years (volunteers aged 16–17 can also participate in special circumstances), maximum 30 years.

Disability access: Depends on the hosting placement; contact potential hosting organisations directly for further details.

Language requirements: Basic knowledge of language of host country may be required but this is not necessarily a prerequisite.

Educational/professional qualifications: No.

Other requirements: No.

Application procedure: A volunteer can search the project database (see above), by theme and by country, to find a list of all approved hosting projects. Direct contact between the volunteer and hosting project must then be made to determine if there is a vacancy in the organisation within the appropriate time frame. Volunteers must also find a sending organisation to support them during the project. Applications must be submitted to the national agency (i.e. Léargas in Ireland or another national agency in partner country) for consideration by one of the five annual deadlines (1 February, 1 April, 1 June, 1 September, 1 November) and, if approved, the volunteering placement can start 3 months afterwards.

Costs: No.

Benefits: Some preparation costs, travel, food, accommodation, some pocket money.

Work individually/in teams: Both.

Code of Practice	Volunteer Charter	In-country support for volunteers	Pre-programme training	Post-programme debriefing	Contact with returned volunteers
Yes, contact the organisation for details.	Yes, contact the organisation for details.	Yes, available full-time.	A one-day training course for groups of 4+; encourages sending organisations to provide pre-departure preparation.	Generally takes place through sending organisations; evaluation event for former volunteers will take place.	Yes, when possible.

Link Community Development

Address: 23 Crofton Road, Dun Laoghaire, Co. Dublin
Telephone number: +353 (0)1 284 1414
Email: info@lcd.ie
Website: www.lcd.ie

Established in the UK in 1989 and in Ireland 2006, LCD is a not-for-profit organisation.

Type: Short-term/intercultural.
Stated mission: 'LCD's vision is of a future where children are given a chance to flourish and fulfil their potential. LCD aims:
- to improve schools and the quality of education they deliver so that children and their communities have better opportunities;
- to build the capacity of district departments of education so that they can better meet the needs of their schools and communities;
- to support government education policy by using lessons learned at the grassroots level to inform national and regional strategies;
- to facilitate partnerships between European and African education sectors for mutually beneficial development and learning.'

Countries: Africa (Uganda).
Activities: Children/young people, education.
Duration: 5 weeks; placements in Africa last approximately 5 weeks, but are part of a 15-month programme, which includes preparatory activities pre-departure and follow-up activities on return home.
Age requirements: There is no specific age limit but teachers should have four years' work experience and also be set to continue working in their own school for at least one year after return home.

Link Community Development – Global Teachers

Want to do something completely different next summer?

Link Community Development invites applications from Irish primary school principals and teachers to take part in its Global Teachers Programme.

Link is an international education-focused development organisation working in Ethiopia, Ghana, Malawi, South Africa and Uganda towards improving education for children, giving them the chance to escape the poverty into which they have been born. In addition to its work in Africa, Link runs programmes in Ireland that have a development education focus.

The Global Teachers Programme is a programme for experienced school principals and teachers, centred around a five-week placement in a primary school in Africa in July/August. The programme aims to help teachers become better development educators, and also develops their leadership, management and training skills.

This programme receives support from Irish Aid. For more information and an application pack, email info@lcd.ie or call 01 2841414. www.lcd.ie

CHY No. 17232

Disability access: Contact the organisation for further information.

Language requirements: Fluent English.

Educational/professional qualifications: Qualified primary school teachers with four years' teaching experience. Applications from candidates with less teaching experience may be considered.

Other requirements: No.

Application procedure: An application form and information pack is available from Link Community Development. Two references are required, one of which should be from the candidate's principal (or chairperson of the school's Board of Management if the candidate is the principal). Successful candidates are selected from a shortlist called for interview/selection day.

Costs: Yes. A fee of €1,500 is payable for participation in the programme. Volunteers are encouraged to undertake fundraising in excess of this amount.

Benefits: Pre-placement residential training weekends; return flight; full briefing, covering health, safety and security; food and accommodation with hosts in the local community; support throughout the placement; comprehensive travel insurance.

Work individually/in teams: Individually, but opportunities are provided to meet with other volunteers on the programme.

Code of Practice	Volunteer Charter	In-country support for volunteers	Pre-programme training	Post-programme debriefing	Contact with returned volunteers
Signatory to Comhlámh Code of Good Practice for Sending Organisations.	Supporters of the Comhlámh Volunteer Charter.	Yes, ongoing support is provided throughout the trip from dedicated LCD staff in-country.	Yes, two residential pre-placement training weekends; in-country induction course.	Yes, post-placement training weekend that focuses on follow-up, and a reunion weekend.	Yes.

Médecins Sans Frontières (MSF)

Address: 71 Amiens Street, Dublin 1
Telephone number: +353 (0)1 806 9804
Fax number: +353 (0)1 855 9532
Email: office.dublin@dublin.msf.org
Website: www.msf.ie

Established in 1971, MSF is a not-for-profit organisation.

Type: Relief/emergency
Stated mission: 'Médecins Sans Frontières is a leading non-governmental organisation for emergency medical aid. We provide independent medical relief to victims of war, disasters and epidemics in over 80 countries around the world. We strive to provide assistance to those who need it most, regardless of ethnic origin, religion or political affiliation. MSF insists on exercising its responsibility to speak out when it sees that those that we are trying to help are being abused. MSF is a voluntary organisation. Each year, about 2,500 doctors, nurses, logistics specialists and engineers from around the world leave on field assignments. They work closely with thousands of national staff.'
Countries: Africa, Asia, Europe, Latin America (various).
Activities: Administration/management, capacity building, construction, health/medical, human rights, technical support, other.

Duration: 6–9 months (depending on experience and role).

Age requirements: 25 years plus, due to requirement for previous professional experience.

Language requirements: English. Fluency in French, Spanish, Portuguese, Arabic or Russian is an advantage.

Educational/professional qualifications: Yes. Contact organisation for details of qualifications required for doctors, surgeons, anaesthetists, biomedical scientists, midwives, mental health professionals, nurses, logistical and technical experts, nutritionists and epidemiologists. A minimum of two years' post-qualification experience needed.

Other requirements: Proven ability to train others and the ability to organise yourself and others; ability to work in a team and to manage/supervise staff; ability to cope with stress; minimum of three months travelling and/or work experience in a developing country.

Application procedure: Initial enquiry; application form and CV submission; screening process; if successful, interview in Dublin; two good references; statutory declaration; then matching to a project.

Costs: No. However, potential volunteers must cover the cost of travel to interview.

Benefits: Return ticket, monthly allowance, living and accommodation costs, transport in project country, insurance and cost of vaccinations.

Work individually/in teams: In teams.

Code of Practice	Volunteer Charter	In-country support for volunteers	Pre-programme training	Post-programme debriefing	Contact with returned volunteers
		Yes, available full-time.	Week-long 'Preparation Primary Departure Course' covering organisational, technical and teamwork topics.	Includes field evaluations, debriefing at MSF operational centre, debriefing in UK.	Yes.

Medical Missionaries of Mary

Address: 'Rosemount', Booterstown Avenue, Blackrock, Co. Dublin
Telephone number: +353 (0)1 288 2722
Fax number: +353 (0)1 283 4626
Email: usharpe@indigo.ie
Website: www.mmmworldwide.org

Established in 1937, Medical Missionaries of Mary is a not-for-profit organisation.

Type: Long-term development.
Stated mission: 'As Medical Missionaries of Mary, in a world deeply and violently divided, we are women on fire with the healing love of God. Engaging our own pain and vulnerability, we go to peoples of different cultures, where human needs are greatest. Our belief in the inter-relatedness of God's creation urges us to embrace holistic healing and to work for reconciliation, justice and peace.'
Countries: Africa (Angola, Benin, Ethiopia, Kenya, Malawi, Nigeria, Rwanda, Tanzania, Uganda), Latin America (Brazil, Honduras)
Activities: Administration/management, agriculture, business, capacity building, children/young people, community development, health/medical, human rights, women, other.
Duration: 2 years (negotiable).
Age requirements: Minimum 24 years.
Disability access: Depends on placement; contact organisation for further details.
Language requirements: Depends on placement, e.g., French is required for francophone countries.
Educational/professional qualifications: Yes. Professional qualifications should be in the medical, social welfare, community development, agriculture, financial or administration/management fields.
Other requirements: Sound physical and mental health.
Application procedure: Apply with a CV and two named referees. After an interview, the applicant's CV is circulated to the MMM's country programmes to find a suitable placement.
Costs: No.
Benefits: Travel costs, accommodation and allowance.
Work individually/in teams: In teams.

Code of Practice	Volunteer Charter	In-country support for volunteers	Pre-programme training	Post-programme debriefing	Contact with returned volunteers
Signatory to Comhlámh Code of Good Practice for Sending Organisations.	Supporters of the Comhlámh Volunteer Charter.	Yes, available part-time.	Yes, new training schedule is in development.	Individual meeting with returned volunteers; volunteers are encouraged to avail of Irish Aid services.	Yes.

Niall Mellon Township Trust

Address: Taylors Three Rock, Grange Road, Rathfarnham, Dublin 16, Ireland
Telephone number: +353 (0)1 494 8200
Fax number: +353 (0)1 494 8250
Email: info@irishtownship.com
Website: www.irishtownship.com

Established in 2003, Niall Mellon Township Trust is a not-for-profit organisation.

Stated mission: 'Our mission is to build sustainable communities. We aim to improve the quality of life for disadvantaged people living in the townships of South Africa by replacing shacks with decent low cost housing and providing community facilities. We aim to increase the spirit of volunteerism and philanthropy in Ireland.'
Countries: Africa (South Africa).
Activities: Construction.
Duration: One week; in special circumstances, longer placements can be arranged.
Age requirements: Minimum of 18 years, maximum of 65 years.
Disability access: No.
Language requirements: English.
Educational/professional qualifications: No.
Other requirements: 80% of volunteers must be from the construction industry, while 20% are non-trade.
Application procedure: Complete an application form and submit a medical certificate.
Costs: Yes, programme costs start from €5,000.
Benefits: Flights; accommodation; breakfast, lunch and water during the day.
Work individually/in teams: In teams of 70 to 100.

Code of Practice	Volunteer Charter	In-country support for volunteers	Pre-programme training	Post-programme debriefing	Contact with returned volunteers
Signatory to Comhlámh Code of Good Practice for Sending Organisations	Supporters of the Comhlámh Volunteer Charter.	Yes, available full-time.	No.	No.	Yes.

Progressio Ireland

Address: c/o CORI, Bloomfield Avenue, Donnybrook, Dublin 4
Telephone number: +353 (0)1 614 4966
Email: progressio@eircom.net
Website: www.progressio.ie

Progressio Ireland was established in 2004 as a not-for-profit organisation.

Type: Long-term development
Stated mission: 'Progressio Ireland is an independent charity, with strong roots and stakeholders amongst radical Christians. It works with people of any religious belief or none to overcome poverty and injustice internationally. Progressio Ireland is committed to the pursuit of development based on democratic political and economic participation, social justice and gender equality. Whether through placing development workers overseas, or in our policy and advocacy achievements, Progressio Ireland has a track record of making a difference. We work with people of all faiths and none.'
Countries: Africa (Malawi, Somaliland, Zimbabwe), Asia (East Timor, Yemen), Latin America (Dominican Republic, Ecuador, El Salvador, Honduras, Nicaragua, Peru).
Activities: Administration/management, agriculture, business, capacity building, community development, education, health/medical, technical support.
Duration: 1 year plus.
Age requirements: No.
Disability access: Depends on placement; contact organisation for further details.
Language requirements: Depends on placement. Spanish is required for placements in Latin America, Arabic is essential for posts in Yemen, Somali is desirable for posts in Somaliland, and Tetum, Bahasa Indonesia and Portuguese are desirable for posts in East Timor. Language training is provided.
Educational/professional qualifications: Yes. Volunteers tend to have relevant degrees or qualifications.
Other requirements: Progressio does not recruit candidates who are nationals of the country of posting.
Application procedure: Posts are advertised on website. The applicant can download an application form and email it – CVs are not considered. Only shortlisted candidates are contacted. Candidates may travel to Progressio's country offices for interviews. References are checked after a provisional offer is made.
Costs: No.
Benefits: Pre-departure grant, travel costs, salary, accommodation, insurance cover.
Work individually/in teams: In teams.

Code of Practice	Volunteer Charter	In-country support for volunteers	Pre-programme training	Post-programme debriefing	Contact with returned volunteers
Contact organisation for details.	Contact organisation for details.	Yes, available on a full-time basis.	Ye, topics include gender training, HIV training, briefings about the country and the project/partners, information about Progressio.	Yes.	Yes.

Raleigh Ireland/Raleigh International Youth Development

Address: 20 Faughart Terrace, St Mary's Road, Dundalk, Co. Louth
Telephone number: +353 (0)85 725 3444
Email: info@raleighireland.org
Website: www.raleighireland.org and www.raleighinternational.org

A not-for-profit organisation, Raleigh International was established in the UK in 1978 and Raleigh Ireland was established in 2002.

Type: Short-term/intercultural.
Stated mission: 'Raleigh International, Ireland aims to: inspire young people from different nationalities and backgrounds to discover their full potential by working together on challenging and sustainable community, environmental and adventure projects around the world.'
Countries: Africa (Namibia), Asia (Malaysia), Latin America (Costa Rica/Nicaragua).
Activities: Community development, conservation/environment, construction, other.
Duration: 2/3 weeks – 10 weeks.
Age requirements: Volunteers must be between the ages of 17 and 25 and volunteer staff members aged 25+.
Disability access: Yes, check with organisation beforehand.
Language requirements: Basic understanding of English.
Educational/professional qualifications: No, but participants with various skills such as medical, construction etc. are always needed.
Other requirements: No.
Application procedure: An application is made to Raleigh International. There are no references needed, just general information. International volunteers are then given the option of participating in an introductory weekend in the UK or having a telephone conversation with a member of Raleigh HQ staff. Volunteers choose their expedition country and begin fundraising.
Costs: Yes. Volunteers are asked to fundraise a minimum of: 10 weeks €4,413; 7 weeks €3,315; 5 weeks €2,579; 4 weeks €2,210. Contact Raleigh International for updated fundraising targets.
Benefits: Food and accommodation, travel and emergency medical insurance, specialist equipment, in-country transport, training.
Work individually/in teams: In teams.

Code of Practice	Volunteer Charter	In-country support for volunteers	Pre-programme training	Post-programme debriefing	Contact with returned volunteers
Signatory to Comhlámh Code of Good Practice for Sending Organisations.	Supporters of the Comhlámh Volunteer Charter.	Yes. generally available full-time.	Optional introductory weekend in the UK; week-long in-country team work and skills training.	Volunteers are provided with an individual and overall project assessment.	Yes.

SERVE

Address: Cork Office: SERVE Volunteer Office, Enterprise Centre, Bessboro, Blackrock, Cork; Dublin Office: SERVE, Marianella, 75 Orwell Road, Rathgar, Dublin 6
Telephone numbers: +353 (0)21 461 4688; (0)1 643 4601; (0)87 232 0295
Fax number: +353 (0)1 492 9635
Email: info@serve.ie; david@serve.ie; gerry.oc@oceanfree.net
Website: www.serve.ie

Established in 2002, SERVE is a not-for-profit organisation.

Type: Short-term/intercultural.
Stated mission: 'SERVE is an initiative committed to tackling world poverty. In particular SERVE strives to combat both youth poverty and pro-actively unleash, nurture and retain youth capacity. Working in partnership with young Irish adults, the Irish Redemptorists and marginalised communities in the developing world, SERVE aims to support development projects that work to transform the lives of those who are poor and to overcome acute injustices. SERVE achieves this by: volunteering projects in Ireland, Brazil, India, the Philippines, Thailand, South Africa, Zimbabwe and Mozambique; fostering global citizenship by opening opportunities for volunteers from developing countries to participate in service

Development Volunteering Programme
To:
Brazil, the Philippines, India, Thailand, Ireland, South Africa, Mozambique, Zimbabwe

House building programmes for homeless, youth leadership training, skills development, care of carers, street children programmes, rural communities, rural community water cisterns, women in prostitution, community development, support to orphanages, outreach to the poorest of the poor, promoting partnership, challenging abusive sex tourism, fair trade development.

Short term placements, global citizenship, shared advocacy, capacity building of the youth sector.

www.serve.ie

projects in Ireland; offering a Development Education Programme to all participants; and providing an outreach service to youth organisations helping them to creatively engage with Development Issues; engaging in advocacy initiatives, and supporting Fair Trade projects.'

Countries: Africa (Mozambique, South Africa, Zimbabwe) Asia (India, Philippines, Thailand), Latin America (Brazil).

Activities: Children/young people, community development, construction, disability/special needs, education, health/medical, women, other.

Duration: 6 weeks to 6 months.

Age requirements: Minimum 20 years, maximum age is flexible.

Disability access: Depends on placement; contact organisation for further details.

Language requirements: No. Some in-country language training is offered. Some placements may be influenced by language skills.

Educational/professional qualifications: No. However, preference will be given to people involved in voluntary movements and people with transferable skills.

Other requirements: Volunteers must have a spirit of adventure, be interested in development, be ready to rough it, be willing to learn from another culture, be happy to be of service to the poor, be a team player, and respect the traditions and customs of host communities. As many host communities will be linked to the Catholic Church, it is important that volunteers are comfortable with this. They must be willing to enter into a group contract and identify with SERVE's mission statement.

Application procedure: Applicants attend an information day, submit an application form and attend an interview. References are then requested. Successful applicants take part in group preparation days and sign up to a group contract.

Costs: Yes. Volunteers cover travel costs and fundraise for the host community.

Benefits: Food costs, most accommodation costs, training costs.

Work individually/in groups: Both.

Code of Practice	Volunteer Charter	In-country support for volunteers	Pre-programme training	Post-programme debriefing	Contact with returned volunteers
Signatory to Comhlámh Code of Good Practice for Sending Organisations.	Supporters of the Comhlámh Volunteer Charter; has a group contract for volunteers.	Yes, available full-time.	3 pre-departure training days, an in-country orientation week, a mid-term group evaluation and an end-term group evaluation.	Pre-return evaluation, individual meetings with returned volunteers, a weekend evaluation course, and links to other SERVE activities. Also holds evaluations with host communities.	Yes.

Skillshare International Ireland

Address: Dominick Court, 40 Lower Dominick Street, Dublin 1
Telephone number: +353 (0)1 874 8188
Fax number: +353 (0)1 874 8960
Email: fran.flood@skillshare.org
Website: www.skillshare.ie

Established in 2003, Skillshare International Ireland is a not-for-profit organisation.

Type: Long-term development.

Stated mission: 'Skillshare International works to reduce poverty, injustice and inequality and to further economic and social development in partnership with people and communities throughout the world. We do this by sharing and developing skills and ideas, facilitating organisational and social change and building awareness of development issues.'

Countries: Africa (Botswana, Kenya, Lesotho, Malawi, Mozambique, Namibia, South Africa, Swaziland, Tanzania, Uganda), Asia (Cambodia, India, Nepal, Sri Lanka).

Activities: Agriculture, business, capacity building, community development, education, health/medical, other.

Duration: Normally 2 years; consultants and specialists are also recruited for 1 to 3 months.

Age requirements: Minimum 22 years, maximum 65 years.

Disability access: Depends on project; contact organisation for further details.

Educational/professional qualifications: Yes. Specific requirements will depend on the placement.

Other requirements: Depends on placement: volunteers must meet the criteria set out in the job description and job specification.

Application procedure: Complete application form (with three references – personal, professional and other); attend a selection day; attend a four-day pre-departure training event.

Costs: No.

Benefits: Include travel costs, insurance (medical and social), and a subsistence allowance.

Work individually/in teams: In teams, with local partners.

Code of Practice	Volunteer Charter	In-country support for volunteers	Pre-programme training	Post-programme debriefing	Contact with returned volunteers
Signatory to Comhlámh Code of Good Practice for Sending Organisations.	Supporters of the Comhlámh Volunteer Charter.	Yes, available full-time.	Yes, week-long pre-departure training that covers issues including intercultural training, country-specific information, and general and specific info relating to the placement.	Yes, a comprehensive debriefing programme takes place in country of origin. This programme is tailored to suit the needs of individual returnees.	Yes, including as part of pre-departure training.

Slí Eile – Jesuits' Outreach to Young Adults

Address: 20 Upper Gardiner Street, Dublin 1
Telephone numbers: +353 (0)1 888 0607; (0)86 232 1768
Email: openevents@sli-eile.com
Website: www.sli-eile.com

Established in 2000, Slí Eile is a not-for-profit organisation.

Type: Short-term/intercultural
Stated mission: 'To foster the growth of the already existing informal association of adults (18–35) who are interested or have been involved in our faith and justice activities. To maintain the following characteristics of Slí Eile: open community, faith continuum, inclusive spectrum and committed service, while we respond effectively to Irish young adult reality. To engage young adults with the three core values: Spirituality (Ignatian), Community and Social Justice. To create conditions whereby some of those participating in Slí Eile activities engage actively and join in real co-ownership (as/with trustees, board) of Slí Eile, even committing themselves to leadership within the community.'
Countries: Africa (Zambia), Latin America (Colombia).
Activities: Children/young people, community development, education, other.
Duration: 3 weeks.
Age requirements: Minimum 18 years, maximum 35 years.
Disability access: No.
Language requirements: Depends on placement; Spanish is an advantage for Colombia.
Educational/professional qualifications: No.
Other requirements: No.
Application procedure: Complete an application form, available from the organisation. This is followed by an interview, after which references are requested.
Costs: Yes. A fundraising minimum of €1,000 is required.
Benefits: Travel, food, accommodation.
Work individually/in teams: In teams.

Code of Practice	Volunteer Charter	In-country support for volunteers	Pre-programme training	Post-programme debriefing	Contact with returned volunteers
Signatory to Comhlámh Code of Good Practice for Sending Organisations.	Supporters of the Comhlámh Volunteer Charter.	Yes, available part-time.	Orientation takes place over 6 months.	Takes place every September.	Yes, ex-volunteers attend pre-departure training; online forum.

Suas Educational Development

Address: Suas, 14 St Stephen's Green, Dublin 2
Telephone number: +353 (0)1 662 1412
Email: vp@suas.ie
Website: www.suas.ie

Established in 2002, Suas is a not-for-profit organisation.

Type: Short-term/intercultural.
Stated mission: 'Founded in 2002, Suas is a youth and education focused organisation, with programmes in India, Ireland and Kenya. We are committed to helping individuals fulfill their potential and play meaningful roles in shaping our world. Suas is secular and is a registered charity (CHY 14931).The volunteer programme provides an opportunity to volunteer in a community-based school, or educational project, in India or Kenya, for ten weeks, while learning about different cultures. It offers the possibility to develop personal and professional skills, to work in a team, and to learn about the challenges and opportunities of development in our interconnected world.'
Countries: Africa (Kenya), Asia (India).
Activities: Children/young people, community development, education, other.
Duration: 10 months part-time programme; 10-week full-time overseas placement.
Age requirements: Minimum 18 years, maximum 25 years (applications from people over 25 will be considered).
Language requirements: English.
Educational/professional qualifications: No.
Other requirements: Selected volunteers are required to be resident in Ireland during the year of the programme in order to be able to participate fully in pre- and post-departure training.
Application procedure: Candidates submit a completed application form by the December deadline. They are required to provide the names of two referees. Assessment centres are run in January to select suitable candidates. Individuals are evaluated on a competency model through a combination of group and individual interviews.
Costs: Yes, participation fee from €2,950 to €3,100.
Benefits: Flights, accommodation, pre-departure preparation and post-return debriefing, insurance, contribution towards vaccinations and malaria tablets, one week in-country global perspectives workshop, a stipend for each volunteer and a donation to the partner school/organisation.
Work individually/in teams: In teams of up to 13.

Suas Volunteer Programme

Release Potential

The Suas Volunteer Programme is a 10 month programme with a 10 week overseas placement. It offers enthusiastic young people the chance to make a difference. It is an opportunity to volunteer with schools and community projects in India or Kenya, and to learn about different cultures and global perspectives. It's about putting yourself forward and giving your all. It is a way to meet and work with like-minded individuals working for change, in Ireland and overseas. The programme is a demanding, challenging experience. It's about leadership and making a contribution. In essence, it's about 'releasing your potential' in order help others to release theirs.

Recruitment for the programme takes place from November.

For further information, see www.suas.ie
email vp@suas.ie or phone +353 1 662 1412

Suas

Code of Practice	Volunteer Charter	In-country support for volunteers	Pre-programme training	Post-programme debriefing	Contact with returned volunteers
Signatory to Comhlámh Code of Good Practice for Sending Organisations. Signatory to Dóchas Code of Conduct on Images and Messages. Legal contract. Team contract.	Supporters of the Comhlámh Volunteer Charter.	Yes, team leader available full-time; 24-hour emergency hotline based in Ireland.	Three weekends of pre-placement preparation, covering issues including cultural awareness, personal and team development, language and teacher introduction, global perspectives.	Post-programme return weekend covering learning from the experience and looking forward.	Each year 60 return volunteers help to run the programme through marketing, recruitment, pre-departure preparation weekend delivery and internships.

Working for a better world

Tekera Resource Centre

Address: 1 Foxrock Green, Foxrock, Dublin 18
Telephone number: +353 (0)85 168 0390
Email: killiankehoe@gmail.com
Website: www.ugandavillage.org

Established in 2005, Tekera Resource Centre is a not-for-profit organisation.

Type: Short-term/intercultural/long-term development.
Stated mission: 'Tekera Resource Centre is an organisation that seeks to assist the local community of Tekera village in southern Uganda through a number of methods. First, the Centre provides health care, disease screening, and referral services. Second, the Centre organises education programmes relevant to the needs of the community. Third, the Centre develops local initiative through operating a demonstration farm. The Centre encourages community investment and dynamism through a Community Work Programme which offers work to the local population and access to our services in return. This results in maximum benefit to individuals by helping them to help themselves.'
Countries: Africa (Uganda)
Activities: Agriculture, community development, education, health/medical.
Duration: Three months plus.
Age requirements: Minimum 18 years.
Disability access: Yes, contact the organisation for further details.
Language requirements: Volunteers must have good English.
Educational/professional qualifications: Yes, qualifications required depend on the particular placement. Professional medical qualifications are usually necessary for volunteer involvement with the clinic, but volunteers with other qualifications can be involved in other projects at the centre, in administration, development, education and agriculture.
Other requirements: No.
Application procedure: Volunteers must email a covering email and their CV to killiankehoe@gmail.com. Volunteers are advised to focus on what they can bring to the centre and to outline in which period they are interested in working. Shortlisted candidates are then interviewed.
Costs: No. There are no specific programme charges. Volunteers are expected to pay the cost of their own flight, the cost of their own food, and the cost of their transport. There are no obligatory contributions, but donations are very welcome.
Benefits: Accommodation, opportunity to design work plans in consultation with staff.
Work individually/in teams: In teams with the project staff.

Code of Practice	Volunteer Charter	In-country support for volunteers	Pre-programme training	Post-programme debriefing	Contact with returned volunteers
		Yes, available full-time.	No, but applicants are encouraged to communicate with previous volunteers.	Yes, through a report and meeting with the volunteer co-ordinator	Yes.

To Russia With Love

Address: To Russia With Love, Seaview House, 192 Clontarf Rd, Dublin 3
Telephone number: +353 (0)1 853 2920
Fax number: + 353 (0)1 853 2919
Email: info@torussiawithlove.ie
Website: www.torussiawithlove.ie

Established in 1998, To Russia With Love is a not-for-profit organisation.

Type: Short-term/intercultural.
Stated mission: 'To Russia with Love (TRWL) is a registered Irish charity dedicated to improving the physical and emotional care provided to children in Russian State Orphanages. TRWL works in full cooperation with the Russian authorities to deliver comprehensive aid packages to orphanages in the Bryansk region. TRWL's philosophy is based on the premise that every child deserves the right to a decent upbringing and an opportunity to play a positive role in society. The ultimate goal of the charity is to develop a benchmark of excellence in the care of institutionalised children in Bryansk, which will have a ripple effect throughout Russia.'
Countries: Europe (Russia)
Activities: Children/young people, education, other.
Duration: Three months. Changes to the standard duration can be discussed with management.
Age requirements: Minimum 21 years.

To Russia with Love
Volunteer Carers Needed

We are currently recruiting volunteer carers to work for three month periods in Khortolova Orphanage in Western Russia.

Open your eyes to a life changing experience and help to transform dreams to reality.

For the protection of our children a comprehensive interview process applies.

To Russia with Love is a registered Irish Charity.

For further information and application form contact

Phone: + 353 1 8532920
         + 353 1 8532918
Email: **info@torussiawithlove.ie**
Web: **www.torussiawithlove.ie**

Disability access: Contact organisation for further information.
Language requirements: No. However, basic Russian is very useful.
Educational/professional qualifications: No. Volunteers from different backgrounds are encouraged to apply.
Other requirements: No.
Application procedure: Potential volunteers should contact the Dublin office to express an interest. If a vacancy exists, candidates will be sent an application form along with detailed information about the volunteer programme. Candidates should submit this form to the Dublin office along with at least two references. They are required to provide evidence of a clean police record. A comprehensive interview process applies, which is used both to assess the suitability of the candidate and answer any queries they may have.
Costs: Yes. Volunteers are required to fundraise a minimum of €2,000 for the period of their placement.
Benefits: Airfare, accommodation, food and travel insurance.
Work individually/in teams: Both.

Code of Practice	Volunteer Charter	In-country support for volunteers	Pre-programme training	Post-programme debriefing	Contact with returned volunteers
Signatory to Comhlámh Code of Good Practice for Sending Organisations; service standards are based on the annually updated Development Plan.	Supporters of the Comhlámh Volunteer Charter; also has own set of rules and policies for volunteers.	Yes, available full-time.	Induction booklet, discussions with previous volunteers, in-country induction.	Post-return debriefing session; counselling, when appropriate.	Yes.

UCD Volunteers Overseas

Address: Library Building, University College Dublin, Belfield, Dublin 4
Telephone number: +353 (0)1 716 7126
Email: info@ucdvo.org
Website: www.ucdvo.org

Established in 2003, UCD Volunteers Overseas is a not-for-profit organisation.

Type: Short-term/intercultural.
Stated mission: 'UCD Volunteers Overseas has been established to offer students the opportunity to engage in voluntary work in the developing world. We believe in the need to listen to the wisdom of local knowledge and learn from the expertise of local people in all the community projects where we work. We fundraise to support these projects financially on a once off and continuing basis. Those funds are directed according to need to projects identified by local groups, which will most benefit the community. Central to the work of the charity is the belief that students benefit greatly by volunteering their time and energy in these projects. The challenge for students and local people is to learn a mutual respect and understanding of each others' cultural identities, maintaining the hope that we can alleviate some of the causes of disadvantage.'
Countries: Asia (India), Latin America (Haiti, Nicaragua).
Activities: Conservation/environment, construction, education, health/medical.
Duration: 4–5 weeks.
Age requirements: No.
Disability access: No.
Language requirements: No.
Educational/professional qualifications: No.
Other requirements: Applicants must be students of University College Dublin.
Application procedure: An application form with an explanatory sheet can be downloaded from the organisation's website when the programme is advertised. Two referees are needed, and all applicants are interviewed.
Costs: Yes; €1,600.
Benefits: Travel, food, accommodation, training.
Work individually/in teams: In teams.

Code of Practice	Volunteer Charter	In-country support for volunteers	Pre-programme training	Post-programme debriefing	Contact with returned volunteers
Signatory to Comhlámh's Code of Good Practice for Sending Organisations.	Supporters of the Comhlámh Volunteer Charter.	No, but all teams work with a local NGO.	Yes, four training days, in conjunction with Comhlámh and Dtalk.	Yes.	Yes.

USIT

Address: 19–21 Aston Quay, Dublin 2
Telephone number: +353 (0)1 602 1600
Fax number: +353 (0)1 677 8908
Email: workandtravel@usit.ie
Website: www.usit.ie

Established in 1959, USIT is a for-profit organisation.

Type: Short-term/intercultural.
Stated mission: 'In addition to the full range of products offered by any travel agent, we have developed a unique range of products specifically for student and youth travellers, including low cost flexible fares, work, travel & volunteer programmes, tailor-made insurance policies, budget accommodation, TEFL and much much more. USIT is also a specialist in student and youth work exchange programmes, offering all the information, administration and support needed to work around the world.'
Countries: Africa (Ghana, Kenya, South Africa), Asia (China, India, Mongolia, Nepal, Sri Lanka, Thailand,Vietnam), Latin America (Bolivia, Brazil, Costa Rica, Dominican Republic, Ecuador, Guatemala, Honduras, Mexico, Peru).
Activities: Community development, conservation/environment, construction, education, health/medical.
Duration: 2–18 months
Age requirements: Minimum 18 years; there may be a maximum age limit for some placements.
Disability access: Depends on placement; contact organisation for further information.
Language requirements: Depends on placement. Volunteer Peru and Costa Rica both require that the participant has a basic level of Spanish. Language courses are available prior to both of these programmes.
Educational/professional qualifications: No. However, experience may be useful for some projects.
Other requirements: Volunteers must hold an Irish or UK passport and be permanently resident in Ireland. Previous independent travel experience is desirable.
Application procedure: To apply the applicant simply has to send an application form along with a passport photocopy, CV and full placement fee to USIT. Two reference forms must be filled in by a previous employer/tutor of the applicant. Each participant is then invited to the USIT office for interview to assess their suitability to the programme. Once the applicant is accepted on the programme, their application is then sent to the partner organisation for processing.
Costs: Yes. Programme fees start from €549 depending on the chosen destination. Volunteers also cover travel costs.

Benefits: Pre-departure support, assistance with visa application where applicable, airport pick-up and transfer, hostel accommodation upon arrival, comprehensive orientation, tours, project placement, language courses if required, host family placement, meals, support of local partner throughout stay.

Work individually/in teams: Depends on applicant's chosen project.

Code of Practice	Volunteer Charter	In-country support for volunteers	Pre-programme training	Post-programme debriefing	Contact with returned volunteers
Member of IAEWEP (International Association of Education and Work Exchange Programmes) and of ISTC.	No.	Yes, available full-time.	Formal training not scheduled; however, this occurs during the interview and through regular contact via telephone or email with the participant.	All programme participants are required to submit feedback forms to USIT upon completion of programme.	Yes, via email.

Viatores Christi

Address: 38–39 Upper Gardiner St, Dublin 1
Telephone numbers: +353 (0)1 874 9346; (0)1 872 8027
Fax number: +353 (0)1 874 5731
Email: info@viatoreschristi.com
Website: www.viatoreschristi.com

Established in 1960, Viatores Christi is a not-for-profit organisation.

Stated mission: 'Viatores Christi is a voluntary Catholic lay missionary association which was established in 1960 and recruits, prepares and facilitates the placement of people who wish to work overseas, for one year or more, in areas of need such as Africa, South America, Asia and parts of Canada, USA and Europe. They recruit people aged 21 or over from a diverse range of backgrounds and professions and provide a part-time preparatory training programme over a period of five months.'

Countries: Africa (Ghana, Malawi, Nigeria, South Africa, Swaziland, Zambia), Asia (Cambodia), Latin America (El Salvador, Guatemala, Haiti, Mexico, Peru).

Activities: Administration/management, business, capacity building, education, health/medical, technical support.

Duration: From 1 year to 3 years plus.

Age requirements: Minimum of 21 years.

Disability access: Not at present.

Language requirements: Depends on placement: some positions require the volunteer to have the local language.

Educational/professional qualifications: Contact organisation for further details.

Other requirements: Volunteers are required to be actively involved in a voluntary activity in their local community prior to going overseas.

Application procedure: Attendance at an information seminar followed by a six-month training programme (consisting of one weekend for six consecutive months) is required. On completion of the training programme and having agreed to become a member of Viatores Christi, once a suitable work assignment has been found, references are then sought.

Costs: No. However, volunteers are required to cover the cost of their pre-departure courses.

Benefits: Fixed yearly allowance.

Work individually/in teams: Both.

Code of Practice	Volunteer Charter	In-country support for volunteers	Pre-programme training	Post-programme debriefing	Contact with returned volunteers
Signatory to Comhlámh Code of Good Practice for Sending Organisations.	Supporters of the Comhlámh Volunteer Charter.	No.	Takes place over 6 weekends; topics include cultural adaptation, health and global awareness.	Through meetings with the administrator and a returned volunteer.	Yes.

Vincentian Lay Missionaries

Address: St Peter's, Phibsborough, Dublin 7
Telephone number: +353 (0)1 838 9708
Fax number: +353 (0)1 838 9950
Email: michaelcm@eircom.net
Website: www.vincentians.ie

Established in 2002, the Vincentian Lay Missionaries is a not-for-profit organisation.

Type: Short-term/intercultural.
Stated mission: 'The Vincentian Lay Missionaries (VLM) was established in Ireland to promote, facilitate, support and coordinate the missionary presence and work of lay Vincentians in those overseas missions already entrusted to the Vincentian Family or animated by them. One of the aims of VLM is to provide young people with short-term missionary experiences. While the volunteers wish to make a contribution to the communities to which they are assigned, it is also hoped that by participating fully in the cultural, economic and religious life of the mission community they will, on their return, enrich the communities in which they live.'
Countries: Africa (Ethiopia)
Activities: Children/young people, education, other.
Duration: 6–12 weeks.
Age requirements: Minimum 20 years.
Language requirements: English; it is recommended that volunteers become familiar with Amharic.
Educational/professional qualifications: Teaching qualification at all three levels (primary, secondary and third level): BA, BEd, HDipEd, TEFL or equivalents; people with IT skills and qualifications in economics and physical education also welcome.
Other requirements: VLM welcomes volunteers who feel at home in the religious milieu of the communities with which they will work closely. It is also accepted that they will worship weekly with those with whom they work.
Application procedure: Contact VLM by phone 8389708 or email michaelcm@eircom.net to request an application form. Return the completed form with references; formal interviews will then be held.
Costs: Yes. Varies to cover travel to, and within, Ethiopia, health, insurance, accommodation overseas, preparation and mentoring.
Benefits: Working in collaboration with the Ethiopian community of the Daughters of Charity.

Code of Practice	Volunteer Charter	In-country support for volunteers	Pre-programme training	Post-programme debriefing	Contact with returned volunteers
Signatory to Comhlámh Code of Good Practice for Sending Organisations.	Supporters of the Comhlámh Volunteer Charter, also has a written contract with volunteers.	Yes, available full-time.	Language course; 3 briefing weekends.	Yes.	Yes.

Volunteer Missionary Movement (VMM)

Address: All Hallows College, Grace Park Road, Drumcondra, Dublin 9
Telephone number: +353 (0)1 837 6565
Fax number: +353 (0)1 836 7122
Email: mission@vmm.ie
Website: www.vmm.ie

Established in 1969, VMM is a not-for-profit organisation.

Type: Long-term development.

Stated mission: 'VMM is an international Christian development organisation whose members share their lives, faith, resources and skills to promote equality, respect and dignity for all. VMM works through supporting community development at home and overseas.'

Countries: Africa (Cameroon, Kenya, Sierra Leone, South Sudan, Tanzania, Uganda, Zambia), Asia (Philippines), Latin America (Guatemala)

Activities: Administration/management; agriculture; business; capacity building; community development; education; health/medical; technical support.

Duration: 1–2 years; contracts can be renewed to a maximum of 6 years on the same project.

Age requirements: Minimum 21 years.

Disability access: Yes; contact organisation for further details.

Language requirements: No, language training is provided in-country.

Educational/professional qualifications: Yes, relevant professional and educational qualifications with experience.

Other requirements: The movement is a Christian-based mission and development organisation, so volunteers must demonstrate a commitment to Christian values.

Application procedure: Applicant applies by email or post. An informal meeting takes place; applicant usually attends an introductory day, before which a CV and application forms are sought. A formal interview then takes place. The applicant is invited to two weeks' training, one with Dtalk and one with VMM. References are sought, along with medical certification and police clearance.

Costs: No.

Benefits: Pre-departure training costs and medical expenses; monthly living allowance; mid-term grant; post-return settlement grant and final medical check.

Work individually/in teams: In teams.

Code of Practice	Volunteer Charter	In-country support for volunteers	Pre-programme training	Post-programme debriefing	Contact with returned volunteers
Signatory to Comhlámh Code of Good Practice for Sending Organisations; also set out in Partner Handbook.	Supporters of the Comhlámh Volunteer Charter; charter also set out in Volunteer Handbook.	Yes, through partner organisation.	Two-week training course prior to departure, including one week with Dtalk.	Takes place as soon as possible after volunteer's return.	Yes.

VSI – Voluntary Service International

Address: 30 Mountjoy Square, Dublin 1
Telephone number: +353 (0)1 855 1011
Fax number: +353 (0)1 855 1012
Email: info@vsi.ie
Website: www.vsi.ie

Established in 1965, VSI is a not-for-profit organisation.

Type: Short-term/intercultural.

Stated mission: 'Voluntary Service International is the Irish branch of Service Civil International, a worldwide movement working for peace and international understanding through the medium of voluntary work projects, international exchanges and education and awareness programmes. We base our work on the following values: volunteering, non-violence, human rights, solidarity, respect for the environment, inclusion, empowerment, and cooperation. VSI has three different volunteer programmes: the International Volunteer Projects Programme (Europe, North America, Japan, South Korea, Australia), the Long Term Volunteering Programme (Europe, North America), and the Africa, Asia Latin America and Middle East Programme.'

Countries: Africa, Asia, Europe, Latin America (various).

Activities: Administration/management, children/young people, conservation/ environment, construction, disability/special needs, education, other.

Duration: From 2 weeks to 6 months +.

Age requirements: Minimum 18 years for International Volunteer Projects and Long Term Volunteering; minimum 21 years for Africa/Asia/Latin America, Middle East Programme.

Disability access: Depends on placement; contact organisation for further information.

Language requirements: In general, volunteers should speak the common local language, for example, Spanish for Latin American projects.

Educational/professional qualifications: No.

Other requirements: For the International Volunteer Projects Programme, volunteers need an interest in the project. Any specific skills required are outlined in VSI's annual publication; these differ from project to project. For the Long Term Volunteering Programme and the Africa/Asia/Latin America Programme, previous voluntary work experience is required.

Application procedure: International Volunteer Projects Programme: download and complete forms from web, from VSI annual book or from VSI office and send to VSI with application fee to cover insurance and administration. Long Term Volunteering: download and complete forms from web or from the VSI office and send to VSI with application fee. Africa/Asia/Latin America, Middle East Programme: Volunteers get application form at the Information Workshops run in January/February around the country, or from the VSI office; complete and return to the VSI office with appropriate fees.

Voluntary Service International
0 Mountjoy Square
Dublin 1

www.vsi.ie

VSi
local and global
volunteering
for peace

Costs: Yes. Volunteers cover programme and travel costs.
Benefits: Accommodation and food are provided on projects.
Work individually/in teams: In teams.

Code of Practice	Volunteer Charter	In-country support for volunteers	Pre-programme training	Post-programme debriefing	Contact with returned volunteers
Signatory to Comhlámh Code of Good Practice for Sending Organisations.	Supporters of the Comhlámh Volunteer Charter.	Yes, available full-time.	Training is provided for all placements; duration depends on type of placement.	Through workshops and evaluation forms.	Yes.

VSO Ireland

Address: Office 335, The Capel Building, Mary's Abbey, Dublin 7
Telephone number: +353 (0)1 872 7173
Fax number: + 353 (0)1 887 4458
Email: info@vso.ie
Website: www.vso.ie

Established in 1958, VSO is an independent not-for-profit organisation.

Type: Long-term development.
Stated mission: 'VSO is an international development charity that works through volunteers. Our vision is a world without poverty in which people work together to fulfill their potential. We bring people together to share skills, creativity and learning to build a fairer world. VSO welcomes volunteers from an ever-increasing range of countries, backgrounds and ages. National agencies in Canada, Ireland, India, Kenya, the Netherlands, the Philippines, and the UK recruit volunteers from many different countries worldwide and this international approach allows us to combine and learn from a rich variety of perspectives.'
Countries: Africa (Cameroon, Eritrea, Ethiopia, Gambia, Ghana, Kenya, Malawi, Mozambique, Namibia, Nigeria, Rwanda, Sierra Leone, South Africa, Tanzania, Uganda, Zambia), Asia (Bangladesh, Cambodia, China, India, Indonesia, Kazakhstan, Maldives, Mongolia, Nepal, Pakistan, Papua New Guinea, Philippines, Sri Lanka, Thailand, Vanuatu, Vietnam), Latin America (Guyana).
Activities: Administration/management, agriculture, business, capacity building, children/young people, community development, conservation/environment, disability/special needs, education, health/medical, human rights, internships, technical support, women, other.
Duration: 2 months to 2 years.
Age requirements: Ages 25 to 75.
Disability access: Yes, contact organisation for further details.
Language requirements: No.
Educational/professional qualifications: Yes, 2 years' post-qualification experience. In most cases volunteers need a minimum of four years' work experience in the field of their formal academic qualification.
Application procedure: First, speak to representative in VSO Ireland. Then fill out application form online or on paper and forward to VSO Ireland. Two references will be required, one professional and one personal. If the candidate is successful on first screening of application they will be invited to an assessment day, which involves individual interviews, teamwork and team dilemmas. If the candidate passes the assessment, he/she will be contacted by a placement advisor to speak about the possible opportunities available. Following this, the candidate attends three weekend workshops as part of pre-departure training. When the candidate accepts a placement he/she then goes overseas for more placement-specific training before taking up post with VSO partner.
Costs: No. Volunteers are encouraged to fundraise, but this is not a requirement.

Sharing skills
Changing lives

CHANGE MORE THAN JUST YOUR JOB – CHANGE LIVES

VSO is a development charity that urgently needs professionals to work with the world's most disadvantaged communities for 1-2 years. You'll work at grassroots level, sharing your skills to help bring about lasting change.

If you are a qualified education, health, business or NGO professional with at least two years work experience, then we want to hear from you. VSO will provide all the training and support you need, plus pay for your flights, accommodation, insurance and medical costs.

To change more than just your job, contact VSO today. Visit www.vso.ie for more details.

Benefits: All expenses are covered from pre-departure to post-service. Pre-departure expenses covered include: travel to and from assessment day; lodging and food during assessment day; travel to pre-departure training and lodging and food during training sessions; moving allowance before departure; and flights and accommodation on arrival overseas. In-service benefits include: monthly salary equivalent to colleagues in partner organisation; travel for VSO business; language learning allowance; accommodation; mid-service holiday payment. Post-service benefits include flights home and a resettlement grant of approximately €100 per month of service.
Work individually/in teams: Both.

Code of Practice	Volunteer Charter	In-country support for volunteers	Pre-programme training	Post-programme debriefing	Contact with returned volunteers
Signatory to Comhlámh Code of Good Practice for Sending Organisations.	Supporters of the Comhlámh Volunteer Charter.	Yes, available full-time.	Covers areas such as preparation for going overseas, health and safety, development issues, etc.	In-country exit interview and returned volunteer weekend.	Yes, VSO actively encourages potential volunteers to get in touch with returned volunteers.

ucc

Coláiste na hOllscoile Corcaigh, Éire
University College Cork, Ireland

The Department of Food Business & Development & Centre for Co-operative Studies, UCC offer the following programmes that may be of interest to readers:

For further information and application forms please contact:

Bridget Carroll
Centre for Co-operative Studies
O'Rahilly Building
University College Cork
Western Road
Cork

T: +353 (0)21 4902070
E: b.carroll@ucc.ie
W: http://www.ucc.ie/ccs

- Diploma in Social Integration & Enterprise for Community Development Workers (by distance learning)

- MBS in Co-operative & Social Enterprise (on-line)

- Postgraduate Diploma/MSc in Co-operative organisation, Food Marketing & Rural Development (full-time)

7.3 Volunteer placement organisations: international

2Way Development

Address: Unit 4, 25a Vyner Street, Bethnal Green, London E2 9DG, UK
Telephone number: +44 (0)20 8980 9074
Email: volunteer@2way.org.uk
Website: www.2way.org.uk

Established in 2003, 2Way Development is a not-for-profit organisation.

Type: Recruitment/placement.
Stated mission: '2Way Development offers a unique tailor-made service, arranging individual, long-term volunteer placements across the developing world. 2Way Development matches the skills of volunteers to the needs of locally run organisations that work towards poverty reduction, sustainable development and social justice. In assisting with project development, training or research, volunteers can empower local NGOs or not-for-profit organisations to successfully engage in projects that offer long-term sustainable solutions to local development issues.'
Countries: Africa, Asia, Latin America (various)
Activities: Administration/management, agriculture, capacity building, community development, conservation/environment, education, human rights, internships, technical support, other.
Duration: 3–24 months
Age requirements: Minimum 21 years.
Disability access: Check with organisation.
Language requirements: Depends on project; Spanish for Latin America.
Educational/professional qualifications: Yes. University degree and/or work experience.
Other requirements: No.
Application procedure: Complete an online enquiry form and attend an interview.
Costs: A set fee of £850 covers research costs, accommodation and work-related expenses. Volunteers also cover travel costs.
Benefits: Provision of information and advice; visa assistance; arranging customised placement; support throughout placement.
Work individually/in teams: Both.

In-country support for volunteers	Pre-departure training	Post-return debriefing	Contact with returned volunteers
Limited.	Provides written handbook on volunteering overseas and health literature.	Yes.	Yes.

Abandoned Street Kids of Brazil Trust – Task Brasil

Address: Task Brasil, PO Box 4901, London SE16 3PP, UK
Telephone number: +44 (0)20 7735 5545
Fax number: +44 (0)20 7735 5675
Email: info@taskbrasil.org.uk
Website: www.taskbrasil.org.uk

Established in 1992, Task Brasil is a not-for-profit organisation.

Type: Short-term/intercultural.

Stated mission: 'Task Brasil's mission is to provide a loving and supportive home environment for street children and adolescents in Brazil, ensuring that all of their basic needs are met and that they are provided with the necessary tools to go on to lead rich and fulfilling lives, and to operate "outreach" programmes for children still living on the streets. Task Brasil acts to advance the education and well-being of impoverished children in Brazil. Task Brasil is a non-partisan organisation operating on ethical and humane principles shared by people of any or no religious faith. It does not engage in political activity.'

Countries: Latin America (Brazil)

Activities: Agriculture, children/young people, education.

Duration: 1–12 months.

Age requirements: Minimum 21 years.

Disability access: No.

Language requirements: Basic level of Portuguese is required. Volunteers with good knowledge of Spanish are also accepted.

Educational/professional qualifications: No.

Other requirements: Volunteers should have experience of working with children. Desirable qualifications include TEFL certificate and life-saving certificate (for swimming activities). Task Brasil does not offer places for married couples and prefers people to go out separately to projects.

Application procedure: Volunteers should get in touch with Task Brasil for an information pack about the placements and then return the relevant documents with two references. Applicants will then be invited to Task Brasil for an interview. The procedure normally takes about two months to complete.

Costs: Yes, from £1,000 for up to 3 months. Volunteers also cover travel costs.

Benefits: Accommodation, food, and in-country work-related travel expenses.

Work individually/in teams: Both.

In-country support for volunteers	Pre-programme training	Post-programme debriefing	Contact with returned volunteers
Yes, available full-time.	Through an informal briefing.	Volunteers are asked to complete a questionnaire.	Contact with volunteer leaders.

African Conservation Experience

Address: PO Box 206, Faversham, Kent ME13 8WZ, UK
Telephone number: +44 (0)870 241 5816
Fax number: +44 (0)870 241 5816
Email: info@ConservationAfrica.net
Website: www.ConservationAfrica.net

Established in 1999, African Conservation Experience is a for-profit organisation.

Type: Conservation/environment.

Stated mission: African Conservation Experience establishes, maintains and supports conservation projects in Southern Africa. Projects are selected on the basis of real conservation value, the genuine wildlife experience that they are able to provide to enthusiastic volunteers and their contribution to the local environment and community.

Countries: Africa (Botswana, South Africa, Zimbabwe).

Activities: Conservation/environment.

Duration: 2–12 weeks, depending on placement.

Age requirements: Minimum 17 years.

Disability access: Contact organisation for further details.

Language requirements: No.

Educational/professional qualifications: No.

Other requirements: No.

Application procedure: Application form and information pack available from organisation.

Costs: Yes. Programme costs begin at £2,890 for 4 weeks.

Benefits: Flights from London Heathrow, all meals, transfers, accommodation and full back-up.

Work individually/in teams: In teams.

In-country support for volunteers	Pre-programme training	Post-programme debriefing	Contact with returned volunteers
Yes; available full-time.	Training provided in-country.	Feedback form is sent to all volunteers.	Yes.

African Conservation Trust

Address: PO Box 310, Link Hills, 3652, South Africa
Telephone number: +27 (0)31 767 5044
Fax number: +27 (0)31 767 5044
Email: info@projectafrica.com
Website: www.projectafrica.com

Established in 2000, African Conservation Trust is a not-for-profit organisation.

Type: Conservation/environment.
Stated mission: 'The mission of the African Conservation Trust is to provide a means for conservation projects to become self funding through active participation by the public. This gives ordinary people a chance to make a positive and real contribution to environmental conservation by funding and participating in the research effort as volunteers.'
Countries: Africa (Botswana, South Africa)
Activities: Conservation/environment, construction.
Duration: 2 weeks to 3 months.
Age requirements: Minimum 18 years.
Disability access: No.
Language requirements: English.
Educational/professional qualifications: No. All required training given on site.
Other requirements: No.
Application procedure: Complete a questionnaire and application form, which are available on the website.
Costs: Yes. Programmes cost from £450 a month; volunteers also cover travel costs.
Benefits: Food, accommodation, activities.
Work individually/in teams: In teams.

In-country support for volunteers	Pre-programme training	Post-programme debriefing	Contact with returned volunteers
Yes, available full-time.	Yes, on-site training is provided for all volunteers.	Volunteers are asked to complete an evaluation form.	Yes.

Africatrust Networks

Address: Africatrust Chambers, PO Box 551, Portsmouth, Hampshire PO5 1ZN, UK
Telephone number: +44 (0)187 381 2453
Email: wales@africatrust.gi or ghana@africatrust.gi
Website: www.africatrust.gi

Established in 1994, Africatrust is a not-for-profit organisation.

Type: Short-term/intercultural
Stated mission: 'Africatrust Networks (ATN) is the successor to St David's (Africa) Trust and is an informal partnership of volunteer programmes in West and North Africa. Each project is managed by an in-country registered Non-Government Organisation (NGO). The first Africatrust volunteer programmes were founded in 1994. The current and future programmes are now each to be managed in-country by a family of good African friends and colleagues.'
Countries: Africa (Cameroon, Ghana, Morocco)
Activities: Children/young people, community development, disability/special needs, education, women.
Duration: 13–26 weeks.
Age requirements: Minimum 18 years.
Disability access: No.
Language requirements: Depends on placement.
Educational/professional qualifications: No.
Other requirements: No.
Application procedure: Application form is available from the organisation's website. References will be requested. Successful applicants are requested to attend an interview.
Costs: Yes, programme costs start at £2,500.
Benefits: Return air tickets, food, accommodation, in-country transport, lecture instruction.
Work individually/in teams: In teams.

In-country support for volunteers	Pre-programme training	Post-project debriefing	Contact with returned volunteers
Yes, available full-time.	2–3 weeks' in-country induction.	Contact organisation for information.	Yes.

AidCamps International

Address: 5 Simone Court, Dartmouth Road, London SE26 4RP, UK
Telephone number: +44 (0)20 8291 6181
Fax number: +44 (0)870 130 3420
Email: info@AidCamps.Org
Website: www.AidCamps.Org

Established in 2002, AidCamps International is a not-for-profit organisation.

Type: Short-term/intercultural.
Stated mission: 'AidCamps International is a registered charity offering volunteers the opportunity to participate in short term voluntary work development aid projects overseas run by local non-governmental organisations in the third world. In addition to the volunteer work involved our three-week projects provide volunteers the chance to meet, live, and work overseas with local people and experience their culture first hand, while providing a solution to a local problem, as requested by the locals.'
Countries: Africa (Cameroon), Asia (India, Nepal, Sri Lanka).
Activities: Construction.
Duration: 3 weeks.
Age requirements: Minimum 18 years, no maximum.
Disability access: No.
Language requirements: English (not necessarily fluent).
Educational/professional qualifications: No.
Other requirements: Normal state of good health.
Application procedure: Simple application form, no references needed.
Costs: Yes, £600. Volunteers also cover travel costs.
Benefits: Accommodation, most food, ground transportation, excursions.
Work individually/in teams: In teams.

In-country support for volunteers	Pre-programme training	Post-programme debriefing	Contact with returned volunteers
Yes, available full-time.	Volunteers are given written and verbal information on placements.	Carried out in field at end of project.	Yes.

Amizade

Address: PO Box 110107, Pittsburgh, PA 15232, USA
Telephone numbers: +1 412 441 6655; 888 973 4443
Fax number: +1 757 257 8358
Email: volunteer@amizade.org
Website: www.amizade.org

Established in 1994, Amizade is a not-for-profit organisation.

Type: Short-term/intercultural, recruitment/placement (2-week minimum placements)

Stated mission: 'Amizade encourages intercultural exploration and understanding through community-driven service-learning courses and volunteer programmes. Amizade collaborates with community-based organisations around the world to participate in projects that are both beneficial to the community and rewarding to the volunteers. Amizade offers volunteer programmes that are a mix of community service, educational opportunities, and recreational activities. We provide volunteers with the unique opportunity to participate first hand in the culture of the region where they are volunteering.'

Countries: Africa (Bolivia, BrazilGhana, , Mexico, Tanzania), Latin America (Bolivia, Brazil, Jamaica, Mexico).

Activities: Children/young people, community development, construction, education, health/medical.

Duration: Programmes are 2 weeks in length. Customised volunteer placements must be a minimum of 2 weeks but can extend up to 6 months.

Age requirements: Minimum 18 years. Volunteers aged 12–17 may participate if accompanied by a parent or guardian.

Disability access: Yes.

Language requirements: No. Mexico placement volunteers must have an intermediate level of Spanish.

Educational/professional qualifications: No.

Other requirements: No.

Application procedure: No references are required. An application, medical form and liability waiver are necessary for participation in a programme and can be downloaded from the website. Volunteers must complete the three forms and mail them to our office along with a $100, non-refundable, check deposit.

Costs: Yes. Programme fees begin at $610 and vary by location. There are separate fees for individual volunteer placements. Volunteers are responsible for covering the costs of airfare, travel documents and immunisations (if needed).

Benefits: Programme fee includes room and board, transportation during the programme, recreational, cultural and educational activities, Amizade administration and staff costs, and a donation to the community.

Work individually/in teams: Both.

In-country support for volunteers	Pre-project training	Post-project debriefing	Contact with returned volunteers
Yes, some full-time, some part-time.	No.	No.	Yes.

ARCAS (Wildlife Rescue and Conservation Association)

Address: 4 Ave. 2-47, Sector B5, Zona 8 Mixco, San Cristobal, Guatemala
Telephone numbers: +502 2478 4096; 2480 7270; 5704 2563
Email: arcas@intelnet.net.gt
Website: www.arcasguatemala.com

Established in 1989, ARCAS is a not-for-profit organisation.

Type: Conservation/environment.
Stated mission: 'To strive for the conservation, preservation and research of wildlife; to rescue, rehabilitate and reintroduce into their natural habitat wild animals seized from illegal traffickers; to promote and assist in the creation and management of protected habitat areas for wild animals; to support tropical wild animal veterinary medicine and research; to reproduce and re-introduce endangered wildlife; to raise awareness among Guatemalans about the need to conserve natural resources through a program of education and information dissemination; to develop and promote economic alternatives in rural communities to the unsustainable consumption of natural resources.'
Countries: Latin America (Guatemala)
Activities: Conservation/environment, education, internships.
Duration: Completely flexible.
Age requirements: No.
Disability access: Depends on placement; contact organisation for further details.
Language requirements: No. However, some Spanish language ability is advised.
Educational/professional qualifications: No.
Other requirements: No.
Application procedure: Send an email. For internships or longer-term volunteers, each case is handled separately.
Costs: Yes. US$50–100 per week. Volunteers also cover travel costs.
Benefits: Food and accommodation.
Work individually/in teams: Teams.

In-country support for volunteers	Pre-programme training	Post-programme debriefing	Contact with returned volunteers
Yes, available full-time.	Can provide in-country training if remunerated.	No.	Yes.

Ard El Insan Palestinian Benevolent Association

Address: Nasr Street, PO Box 1099, Gaza, Palestinian Territory
Telephone numbers: + 970 8286 8138; 599 183 326
Fax number: +970 8284 2516
Email: telephonehusam@yahoo.co.uk and husam@ardelinsan.org
Website: www.ardelinsan.org

Established in 1984, Ard El Insan is a not-for-profit organisation.

Type: Long-term development
Stated mission: 'Ard El Insan (AEI) provides nutritional and health services to the most needy and marginalised children under five, their mothers and families. Two community health and nutrition centers in Gaza Strip (one in Gaza and another in Khan Younis) provide preventive, curative and community health mobilization to beneficiaries in these areas. In addition, each center conducts a community based programme targeting vulnerable areas in different locations such as refugees' camps, villages and deprived and rural areas. Over the years, AEI has become the leading health community and nutrition services provider in the Gaza Strip.'
Countries: Asia (Palestinian Territory).
Activities: Administration/management, capacity building, children/young people, community development, education, health/medical, women, other.
Duration: 2 weeks +.
Age requirements: No.
Disability access: No.
Language requirements: In general, English is the main language.
Educational/professional qualifications: Yes, in line with the role the volunteer will be undertaking (e.g. medical qualifications).
Other requirements: No.
Application procedure: Contact the organisation to provide details of availability, areas of interest, CV, etc.
Costs: No.
Benefits: Depends on the placement; further information is available from the organisation.
Work individually/in teams: Both.

In-country support for volunteers	Pre-programme training	Post-programme debriefing	Contact with returned volunteers
Yes, available full time.	No, but volunteers are welcome to join training for local staff.	No.	Yes

Asociación ANAI

Address: Apartado 170 – 2070, Sabanilla, San José, Costa Rica
Telephone numbers: +506 224 3570; 224 6090
Fax number: +506 253 7524
Email: anaicr@racsa.co.cr
Website: www.anaicr.org

Established in 1978, ANAI is a not-for-profit organisation.

Type: Conservation/environment.
Stated mission: 'Our mission is to help the people of Talamanca design and implement a strategy linking socio-economic development, cultural strengthening and biodiversity conservation. We seek the emergence of a truly grassroots process within the local community that achieves a healthy mix of protected rainforests, wetland and marine areas, managed forests and diverse agro-ecosystems and human services like tourism, and provides Talamanca's current and future inhabitants with economic stability and an attractive quality of life.'
Countries: Latin America (Costa Rica)
Activities: Agriculture, conservation/environment, internships.
Duration: 1 week to 12 months.
Age requirements: Minimum 18 years.
Disability access: Depends on placement; contact organisation for further details.
Language requirements: No. However, a basic knowledge of English and Spanish is helpful.
Educational/professional qualifications: Depends on placement. Relevant qualifications include in the areas of economics, business administration, agriculture, biology, ecology and post-harvest technology.
Other requirements: No specific requirements, but preference is given to those who have demonstrated interest in environmental issues, speak some Spanish, have worked or volunteered abroad or have spent significant time in challenging situations.
Application procedure: Contact the organisation for details of programmes and a registration form; for internships, applicants must submit a CV and a statement of interest.
Costs: Yes; a registration fee of $30 to $160, plus lodging fees that depend on the placement. There is no fee for the internship. Volunteers also cover travel costs.
Benefits: Depends on placement type. Accommodation and/or food may be provided.
Work individually/in teams: Both.

In-country support for volunteers	Pre-programme training	Post-programme debriefing	Contact with returned volunteers
Yes, available full-time.	In-country orientation programme.	Through written evaluation.	Yes.

Assin Endwa Trust UK

Address: 184 Maldon Road, Great Baddow, Chelmsford, Essex CM2 7DG, UK
Telephone number: +44 (0)1245 475920 (evenings only)
Fax number: +44 (0)1 245 475920
Email: volunteers@endwa.org.uk
Website: www.endwa.org.uk

Established in 1999, Assin Endwa Trust is a not-for-profit organisation.

Type: Short-term/intercultural.
Stated mission: 'A joint Charitable Trust between Ghana and the UK where like-minded people in both countries can help develop the village of Endwa in a manner that would benefit the people of the village without destroying their culture.'
Countries: Africa (Ghana)
Activities: Construction, education, women.
Duration: 3 weeks in general, but longer-term positions can be arranged.
Age requirements: Minimum 18 years; or 16 years if accompanied by a parent/guardian.
Disability access: Contact organisation for specific information.
Language requirements: Good working knowledge of English.
Educational/professional qualifications: Good general level of education.
Other requirements: Sense of humour, enthusiasm, patience and the ability to get along with other people.
Application procedure: Request details through website or by post, fill in form (reference required), return form with deposit. Prospective volunteers are generally contacted within 2 weeks for phone interview, and referees within the month. Volunteer will be accepted if references and interview are satisfactory.
Costs: Yes. Cost begins with deposit specified on website and application, and volunteers must also raise £250 to fund the project work in Ghana. Volunteers also cover travel costs.
Benefits: Accommodation, most meals and internal travel in Ghana, including several weekend trips.
Work individually/in teams: In teams or pairs.

In-country support for volunteers	Pre-departure training	Post-return debriefing	Contact with returned volunteers
Yes, available full time.	Yes, orientation meeting.	Yes, evaluation forms and debriefing meetings.	Yes.

Associação Iko Poran

Address: Rua do Oriente, 280/ 201 – Santa Teresa, Rio de Janeiro – RJ – Brasil,
CEP: 20.240-130
Telephone number: +55 21 3852 2916
Fax number: +55 21 3852 2917
Email: volunt@ikoporan.org
Website: www.ikoporan.org

Established in 2002, Iko Poran is a not-for-profit organisation.

Type: Short-term/intercultural.
Stated mission: 'Our mission is: To implement international volunteer programmes that make a positive impact on the projects in which they take place, promoting a wide experience exchange between cultures and strengthening a constant and growing number of NGOs in Brazil. Iko Poran offers very strong programmes and all of them have very well defined impact evaluation and performance indicators. The volunteers have a unique experience of participating actively on the development of the tended communities and on the construction of a fairer world for all.'
Countries: Latin America (Brazil).
Activities: Administration/management; business; children/young people; community development; conservation/environment; education; health/medical; other.
Duration: 2–24 weeks.
Age requirements: Minimum 18 years, maximum 70 years.
Disability access: Yes; contact organisation for further details.
Language requirements: No. However, it is recommended that volunteers learn some Portuguese. Portuguese classes are available in Brazil.
Educational/professional qualifications: No.
Other requirements: No.
Application procedure: Prospective volunteers are asked to fill out an on-line form, providing references, and also to send forward a copy of their CV. The organisation then develops their work plans, based on the information sent (and verified).
Costs: Yes. Volunteers cover their travel costs to Brazil, individual placement fees and accommodation. Placement fee is R$1,500 (Brazilian reals) and includes 4 weeks' lodging. Additional weeks cost R$180.
Benefits: Organisation of work plan; orientation, programme management and administrative fee; donation to partner organisation (50% of fee), 24/7 emergency support, airport pick-up, accommodation (first 4 weeks).
Work individually/in teams: Both.

In-country support for volunteers	Pre-programme training	Post-programme debriefing	Contact with returned volunteers
Yes, available full-time, Monday–Friday.	Through the development of individual work plans.	No.	Yes.

Associazione Oikos

Address: Via Paolo Renzi, 55 00128 Roma, Italy
Telephone number: +39 (0)6 508 0280
Fax number: +39 (0)6 507 3233
Email: volontariato@oikos.org
Website: www.oikos.org; www.volontariato.org

Established in 1979, Oikos is a not-for-profit organisation.

Type: Short-term/intercultural
Stated mission: 'Oikos is an organisation involved in preservation of forest heritage, and themes connected with the young reality. The experience of workcamps started in 1980 as a programme of international exchange. Our volunteers are involved in projects that help people in trouble, where there is a lack of resources.'
Countries: Africa (Burkina Faso, Ghana, Kenya, Lesotho, Morocco, Tanzania, Uganda), Asia (Bangladesh, India, Korea, Nepal, Palestine), Latin America (Costa Rica, Ecuador, Guatemala, Haiti, Mexico, Peru, Argentina).
Activities: Children/young people, community development, conservation/ environment, construction, education.
Duration: 2 weeks to 12 months +.
Age requirements: Minimum 18 years.
Disability access: Depends on placement; contact organisation for further details.
Language requirements: No. However, where there is a lot of interaction with local people, a basic knowledge of the local language can be very useful.
Educational/professional qualifications: No.
Other requirements: No.
Application procedure: Complete an application form and pay the participation fee.
Costs: Yes. See website for programme fees. Volunteers also cover travel costs.
Benefits: Food and accommodation.

In-country support for volunteers	Pre-programme training	Post-programme debriefing	Contact with returned volunteers
Yes, available full-time.	No.	Yes, volunteers are asked to share their experiences with others.	Yes.

Azafady

Address: Studio 7, 1a Beethoven Street, London W10 4LG, UK
Telephone number: +44 (0)20 8960 6629
Fax number: +44 (0)20 8962 0126
Email: mark@azafady.org
Website: www.madagascar.co.uk

Established in 1994, Azafady is a not-for-profit organisation.

Type: Conservation/environment
Stated mission: 'Azafady is a registered UK charity and Malagasy NGO working to alleviate poverty, improve well-being and preserve beautiful unique environments in southeast Madagascar. Its aims are: (1) to support local communities by providing appropriate health and sanitation infrastructure and education; and by helping to develop alternative sustainable livelihood strategies to improve their well-being; (2) to protect and enhance the unique environment of Madagascar; and (3) to provide an opportunity for people from "developed" countries to get an understanding of the complex issues in conservation and development, gaining skills and experience at a grassroots level.'
Countries: Africa (Madagascar).
Activities: Business, conservation/environment, education, health/medical.
Duration: 3–10 weeks.
Age requirements: Minimum 18 years.
Disability access: Contact the organisation for further information.
Language requirements: No.
Educational/professional qualifications: No.
Other requirements: No.
Application procedure: Once an application is received, the London office does a risk assessment of the potential volunteer and if there are places available will offer them a place if they pass. Further personal/medical references may be required in some cases. Places are on a first-come, first-served basis.
Costs: Yes. Minimum donation of £2,000 is required, of which 90% goes to projects in Madagascar. Volunteers also cover travel costs.
Benefits: In-country field and office support, in-country travel, food, accommodation, training for activities, language training, trip to national park on weekend during orientation.
Work individually/in teams: In teams

In-country support for volunteers	Pre-programme training	Post-programme debriefing	Contact with returned volunteers
Yes, available on a full-time basis.	No.	Yes, informal debriefing though phone contact and a written feedback form.	Yes.

Balkan Sunflowers

Address: Youth, Culture and Sports Hall 114, Luan Haradinaj Street Prishtina, Kosovo
Telephone number: +381 38 246299
Fax number: +381 38 246299
Email: applications@balkansunflowers.org
Website: www.balkansunflowers.org

Established in 1999, Balkan Sunflowers is a not-for-profit organisation.

Type: Short-term/intercultural.
Stated mission: 'Balkan Sunflowers brings volunteers from around the world to work as neighbours and friends in social reconstruction and renewal. By organising social and cultural activities, we promote understanding, further non-violent conflict, transformation, and celebrate the diversity of the lives and cultures of the Balkan region.'
Countries: Europe (Kosovo)
Activities: Children/young people, community development, conservation/ environment, human rights, other.
Duration: 6 months +.
Age requirements: Minimum 21 years.
Disability access: Depends on placement; contact organisation for further details.
Language requirements: Competency in English.
Educational/professional qualifications: No. However, special competencies are useful and welcome.
Other requirements: No.
Application procedure: Application form is available on the organisation's website; two references are required.
Costs: Yes. Volunteers pay €150 on their arrival. Additionally, they cover travel costs and all incidental expenses.
Benefits: Accommodation and food; the organisation has insurance, but it is recommended that volunteers have their own.
Work individually/in teams: Individually.

In-country support for volunteers	Pre-programme training	Post-programme debriefing	Contact with returned volunteers
Yes, available full-time.	Yes, provided on arrival, and can be up to a week.	Through final evaluation.	Yes.

Bangladesh Work Camps Association (BWCA)

Address: 289/2, Work Camp Road, North Shajahanpur, Dhaka-1217, Bangladesh
Telephone numbers: +88 2 935 8206; 2 935 6814; (mobile) 0175 021 918
Fax numbers: + 88 2 956 5506; 2 956 5483 (Attn: BWCA)
Email: bwca@bangla.net
Website: www.mybwca.org

Established in 1958, BWCA is a not-for-profit organisation.

Type: Short-term/intercultural.
Stated mission: 'Bangladesh Work Camps Association (BWCA) promotes international solidarity and peace through organising community development works which takes the form of national/international workcamps for volunteers in rural and urban areas of Bangladesh. The projects organised include environment and health education, literacy, sanitation, forestation, community work, development and construction, etc. Volunteers work 30 hours a week on placements which last from 1 to 2 weeks from October to February. A RTYP (Round The Year Programme) is also available to medium-term volunteers staying for a minimum period of three months. Volunteers should be 18–35, able to speak English, non skilled, be adaptable to any situation and be team-spirited accepted.'
Countries: Asia (Bangladesh)
Activities: Agriculture, community development, conservation/environment, construction, disability/special needs, education, health/medical, other.
Duration: 12 days to 6 months +; depends on type of programme.
Age requirements: 18–35 years.
Disability access: No.
Language requirements: English. Volunteers have the opportunity to learn Bengali.
Educational/professional qualifications: No.
Other requirements: Must agree with the BWCA's 'Policy of Volunteering'. Must be well orientated and self motivated about the programme and about Bangladeshi culture.
Application procedure: Irish volunteers should contact the organisation direct with a letter of motivation. This procedure may change in the future – contact organisation for details.
Costs: Yes. Starts from US$150 for a short-term programme. Volunteers pay a registration fee and a daily food subsidy; an extension fee is charged for people who stay longer than 3 months. Volunteers also cover travel costs.
Benefits: Accommodation, internal transportation cost (within host country) and cost of sightseeing are covered by programme fee; daily food subsidy is paid directly to host organisation.
Work individually/in teams: Both.

In-country support for volunteers	Pre-programme training	Post-programme debriefing	Contact with returned volunteers
Yes; available full-time.	Yes; provides in-country orientation.	Welcome session for returning volunteers.	Yes.

Bruce Peru

Address: 444 Jr San Martin, Trujillo, Peru
Telephone number: +51 44 992 4445
Email: info@bruceperu.com
Website: www.bruceperu.org

Established in 2000, Bruce Peru is a not-for-profit organisation.

Type: Short-term/intercultural
Stated mission: 'Children have the right to be fed and clothed and sheltered and educated by their parents. When parents are unable or refuse to do this, then society must intervene. Bruce Organisation exists to feed, clothe and educate children who have been let down by their parents.'
Countries: Latin America (Argentina, Bolivia, Chile, Ecuador, Panama, Peru).
Activities: Children/young people, construction, education, health/medical, other.
Duration: One month plus.
Age requirements: Minimum 19/20 years; maximum 70.
Disability access: Yes.
Language requirements: Spanish; classes are provided.
Educational/professional qualifications: Professional qualifications are required for medical and health care placements.
Other requirements: No.
Application procedure: An application form is available on the organisation's website.
Costs: Yes. Programme costs of €267 per month for the first 3 months; €215 for the next 3 months, and €110 per month after that. Volunteers also cover travel costs.
Benefits: Full-time accommodation, all meals on weekdays, Spanish language classes.
Work individually/in teams: In teams.

In-country support for volunteers	Pre-programme training	Post-programme debriefing	Contact with returned volunteers
Yes.	Yes, volunteers are encouraged to make contact before their placement: induction, orientation and training are provided in-country.	Yes, exit interviews are provided and former volunteers are encouraged to stay in contact.	Yes, provided on a regular basis.

Casa Guatemala

Address: 14 Calle 10-63, Zona 1, Guatemala City, Guatemala
Telephone number: + 502 2331 9408
Fax number: + 502 2331 9408
Email: casaguatemal@guate.net.gt
Website: www.casa-guatemala.org

Established in 1977, Casa Guatemala is a not-for-profit organisation.

Type: Short-term/intercultural.
Stated mission: 'Casa Guatemala is an orphanage that cares for the nurturing, health and education of over 250 children. These children come from a variety of backgrounds; some have been abandoned, some have been abused, while still others come from families too poor to even provide the basics of a child's needs.'
Countries: Latin America (Guatemala)
Activities: Administration/management, agriculture, business, children/young people, construction, education, health, other.
Duration: 6 months +; shorter placements may be organised in some cases.
Age requirements: Minimum 21 years.
Disability access: No.
Language requirements: Basic Spanish is required for any positions that involve working with children.
Educational/professional qualifications: Depends on placement. Includes professional qualifications as teachers, doctors, nurses, dentists, agronomists, etc. General managers and staff may also be required for work in the organisation's bar, restaurant and shop.
Other requirements: No.
Application procedure: A volunteer application form is available on the organisation's website.
Costs: Yes. Six-month placements cost $180; short-term solidarity tourism packages cost $100 a week. Volunteers also cover travel costs.
Benefits: Accommodation and food.
Work individually/in teams: In teams.

In-country support for volunteers	Pre-programme training	Post-programme debriefing	Contact with returned volunteers
Yes, available part-time.	Some induction training provided.	Yes.	Yes.

Christians Abroad

Address: Room 237, Bon Marché Centre, 241 Ferndale Road, London SW9 8BJ, UK
Telephone number: +44 (0)870 770 7990
Fax number: +44 (0)870 770 7991
Email: recruitment@cabroad.org.uk
Website: www.cabroad.org.uk

Established in 1973, Christians Abroad is a not-for-profit organisation

Type: Recruitment/placement.
Stated mission: 'Christians Abroad offers advice and information on volunteering and working overseas through World Service Enquiry (www.wse.org.uk). We recruit volunteers and professionals willing to work across the whole spectrum of Christian belief for churches and Christian institutions with the same breadth of focus – for our own volunteer programme and on behalf of other agencies. We also give other support, from career advice to practical help, a monthly job list, CV advice and an on-line coaching service'
Countries: Africa (Cameroon, Kenya, Nigeria, Tanzania), Asia (China, India), Latin America (Argentina).
Activities: Education, health/medical, other.
Duration: 6 weeks for elective medical students; 3 months + for others.
Age requirements: Minimum 21 years; also depends on project.
Disability access: No.
Language requirements: Depends on placement; e.g., Spanish is required for Argentina.
Educational/professional qualifications: Depends on placement
Other requirements: Christian faith, evidence of commitment, and potential ability to live cross-culturally.
Application procedure: Applicants complete an application form; three references (friend, academic/work, spiritual) required; face-to-face interview.
Costs: Yes, fee of £150.
Benefits: Support, briefing and de-briefing.
Work individually/in teams: Individually.

In-country support for volunteers	Pre-programme training	Post-programme debriefing	Contact with returned volunteers
Depends on placement; not available full-time.	Yes, country briefing, practical matters, health advice.	Yes.	Yes.

CIS (Centro de Intercambio y Solidaridad)

Address: Colonia Libertad Avenida Bolivar numero 103 San Salvador, El Salvador
Telephone number: +503 2226 5362
Fax number: +503 2235 1330
Email: cis_elsalvador@yahoo.com
Website: www.cis-elsalvador.org

Established in 1993, CIS is a not-for-profit organisation.

Type: Recruitment/placement.
Stated mission: 'The mission of the Centro de Intercambio y Solidaridad (the CIS) is to promote solidarity and exchange across borders between Salvadoran people and others in the search for development and dignity. The CIS works to promote and strengthen a culture of solidarity that implies accompaniment, respect for the equality of different cultures, and mutual support between people. We focus on using different strategies to promote a solidarity that creates the space for grassroots organisation for JUSTICE and DIGNITY. We operate on a model of innovation and participation.'
Countries: Latin America (El Salvador)
Activities: Education.
Duration: 9 weeks.
Age requirements: Minimum 18 years, no maximum.
Disability access: Yes.
Language requirements: English. Spanish is not required, but is useful.
Educational/professional qualifications: No.
Other requirements: CIS welcomes people who are open to new experiences and have a commitment to progressive politics and social justice.
Application procedure: Prospective volunteers should send their CV, a letter of interest, and one letter of recommendation to cis_elsalvador@yahoo.com. All application material should be received at least one month prior to the beginning of the volunteer cycle for which they are applying.
Costs: Yes; US$100 fee to cover human resource costs. Volunteers cover travel costs and living expenses.
Benefits: Training in teaching English and popular education methodology; political-cultural programme. For a fee, CIS can organise accommodation and food, and Spanish classes.
Work individually/in teams: Both.

In-country support for volunteers	Pre-departure training	Post-return debriefing	Contact with returned volunteers
Yes, available full-time.	Volunteers are provided with a written orientation guide and participate in a teacher training programme.	Through collective teachers evaluation; individual debriefing is also available.	Yes.

Coral Cay Conservation

Address: Elizabeth House, 39 York Road, London SE1 7NJ, UK
Telephone number: +44 (0)20 7620 1411
Fax number: +44 (0)20 7921 0469
Email: recintern@coralcay.org
Skype name: recintern (chat only)
Website: www.coralcay.org

Established in 1986, Coral Cay is a not-for-profit organisation.

Type: Conservation/environment.
Stated mission: 'Coral Cay Conservation is the international award-winning, not-for-profit organization, dedicated to providing resources to help sustain livelihoods and alleviate poverty through the protection, restoration and management of coral reefs and tropical forests. Since the establishment of CCC in 1986, thousands of Volunteers have participated on CCC marine and terrestrial expeditions. Volunteers play a crucial role in the conservation of threatened tropical environments through the collection of scientific data. CCC has helped establish several marine reserves and wildlife sanctuaries, including the Belize Barrier Reef as a World Heritage Site and Danjugan Island, Philippines as a Marine Reserve and Wildlife Sanctuary.'
Countries: Asia (Fiji, Philippines, Malaysia), Latin America (Honduras).
Activities: Conservation/environment.
Duration: 2 weeks +.
Age requirements: Minimum 16 years.
Disability access: Depends on placement; contact organisation for further details.
Language requirements: English.
Educational/professional qualifications: No. On-site training provided, where necessary.
Other requirements: Enthusiasm, dedication, keen interest in conservation, team spirit, sense of adventure and fun, moderate level of fitness.
Application procedure: An enrolment pack can be downloaded from the CCC website, or by post from the head office.
Costs: Yes. Programme costs begin at £550 for forest expeditions, and £700 for marine expeditions. Volunteers also cover travel costs.
Benefits: Accommodation, food, training, advice with fundraising.
Work individually/in teams: In teams.

In-country support for volunteers	Pre-programme training	Post-programme debriefing	Contact with returned volunteers
Yes, available full-time.	Pre-departure meeting at Head Office; in-country training provided.	No.	Yes.

Cross-Cultural Solutions

Address: (UK Office) 44 Tower Point, North Road, Brighton BN1 1YR, UK
Telephone numbers: +44 (0)845 458 2781/2782; (0)1273 666392
Fax number: +44 (0)845 458 2783
Email: infouk@crossculturalsolutions.org
Website: www.crossculturalsolutions.org

Established in 1995, Cross-Cultural Solutions is a not-for-profit organisation.

Type: Short-term/intercultural.
Stated mission: 'Our vision is of a world where people value cultures different from their own, are aware of global issues, and are empowered to effect positive change. Our mission is to operate volunteer programmes around the world in partnership with sustainable community initiatives, bringing people together to work side-by-side while sharing perspectives and fostering cultural understanding. We are an international not-for-profit organisation with no political or religious affiliations. Our values are: shared humanity, respect and integrity.'
Countries: Africa (Ghana, Morocco, South Africa, Tanzania), Asia (China, India, Thailand), Europe (Russia), Latin America (Brazil, Costa Rica, Guatemala, Peru)
Activities: Children/young people, community development, disability/special needs, education, health/medical, internships, women, other.
Duration: 1–12 weeks.
Age requirements: For children travelling with a parent/guardian, the minimum is 8 years. For volunteers travelling alone, the minimum is 18 years. There is no maximum age limit. Family participation is welcomed.
Disability access: Depends on placement; contact organisation for further details.
Language requirements: Basic knowledge of English.
Educational/professional qualifications: No.
Other requirements: No.
Application procedure: Talk to a Programme Enrolment Manager to identify a suitable programme; a deposit of £150 is required to secure a place on the programme.
Costs: Yes, from £1,422 for two weeks. Volunteers also cover travel costs.
Benefits: Includes food, accommodation, ground transportation, administrative support, travel and medical insurance, cultural programme activities.
Work individually/in teams: Both.

In-country support for volunteers	Pre-programme training	Post-programme debriefing	Contact with returned volunteers
Yes, full-time support from staff who are locally born and based in-country.	Volunteer handbooks, one-to-one guidance, in-country orientation.	'Re-entry' interview with programme manager.	Yes, this is encouraged.

Development in Action (DiA)

Address: 78 York Street, London W1H 1DP, United Kingdom
Telephone number: +44 7813 395 957
Email: info@developmentinaction.org
Website: www.developmentinaction.org

Established in 1994, Development in Action is a not-for-profit organisation.

Type: Short-term/intercultural.
Stated mission: 'Development in Action aims to: (1) encourage young people to take an interest in global issues by offering them the opportunity to work with development organisations in India; (2) improve understanding of global issues among young people by giving them the chance to explore particular issues and create a project and/or write for our newsletter and magazine; (3) engage with the question of Global Citizenship and contribute in a practical way to the promotion of this idea in the UK.'
Countries: Asia (India).
Activities: Administration/management, business, conservation/environment, disability/special needs, education, women, other.
Duration: Summer scheme involves a two-month placement and Year-Out scheme involves a five-month placement.
Age requirements: Minimum 18 years.
Disability access: Depends on project; contact organisation for further details.
Language requirements: English.
Educational/professional qualifications: Depends on project. Not required for standard placements, but there are specialist openings for those qualified in natural resource management, agriculture, IT and geographical information systems.
Other requirements: Cultural sensitivity, enthusiasm and humility. An interest in global issues and commitment to DiA's development education goals are also desirable.
Application procedure: Candidates apply by application form (including references) and are called to a selection day made up of workshops and interviews.
Costs: Yes. Volunteers have to make a minimum fundraising contribution of £660 for a two-month placement and £1,210 for a five-month placement. Volunteers also cover travel costs, insurance and food.
Benefits: Training in the UK, orientation and accommodation in India.
Work individually/in teams: Individually, in general, but are placed in pairs.

In-country support for volunteers	Pre-departure training	Post-return debriefing	Contact with returned volunteers
Yes, available full-time.	Yes, focuses on development issues. Orientation week provided in-country.	Yes, feedback sessions including workshops and discussions.	Yes.

Ecologia Youth Trust

Address: The Park, Forres, Moray IV36 3TD, Scotland
Telephone number: +44 (0)1309 690995
Fax number: +44 (0)1309 690995
Email: volunteer@ecologia.org.uk
Website: www.ecologia.org.uk

Established in 1995, Ecologia Trust is a not-for-profit organisation

Type: Short-term/intercultural.
Stated mission: 'Kitezh Community of foster families for orphans is the cornerstone of Ecologia Youth Trust's work in Russia. We support social initiatives in the fields of youth empowerment, rehabilitation of orphans, ecological education and nature protection. Kitezh Children's Community consists of a group of foster families who provide a loving home and education to children who have been abandoned or orphaned. It is a place of happiness and joyful refuge for Russian children in contrast to the grim and institutionalized environment of Russian orphanages.'
Countries: Europe (Russia).
Activities: Children/young people, conservation/environment, construction, education.
Duration: 1 month to 1 year.
Age requirements: Minimum 17 years.
Disability access: No.
Language requirements: No.
Educational/professional qualifications: No.
Other requirements: Volunteers should be independent and self-sufficient.
Application procedure: Potential volunteers fill out a preliminary questionnaire which is sent to Kitezh for their approval. If accepted, an official invitation is obtained, which is needed to get visas. Visas are arranged for UK residents; volunteers from other countries must apply in their own countries, but the organisation gives advice on how to do this. No references are required but all volunteers must get a police background check before they go.
Costs: Yes. Costs start at £555 for one month. Volunteers also cover travel costs.
Benefits: Costs include visas and registrations, internal transfers to and from Moscow, food and accommodation, support and practical advice.
Work individually/in teams: Both.

In-country support for volunteers	Pre-programme training	Post-programme debriefing	Contact with returned volunteers
Yes, available half-time.	Volunteers are given a pack pre-departure.	Carried out through a feedback form.	Yes.

Ecuador Volunteer

Address: Reina Victoria, 1325 y Lizardo García, Quito, Ecuador
Telephone number: +593 2 256 4488
Fax number: +593 2 256 4488
Email: info@ecuadorvolunteer.org
Website: www.ecuadorvolunteer.org

Ecuador Volunteer is a not-for-profit organisation.

Type: Short-term/intercultural; long-term development
Stated mission: 'To help the development of social and conservation programmes, to improve the quality of life to local people in need.'
Countries: Latin America (Ecuador)
Activities: Children/young people, community development, conservation/ environment, education, health/medical.
Duration: 2 weeks to 1 year.
Age requirements: Minimum 18 years, maximum 40 years.
Disability access: No.
Language requirements: Yes; intermediate-level Spanish is required. The organisation can help volunteers find a programme to improve their abilities in Spanish before starting the project.
Educational/professional qualifications: Depends on project; contact organisation for further information.
Other requirements: No.
Application procedure: Complete the online application form on the organisation's website; submit a CV, obtain a 12-VII volunteer visa (if staying in Ecuador for more than 3 months); obtain travel insurance; get a police clearance form.
Cost: Yes; costs start from $150 for the programme application fee.
Benefits: Accommodation and food.
Work individually/in teams: Both, depending on the project.

In-country support for volunteers	Pre-programme training	Post-programme debriefing	Contact with returned volunteers
No.	Yes, cultural immersion, safety, information on each programme, tourist information, policies and rules.	No.	Yes.

Frontier

Address: 50–52 Rivington Street, London EC2A 3QP, UK
Telephone number: +44(0)20 7613 2422
Fax number: +44 (0)20 7613 2992
Email: info@frontier.ac.uk
Website: www.frontier.ac.uk

Established in 1989, Frontier is a not-for-profit organisation.

Type: Conservation/environment
Stated mission: 'To promote and advance tropical field research and to implement practical projects contributing to the conservation of natural resources and the development of sustainable livelihoods.'
Countries: Africa (Cameroon, Egypt, Ghana, Kenya, Madagascar, Namibia, South Africa, Tanzania, Uganda), Asia (Cambodia, China, Fiji, India, Indonesia, Mongolia, Nepal, Thailand), Latin America (Argentina, Costa Rica, Ecuador, Guatemala, Nicaragua, Peru).
Activities: Conservation/environment, education.
Duration: 4, 8, 10 or 20 weeks.
Age requirements: Minimum 17 years, no maximum age.
Disability access: Depends on placement; contact organisation for further details.
Language requirements: English.
Educational/professional qualifications: No.
Other requirements: No.
Application procedure: Apply online, or request a postal application form. Volunteers are required to successfully complete a short telephone interview.
Costs: Yes. Four-week places cost from £1,100. Volunteers also cover travel costs.
Benefits: Briefing weekend in the UK, fundraising advice, administration, full travel and medical documentation. In-country costs include accommodation, transfers, food, group expedition equipment, expedition and research training, and staff.
Work individually/in teams: In teams.

In-country support for volunteers	Pre-programme training	Post-programme debriefing	Contact with returned volunteers
Yes, available full-time.	Briefing weekend prior to departure; in-country induction and full training, including health and safety, etc.	No.	Yes.

Fundación Jatun Sacha

Address: Pasaje Eugenio de Santillán N34-248 y Maurián, Urbanización Rumipamba, Quito, Ecuador
Telephone numbers: +593 2 243 2240; 243 2246; 243 2173
Fax number: +593 2 331 8156
Email: volunteer@jatunsacha.org; jatunsacha@jatunsacha.org
Website: www.jatunsacha.org

Established in 1989, Jatun Sacha is a not-for-profit organisation.

Type: Conservation/environment.
Stated mission: 'Jatun Sacha Foundation is a non-governmental, non-profit organization dedicated to promoting the conservation of forest, aquatic and páramo ecosystems of Ecuador through technical training, scientific research, environmental education, community development, sustainable management of natural resources, and the development of leaders with a high participation of ethnic groups and women, to improve the quality of life of the community.'
Countries: Latin America (Ecuador)
Activities: Agriculture, community development, conservation/environment, education, internships.
Duration: 14 days upwards.
Age requirements: Minimum 18 years.
Disability access: Depends on placement; contact organisation for further details.
Language requirements: No. However, volunteers are encouraged to gain a basic level of Spanish before or during their volunteer experience.
Educational/professional qualifications: No.
Other requirements: Each volunteer is required, as part of the application process, to verify through a doctor's certificate that they are in good health and can carry out all the duties expected of them as a volunteer. Volunteers should also have the desire to learn, be adaptable and be conservation-minded.
Application: Submit an application to the organisation, with an application fee ($35 or $50, depending on placement). Include an application letter detailing your interest in the placement for which you are applying, a CV, a recent health certificate, a police record stating previous (if any) offences. Further details of application requirements are available from the organisation.
Costs: Yes. Application fees start from $35, programme costs start from $395. Volunteers also cover travel costs.
Benefits: Orientation, accommodation, food and training.
Work individually/in teams: Both.

In-country support for volunteers	Pre-programme training	Post-programme debriefing	Contact with returned volunteers
Yes, available full-time.	Has volunteer orientation programme.	Feedback is elicited through an evaluation form.	Yes.

GAP Activity Projects

Address: GAP House, 44 Queens Road, Reading, Berkshire RG1 4BB, UK
Telephone number: +44 (0)118 959 4914
Fax number: +44 (0)118 957 6634
Email: volunteer@gap.org.uk
Website: www.gap.org.uk

Established in 1972, GAP Activity Projects is a not-for-profit organisation.

Type: Short-term/intercultural.
Stated mission: 'GAP Activity Projects' mission is to provide a distinctive and international volunteering experience, which is inclusive to all young people. We will do this through a journey of discovery that fosters independence, helps others and promotes global understanding.'
Countries: Africa (Ghana, Malawi, South Africa, Tanzania), Asia (China, Fiji, India, Malaysia, Thailand, Vanuatu, Vietnam), Europe (Russia), Latin America (Argentina, Brazil, Chile, Ecuador, Mexico, Paraguay).
Activities: Children/young people, community development, conservation/environment, disability/special needs, education, health/medical.
Duration: 3–12 months
Age requirements: Minimum 17 years; maximum 25 years.
Disability access: Yes; GAP Activity Projects welcome applications from young people with disabilities.
Language requirements: Depends on placement; Spanish, French or German may be required.
Educational/professional qualifications: Depends on placement. Volunteers are required to attend a Teaching Skills Course before teaching placements – this is arranged through GAP.
Other requirements: Yes. Some opportunities may be restricted to male or female applicants. Overseas hosts are not necessarily subject to UK equal opportunities and disability discrimination legislation and may sometimes request a male or female volunteer for reasons such as availability of accommodation.
Application procedure: Applicants can apply either online or by post using the application form in the brochure/on the website. A reference is also required. Once submitted, the applicant will be informed of an interview date within 28 days. Interviews take place in Dublin or Belfast or on the phone.
Costs: Yes, €1,950. Volunteers also cover costs related to flights, visa, insurance, medical and teaching skills course (where needed)
Benefits: Included in the fee are: a briefing in UK, an orientation in-country, all food and accommodation. Certain placements provide living expenses which vary in amount from country to country.
Work individually/in teams: Both.

In-country support for volunteers	Pre-departure training	Post-return debriefing	Contact with returned volunteers
Yes.	Yes, through briefing day and orientation.	Yes.	Yes.

GAP SPORTS

Address: Thamesbourne Lodge, Station Road, Bourne End, Buckinghamshire SL8 5QH, UK
Telephone number: +44 (0)870 837 9797
Email: info@gapsports.com
Website: www.gapsports.com

Established in 2002, GAP SPORTS is a for-profit organisation.

Type: Short-term/intercultural.
Stated mission: 'GAP SPORTS offers a number of opportunities overseas including sports and non-sports community outreach projects in Africa and Latin America, top-level ski/snowboard instructor courses in Canada, and professional training at international golf, rugby, cricket and scuba academies. No previous experience is required and we welcome applicants from all walks of life.
Countries: Africa (Ghana, South Africa), Latin America (Costa Rica).
Activities: Conservation/environment, construction, health/medical, other.
Duration: 5–52 weeks.
Age requirements: Minimum 18 years.
Disability access: No.
Language requirements: English.
Educational/professional qualifications: No qualifications required for coaching positions; sports psychologists must have relevant academic qualifications; physiotherapists must also have a minimum of 50 hours' clinical experience.
Other requirements: A willingness to work hard and be enthusiastic.
Application procedure: Applicants must download an application form from website, or contact the UK office for information. A deposit and details of previous experience and motives for joining must also be supplied.
Costs: Yes; from £1,295 for a 5-week placement. Volunteers also cover travel costs.
Benefits: Airport transfers; in-country support and project co-ordination; food; accommodation; some social events and recreational activities; donation to host community/organisation.
Work individually/in teams: Both.

In-country support for volunteers	Pre-departure training	Post-return debriefing	Contact with returned volunteers
Yes, available full-time.	Pre-departure training day for all applicants: includes travel safety awareness, travel health, orientation, welcome packs, kit briefings etc.	Through feedback forms and reunions.	Yes.

Geekcorps

Address: 901 15th Street NW, Suite 1010, Washington DC 20005, USA
Telephone number: +1 202 326 0280
Fax number: +1 202 326 0289
Email: geekcorps@iesc.org
Website: www.geekcorps.org

Established in 2001, Geekcorps is a not-for-profit organisation.

Type: Long-term development.
Stated mission: 'IESC Geekcorps is an international nonprofit organisation that promotes stability and prosperity in the developing world through information and communication technology (ICT). Geekcorps' international technology experts teach communities how to be digitally independent by expanding private enterprise with innovative, appropriate, and affordable information and communication technologies. To increase the capacity of small and medium-sized business, local government, and supporting organizations to be more profitable and efficient using technology, Geekcorps draws on a database of more than 3,500 technical experts willing to share their talents and experience in developing nations.'
Countries: Africa, Asia, Europe, Latin America (various).
Activities: Administration/management, business, capacity building, education, technical support, other.
Duration: 1–6 months
Age requirements: No. However, volunteers do need at least 3 to 5 years' professional experience in the subject matter they are to work on.
Disability access: Yes.
Language requirements: Depends on programme. For example, French is required for some placements.
Educational/professional qualifications: Yes. Volunteers need 3–5 years of professional experience in the technical subject matter they are to work on. Specialists required include programmers, graphic designers, public relations and business consultants, database and e-commerce architects, marketing and networking gurus, web developers and designers, and GIS specialists.
Other requirements: No
Application procedure: Applicants fill out an application form that is available on the website. The application is reviewed and included in a skills-bank that is searched when new projects are identified. Candidates are then interviewed in person or by phone.
Costs: No.
Benefits: Airfare, lodging, stipend, health and medical evacuation insurance, and dedicated in-country staff.
Work individually/in teams: Both.

In-country support for volunteers	Pre-programme training	Post-programme debriefing	Contact with returned volunteers
Yes, may be full-time or part-time, depending on project.	Yes, in-country orientation provided. Includes cultural competence and country-specific information.	Involves two sets of interviews with volunteers.	Yes, this is always provided.

Genesis Volunteer Program

Address: Malecon #1312, Bahia de Caraquez, Ecuador
Telephone number: +593 269 2400
Email: vladirvi@yahoo.com
Website: http://www.bahiacity.com/volunteer

Founded in 1999, the Genesis Volunteer Program is a not-for-profit organisation.

Type: Short-term/intercultural.
Stated mission: 'The Genesis Volunteer Program was developed in 1999 and believes that a liberal education is the key to enabling Ecuador to rise above its poverty. The program focuses on giving students a solid education in core concepts as well as the English language. Teaching the children English is the volunteer aspect of this programme. As a result of many volunteers from all over the world, this programme has been running successfully for six years and is essentially about sharing. Share your skills with the children by teaching them English and in turn you will benefit from being immersed in the richness of Ecuadorian culture and the Spanish language.'
Countries: Latin America (Ecuador).
Activities: Children/young people, education.
Duration: 4 weeks +.
Age requirements: Minimum 18 years.
Disability access: Contact organisation for more information
Language requirements: None, but volunteers are asked to learn some basic Spanish phrases.
Educational/professional qualifications: No.
Other requirements: Patience, love and courage.
Application procedure: Application form is available on the website.
Costs: Yes. Programme fee of $990 per month. Volunteers also cover travel costs.
Benefits: Accommodation, food, donation to projects, welcome orientation, TEFL training class, Spanish language classes, unlimited internet access.
Work individually/in teams: In teams.

In-country support for volunteers	Pre-programme training	Post-programme debriefing	Contact with returned volunteers
Yes, through team leaders.	Yes, welcome orientation provided.	No.	Yes.

Global Citizens Network

Address: 130 N. Howell Street, St Paul, Minnesota, 55104 USA
Telephone numbers: +1 651 644 0960; 800 644 9292
Fax number: +1 651 646 6176
Email: info@globalcitizens.org
Website: www.globalcitizens.org

Established in 1992, Global Citizens Network is a not-for-profit organisation.

Type: Short-term/intercultural.
Stated mission: 'The mission of Global Citizens Network (GCN) is to send short-term teams of volunteers to communities in other cultures where participants immerse themselves in the culture and daily life of the community. Each volunteer team is partnered with a local grassroots organization active in meeting local needs. The GCN vision is to create a network of people who are committed to the shared values of peace, justice, tolerance, cross-cultural understanding and global cooperation, to the preservation of indigenous cultures, traditions and ecologies, and to the enhancement of the quality of life around the world.'
Countries: Africa (Kenya, Tanzania), Asia (Nepal, Thailand), Latin America (Brazil, Ecuador, Guatemala, Mexico, Peru).
Activities: Agriculture, children/young people, community development, construction, women, other.
Duration: 1–3 weeks.
Age requirements: Minimum 18 years; people under 18 must be accompanied by an adult. No maximum age. Designated family trips have no age limit.
Disability access: Depends on placement; contact organisation for further details.
Language requirements: No.
Educational/professional qualifications: No.
Other requirements: Willingness to appreciate and accept other cultures. If any expertise is needed for a project, the local community will provide these skills.
Application procedure: To secure a spot on a team, a completed application and money order for US$300 must be received in the office. Complete payment of programme costs is required at least 6 weeks before trip start-date. Applications can be downloaded from website at www.globalcitizens.org. Applications are accepted until trip is filled. Once the trip has been confirmed, volunteer can purchase air ticket and make plans accordingly.
Costs: Yes, starting from $800. Volunteers also cover travel costs.
Benefits: In-country travel and lodging, most meals, orientation materials, medical and emergency evacuation insurance, a share of the team leader's expenses (team leaders are not paid) and a donation to the village project.
Work individually/in teams: In teams.

In-country support for volunteers	Pre-programme training	Post-programme debriefing	Contact with returned volunteers
Yes, usually a member of the host community or an NGO. Varies according to site.	Yes, each volunteer receives an orientation manual.	No.	Yes

Global Service Corps

Address: 300 Broadway, Suite 28, San Francisco, CA 94133, USA
Telephone number: +1 415 788 3666
Fax number: +1 415 788 7324
Email: gsc@earthisland.org
Website: www.globalservicecorps.org

Established in 1993, Global Service Corps is a not-for-profit organisation.

Type: Short-term/intercultural.
Stated mission: 'Global Service Corps (GSC) creates opportunities for adult participants to live in developing nations and work on projects that serve Earth's people and her environment. These projects emphasise grass-roots collaboration on the local level, promote mutual transfer of skills and foster cross-cultural understanding. Our goals are to provide developing communities with the means to function more sustainably and to widen the perspectives of participants as responsible global citizens by revealing the challenges of life in developing nations.'
Countries: Africa (Tanzania), Asia (Thailand).
Activities: Agriculture, education, health/medical.
Duration: 2 weeks to 6 months.
Age requirements: Minimum 18 years for projects in Thailand; minimum 20 years for projects in Tanzania.
Disability access: Depends on project; contact organisation for more details.
Language requirements: English.
Educational/professional qualifications: No.
Other requirements: Volunteers should be flexible and adaptable, and be proficient in English.
Application procedure: Volunteers must send in a copy of their CV, and write a personal statement. They must complete Global Service Corps' application, and send in a $150 refundable application deposit.
Costs: Yes. Two-week programmes begin at US$2,325 plus airfare. Tax-deductible to the full extent of the law.
Benefits: Subsidised airport pick-up and project transport; hotel, hostel or homestay accommodation; all meals; language training; weekend excursion; 24-hour support and project administration.
Work individually/in teams: Depends on project.

In-country support for volunteers	Pre-programme training	Post-programme debriefing	Contact with returned volunteers
Yes, available full time.	Pre-departure written materials; in-country training and orientation.	No.	Yes.

Global Volunteer Network

Address: PO Box 30-968, Lower Hutt, New Zealand, 5040
Telephone number: +64 4 569 9080
Fax number: +64 4 569 9081
Email: info@volunteer.org.nz
Website: www.volunteer.org.nz

Established in 2001, Global Volunteer Network is a for-profit organisation.

Type: Short-term/intercultural.
Stated mission: 'The Global Volunteer Network (GVN) vision is to connect people with communities in need. At GVN we align with the idea of "local solutions to local problems", so we work with local community organisations in each country. We believe that local communities are in the best position to determine their needs, and we provide volunteers to help them achieve their goals.'
Countries: Africa (Ghana, Kenya, Rwanda, South Africa, Tanzania, Uganda), Asia (Cambodia, China, India, Nepal, Philippines, Thailand, Vietnam), Europe (Romania, Russia), Latin America (Costa Rica, Ecuador, El Salvador, Honduras).
Activities: Children/young people, community development, conservation/environment, education, health/medical, other.
Duration: 2 weeks to 6 months.
Age requirements: Minimum normally 18 years.
Disability access: GVN considers volunteers on a case-by-case basis.
Language requirements: No.
Educational/professional qualifications: Depends on placement. Specific medical experience and qualifications are required for all medical programmes.
Other requirements: Volunteers submit application forms through the GVN website, which are considered on a case-by-case basis.
Application procedure: Volunteers fill out the application form at the GVN website. No references are required. Successful volunteers are emailed a letter of acceptance. If they wish, volunteers pay their application fee to secure their place on the programme. Once the application fee is paid, the GVN Volunteer Co-ordinator will contact the volunteer and partner organisation to ensure everything is organised.
Costs: Yes. An application fee of US $350 applies to all GVN programmes. The programme fee varies according to programme, and the cheapest starts at US$400 for two weeks. Volunteers also cover travel costs.
Benefits: Food, accommodation and other costs within the programme.
Work individually/in teams: Both.

In-country support for volunteers	Pre-programme training	Post-programme debriefing	Contact with returned volunteers
Yes.	No.	Offers a separate programme that deals with some of the issues that can be raised post-volunteering.	Yes.

Gram Vikas

Address: Gram Vikas, Mohuda Village, Berhampur, Orissa 760002, India
Telephone numbers: +91 680 226 1866–9
Fax number: +91 680 226 1862
Email: info@gramvikas.org; gramvikas@gmail.com
Website: www.gramvikas.org

Established in 1979, Gram Vikas is a not-for-profit organisation.

Type: Long-term development.
Stated mission: 'The vision of Gram Vikas is: an equitable and sustainable society where people live in peace with dignity. Gram Vikas' mission is to promote processes which are sustainable, socially inclusive and gender equitable, to enable critical masses of poor and marginalised rural people or communities to achieve a dignified quality of life. Gram Vikas leverages the inherent strength of communities to initiate, manage and sustain context-specific development processes. The process is backed up by organising, technical and managerial support by Gram Vikas.'
Countries: Asia (India).
Activities: Agriculture, capacity building, community development, construction, education, technical support, women, other.
Duration: 4 months +.
Age requirements: Volunteers must be graduates or postgraduates who are ready to work in remote rural locations with poor road connections and communication infrastructure.
Disability access: No.
Language requirements: English, and willingness to learn local language.
Educational/professional qualifications: Yes. Minimum qualification: graduate/ postgraduate. Specific areas include: people with strong research and documentation skills, with a background in sociology, political science, development economics; people with ability to teach English to non-English speakers; people from civil/ mechanical engineering background with experience in renewable energy, building technologies; trainers in reproductive health, joyful learning, etc.; people with GIS expertise.
Other requirements: An understanding of the Indian context is desirable; past work experience is also a consideration.
Application procedure: Visit the website, submit a CV detailing past experience and potential contributions to the organisation.
Costs: Yes, accommodation and food cost US$6 per day. Volunteers also cover travel costs.
Benefits: Free accommodation and food for long-term volunteers (1–2 years' service).
Work individually/in teams: In teams.

In-country support for volunteers	Pre-programme training	Post-programme debriefing	Contact with returned volunteers
Yes, not on full-time basis.	Yes, includes an induction programme and an induction manual.	Contact organisation for further information.	Yes.

Greenforce

Address: 11–15 Betterton Street, London WC2H 9 BP, UK
Telephone number: +44 (0)20 7470 8888
Fax number: +44 (0)20 7379 0801
Email: info@greenforce.org
Website: www.greenforce.org

Established in 1996, Greenforce is a not-for-profit organisation.

Type: Conservation/environment.
Stated mission: 'Following the Rio Earth Summit of 1992, Greenforce was formed to meet section 3c. The provision of biodiversity data and management, to ensure areas survive both environmentally and economically.'
Countries: Africa (South Africa, Tanzania), Asia (China, Fiji, India, Nepal/Tibet), Latin America (Bahamas, Ecuador).
Activities: Conservation/environment.
Duration: 1–6 months; average is 3 months.
Age requirements: Minimum 17 years.
Disability access: Yes, subject to disability and insurance cover.
Language requirements: No. If required, language training is provided – Spanish, Nepali, Hindi and Maasai.
Educational/professional qualifications: No.
Other requirements: No.
Application procedure: Obtain brochure; select country; review website information; complete and return application form; advised if accepted within four working days.
Costs: Yes, ten weeks inclusive costs from £2,300. Volunteers also cover travel and insurance costs.
Benefits: Pre-departure training packs; training day; meeting at arrival airport, then three meals per day, all training and transport; medical insurance and accommodation.
Work individually/in teams: In teams.

In-country support for volunteers	Pre-departure training	Post-return debriefing	Contact with returned volunteers
Yes, available full-time.	Provides pre-departure packs, pre-departure training day.	Detailed questionnaire and an annual reunion.	Yes, ex-volunteers attend pre-departure training.

Health and Development Networks (HDN)

Address: P.O. Box 7517, Malahide, Co. Dublin, Ireland or P.O. Box 173, Chiang Mai University Post Office, Huay Kaew Road, Muang Chiang Mai, 50200, Thailand
Telephone number: +66 (0) 53 449055
Fax number: +66 (0) 53 449056
Email: info@hdnet.org
Website: http://www.hdnet.org

Established in 1998, HDN is a not-for-profit organisation.

Type: Long-term development
Mission statement: "Our vision is of reduced transmission, morbidity, mortality and socio-economic impact of the HIV and TB epidemics, as a result of effective alliances among a full range of partners. To help achieve this, the specific mission of the organization is to improve the quality and accountability of HIV and TB responses, by facilitating high-quality information, dialogue and advocacy platforms among affected people and communities."
Countries: Africa (South Africa, Uganda, Zambia, Zimbabwe), Asia (China, Malaysia, Thailand, Vietnam).
Activities: Internships.
Duration: 3 months to one year.
Age requirements: 21 years +.
Disability access: Contact organisation for further details.
Language requirements: Sound written and verbal communication skills in English.
Educational/professional qualifications: Yes. Desirable skills and qualifications include first-year graduate student or candidate with a graduate degree in development and management or health; knowledge in issues of HIV and AIDS, public health and development; strong research and analytical skills.
Other requirements: No.
Application procedure: Please email your CV with two referees and a cover letter to hr@hdnet.org.
Costs: Depends on placement; please contact HDN for information.
Benefits: HDN will provide accommodation and a monthly stipend that should cover basic expenses over the period of the internship.
Work individually/in teams: Both.

In-country support for volunteers	Pre-programme training	Post-programme debriefing	Contact with returned volunteers
Yes, full-time	In-country training provided	Contact organisation for further details	Yes

Himalayan Light Foundation

Address: PO Box 12191, Baluwatar, Kathmandu, Nepal
Telephone number: +977 1 442 5393
Fax number: +977 1 441 2924
Email: info@hlf.org.np
Website: www.hlf.org.np

Established in 1997, HLF is a not-for-profit organisation.

Type: Long-term development.
Stated mission: 'HLF is a non-profit, non-governmental organisation whose main objective is to improve the quality of life of remote populations via the use of and education about environmentally friendly, renewable energy technologies. Environmental: solar energy significantly reduces the use of fuel, wood and petroleum, thus mitigating deforestation and carbon emissions, significant environmental risks in forested regions of South Asia. Social/Economic: HLF fosters community control and alleviates the effects of international tourism in remote communities. Communities, particularly women's groups, receive solar systems and training in schools, community centres, and health posts; providing opportunities for skills development, improved health, and community growth.'
Countries: Asia (India, Nepal, Sri Lanka)
Activities: Capacity building, community development, conservation/environment, construction, education, internships, technical support, women.
Duration: 10 days to 6 months.
Age requirements: No.
Disability access: Depends on placement; contact organisation for further details.
Language requirements: No.
Educational/professional qualifications: No, but volunteers must participate in a solar installation training programme before going into the field.
Other requirements: Sense of cultural awareness and ability to adapt to new surroundings.
Application procedure: Prospective participant must, at least two months before the programme begins, email HLF outlining their interests and experiences, and any details relevant to the programme. HLF will work with applicant to select appropriate site based on applicant's interests and site availability. Once confirmed, participant will complete a Participation Confirmation Form and convey travel itinerary details to HLF so that transport from airport can be arranged. No references are required.
Costs: Yes, from $1,200. Volunteers also cover travel costs.
Benefits: Cost includes: food and accommodation, equipment transportation, one 36-watt solar energy system and accompanying equipment, and all in-country travel costs except flights.
Work individually/in teams: Both.

In-country support for volunteers	Pre-departure training	Post-return debriefing	Contact with returned volunteers
Yes, available full-time.	Yes, pre-project training at HQ or partner organisation.	Yes, 2–3 days' post-project reporting and evaluation.	Yes.

x No 19531, Paknajol, Kathmandu, Nepal
ers: + 977 1 470 0210; (mobile) + 977 985 105 4813
7 1 470 1356
Email: info@infonepal.org; infonepal@mail.com.np
Website: www.infonepal.org

Established in 2000, INFO Nepal is a not-for-profit organisation.

Type: Short-term/intercultural.
Stated mission: 'INFO is a non-governmental organization (NGO), established by 4 Nepalese, and registered with the Social Welfare Council of Nepal since 2000. Our Mission is: develop a challenging volunteer programme for the benefit of both the volunteers and the communities of Nepal; increase awareness of the vital importance of English literacy for Nepali students; educate communities about environmental issues; provide training in the creation of self-employment for the communities; provide language tuition and cultural information for overseas visitors studying, conducting research, and volunteering in Nepal; immerse volunteers in the richness of Nepali culture ensuring a safe, memorable experience in a supportive environment.'
Countries: Asia (Nepal).
Activities: Children/young people, education, health/medical.
Duration: 2 weeks to 10 months.
Age requirements: Minimum 18 years, maximum 80 years.
Disability access: Yes, contact organisation for further details.
Language requirements: English.
Educational/professional qualifications: No.
Other requirements: Patience, sense of humour, tolerance, willingness to share, flexibility, self-motivation, open-mindedness, enthusiasm for learning about new cultures, ability to laugh at yourself. Volunteers must be in good physical health.
Application procedure: Online application form available on website. No references are required.
Costs: Yes, from £400. Volunteers also cover travel costs.
Benefits: Accommodation and meals during training and placement; transportation for volunteers to and from the airport and to and from placement location; supervision during placement.
Work individually/in teams: Both.

In-country support for volunteers	Pre-programme training	Post-programme debriefing	Contact with returned volunteers
Yes, not on full-time basis.	No.	No.	Yes.

Interims for Development

Address: Kingsbury House, 468 Church Lane, London NW9 8UA, UK
Telephone number: +44 (0)20 8200 2373
Fax number: +44 (0)20 8200 2383
Email: info@InterimsFD.com
Website: www.InterimsFD.com

Established in 2002, Interims for Development is a for-profit organisation.

Type: Recruitment/placement.
Stated mission: 'Our mission is to assist the technological and human capacity of African businesses and organizations to meet the challenges of global competition. We aim to direct towards Africa the necessary skills and expertise that will help support African companies in both the private and public sectors in their efforts to transform their economies for the well-being of their citizens. To this end, we focus on the provision of high quality, hands-on human resources, business development and in-house training, primarily through professionals who volunteer their skills on short-term assignments, to companies and organisations based in or operating in Africa.'
Countries: Africa (various).
Activities: Business, capacity building, education, internships, technical support.
Duration: 1 week to 1 year.
Age requirements: No maximum age limit subject to good health and ability to undertake the required role.
Disability access: Depends on project; contact organisation for further information.
Language requirements: English. In some instances French or Portuguese may be required.
Educational/professional qualifications: Yes. Requirements depend on the assignment.
Other requirements: No.
Application procedure: An Interim Application form must be completed in hard copy and submitted with a copy of the applicant's CV. The form can be downloaded from the website. References will be taken up before any assignment is confirmed.
Costs: No.
Benefits: Travel costs, insurance, accommodation and a modest stipend to assist with incidental expenses.
Work individually/in teams: Individually.

In-country support for volunteers	Pre-departure training	Post-return debriefing	Contact with returned volunteers
Limited, depends on country	Cultural training and orientation for volunteers prior to their departure.	Yes.	Yes.

International Relief Friendship Foundation (IRFF)

Address: 307 rue de Rollingergrund, L-2441 Luxembourg City, Luxembourg
Telephone numbers: and +352 220066; (mobile) +352 2174 4973
Email: luxirff@lu.coditel.net
Website: www.irff-europe.org

Established in 1997, the IRFF is a not-for-profit organisation.

Type: Short-term/intercultural.
Stated mission: 'The IRFF is a catalyst for social change and progress. Our service projects stress the importance of cooperative efforts for sustained long-term development. We seek to stimulate individuals and communities by offering a vision of public welfare arising from self-reliance and ethical action. We support short and long terms programmes that encourage the active participation of the intended beneficiaries, who are asked to invest their own time, energy and resources for the achievement of the project. By utilising an international network, we activate local groups and volunteers to initiate shared-work projects that serve the public need.'
Countries: Africa (Kenya, Zambia), Asia (Palestine), Europe (Albania, Bosnia-Herzegovina, Ukraine)
Activities: Agriculture, children/young people, community development, construction, other.
Duration: 1 week to 1 year.
Age requirements: Minimum 18 years.
Disability access: No.
Language requirements: English.
Educational/professional qualifications: No.
Other requirements: No.
Application procedure: Apply through IRFF application forms (contact organisation for these); personal reference required.
Costs: Yes, starting from $250 (depends on location of project). Volunteers also cover travel costs.
Benefits: Food and accommodation.
Work individually/in teams: In teams.

In-country support for volunteers	Pre-programme training	Post-programme debriefing	Contact with returned volunteers
Yes, available full-time.	Yes, two-day orientation programme and in-country training.	Day-long evaluations are carried out at the end of projects.	Yes.

Iracambi Atlantic Rainforest Research and Conservation Center

Address: Fazenda Iracambi, Caixa Postal No 1, Rosário de Limeira, Minas Gerais, CEP 36878-000, Brazil
Telephone number: +55 32 3721 1436
Email: iracambi@iracambi.com
Website: www.iracambi.com

Established in 1999, Iracambi is a not-for-profit organisation.

Type: Conservation/environment.
Stated mission: 'We work with our community to make conservation of the rainforest more attractive than its destruction. Iracambi believes that it is only by working to improve the future of the people who live in the area that we can improve the future of the forest. Volunteers carry out work within our four research priority areas: land use management, forest restoration, income generating alternatives, community understanding and engagement, as well as work which improves the capacity of the Centre.'
Countries: Latin America (Brazil)
Activities: Administration/management, business, children/young people, community development, conservation/environment, internships, technical support, other.
Duration: 1–6 months.
Age requirements: Minimum 18 years.
Disability access: Depends on placement; contact organisation for further information.
Language requirements: Depends on placement; Portuguese may be required for some roles.
Educational/professional qualifications: No.
Other requirements: No.
Application procedure: An up-to-date CV/resumé and a covering letter stating applicant's interests – whether a specific role or a general area of work. The organisation then works with the volunteer to clarify the work that they will be doing. They are also sent more information on the project, and more specific information is requested from them. When a role has been defined an email with this and terms and conditions is sent out. References are preferred.
Costs: Yes; from $550. Volunteers also cover travel costs.
Benefits: Food and accommodation in shared housing.
Work individually/in teams: Depends on placement.

In-country support for volunteers	Pre-programme training	Post-programme debriefing	Contact with returned volunteers
Yes, available full-time.	No.	Through project evaluation.	Yes, by email.

Jubilee Ventures/Africa Development Consortium (AFRIDEC)

Address: PO Box 10477-00100, GPO Nairobi, Kenya.
Telephone number: +254 20 342929
Email: admin@jubileeventures.org
Website: www.jubileeventures.org

Established in 2003, Jubilee Ventures is a not-for-profit organisation.

Type: Short-term/intercultural.
Stated mission: 'Our mission is to work in partnership with local communities to foster community development and nature conservation. We aim at helping less fortunate members of the community including orphans and the disabled and fostering awareness of HIV/AIDS. We seek to explore, develop and promote initiatives to promote environment protection and community understanding in Africa and the world, through volunteer work and other development initiatives.'
Countries: Africa (Kenya, Tanzania)
Activities: Children/young people, conservation/environment, education, health/medical, internships.
Duration: 2 weeks to 6 months.
Age requirements: Minimum 18 years.
Disability access: Depends on placement; contact organisation for further details.
Language requirements: Working knowledge of English.
Educational/professional qualifications: Depends on placement. Medical/nursing volunteers should have medical training background or at least be in the final years of their training. Premedical and beginning medical students applying for medical volunteer work may participate only as student interns.
Other requirements: Co-operative attitude; willingness to learn and help; willingness to live a simple life in a developing country.
Application process: Volunteers write to request an application. They are then sent a response offering available options. Volunteers can email any questions they may have at any point in the application process. References are not required for the application process except in rare cases.
Costs: Yes, from $750 for a two-week stay. Volunteers also cover travel costs.
Benefits: Food, accommodation, in-country transportation, contribution to the hosting project.
Work individually/in teams: In teams.

In-country support for volunteers	Pre-programme training	Post-programme debriefing	Contact with returned volunteers
Yes, available full-time.	All volunteers receive a pre-travel manual and one-day in-country orientation; one week volunteer training for some placements.	Through evaluation reports.	Yes.

Kings World Trust for Children

Address: 7 Deepdene, Haslemere, Surrey GU27 1RE, UK; or Paul Gunton, Carrowntawy House, Ballymote, Co. Sligo
Telephone numbers: +44 (0)71 918 3936; (0)1428 653504
Email: kwtc@haslemere.com
Website: www.kingschildren.org

Established in 1995, Kings World Trust is a not-for-profit organisation.

Type: Short-term/intercultural.
Stated mission: 'The Trust provides a caring home, an education and skills training for orphan and homeless children and young people in South India. The Trust has 2 residential children's villages and one children's home and runs an "outreach" support programme for poor children in their own homes. KWTC has 2 Nurse operated Rural Health Clinics and runs a Health Education Programme in Rural Villages. The Trust also has HIV/AIDS community workers who provide education and counselling to individuals, families and communities. The Trust opened its own English school in 2005 providing a formal education for up to 700 children. We take skilled personnel, gap students and mature individuals taking time out later in their lives.'
Countries: Asia (India)
Activities: Children/young people, education, health/medical.
Duration: 1–6 months, depending on activities.
Age requirements: Minimum 17 years.
Disability access: Contact organisation for further information.
Language requirements: English.
Educational/professional qualifications: No. However, doctors, nurses, teachers and other qualified personnel are welcomed.
Other requirements: No.
Application procedure: Complete Trust's application form (on website or sent by mail); provide three references; all applicants who are not straight out of school must provide a police 'no conviction' certificate.
Costs: Yes. Volunteers must fundraise a minimum of £400 (UK) prior to departure and contribute £10 (UK) a week to living expenses in India. Volunteers also cover travel costs.
Benefits: Accommodation and food.
Work individually/in teams: In teams.

In-country support for volunteers	Pre-departure training	Post-return debriefing	Contact with returned volunteers
Yes, available full-time.	No.	Volunteers are asked to submit a written report.	Yes.

Mafanikio Community Based Organisation

Address: PO BOX 26609, 00504 Nairobi, Kenya
Telephone number: +254 72 082 5340
Email: dchipo@yahoo.com
Website: www.mafanikio.com

Mafanikio Community Based Organisation is a not-for-profit organisation.

Type: Short-term/cultural.
Stated mission: 'Our mission is poverty reduction through empowering communities by supporting their initiatives with possible resources and participation in work camps. This encourages the community to utilise their skills and ability towards their development.
Objectives:

- To afford marginalised communities an opportunity to better their living conditions through developmental projects.
- To create awareness about topical issues such as environmental conservation, girl child education, civic education and HIV/AIDS.
- To foster exchange of useful ideas both locally and internationally through international work camps.
- To promote youth and women development and empowerment.
- To lobby and advocate for peaceful intervention in conflict.'

Countries: Africa (Kenya).
Activities: Community development, conservation/environment, construction, health/medical.
Duration: 4 weeks +.
Age requirements: Minimum 18 years. No maximum age, it is more important to be young at heart.
Disability access: Not at present.
Educational/professional qualifications: No.
Other requirements: No.
Application Procedure: The volunteer must complete an application form which is evaluated by the organisation and matched with a suitable project. The volunteer must be cleared by the government, whether coming for a short- or long-term placement.
Costs: Yes. Work camp charges are €300 to cater for clearance fee, airport transfer, meals and drinking water, administration costs and (in part) project materials. Long-term charges are €480 for three months and cater for airport transfer, food and drinking water, clearance fee, administration. Volunteers also pay for their flights.
Benefits: Accommodation, food, and guide within the country.
Work individually/in teams: In teams, together with the community at the work camp.

In-country support for volunteers	Pre-programme training	Post-programme debriefing	Contact with returned volunteers
Yes.	In-country orientation includes: organisation's responsibilities; community expectations; culture shock; safety precautions in the city and community.	Yes, covering: volunteers' experiences, expectations, feedback and project follow-up.	Yes.

Medair

Address: Medair, Chemin du Croset 9, CH-1007 Lausanne, Switzerland
Telephone number: +41 21 694 3535
Fax number: +41 21 694 3540
Email: personnel@medair.org
Website: www.medair.org

Established in 1988, Medair is a not-for-profit organisation.

Type: Relief/emergency.
Stated mission: 'To respond to human suffering in emergency and disaster situations by implementing multisectorial relief and rehabilitation projects, in a compassionate and serving attitude inspired by its Christian ethos. Primary focus: "Unrecognised" or "forgotten" crises outside media spotlight.'
Countries: Africa (Angola, Congo, Madagascar, Sri Lanka, Sudan, Uganda), Asia (Afghanistan, Iran)
Activities: Administration/management, capacity building, construction, health/medical, other.
Duration: 1 year plus.
Age requirements: Minimum 25 years, maximum 55 years.
Disability access: No.
Language requirements: Fluent English; French may be required for certain projects.
Educational/professional qualifications: Yes. Volunteers should have a degree or relevant professional experience in one of the following areas: project management, financial administration, logistics, health services, water/sanitation, engineering or construction.
Other requirements: Christian commitment and adherence to Medair values; should not have dependant children; able to live and work in a multicultural team under adverse conditions; must successfully complete the Medair Relief/Rehabilitation Orientation Course (ROC).
Application procedure: Apply online at Medair's website (references will be asked for after the application procedure has started)
Costs: No. However, volunteers must cover the cost of the Medair Relief/Rehabilitation Orientation Course (ROC) (?535).
Benefits: Travel, food, accommodation, vaccination and visa costs, health insurance, repatriation coverage, anti-malaria medication, monthly allowance of $100.
Work individually/in teams: In teams.

In-country support for volunteers	Pre-programme training	Post-programme debriefing	Contact with returned volunteers
Yes, not on full-time basis.	Relief/Rehabilitation Orientation Course; three-day briefing prior to each assignment.	Debriefing takes place in international HQ or by phone; professional treatment is also available in certain cases.	Yes.

Nicaragua Solidarity Campaign (NSC)

Address: 129 Seven Sisters Road, London N7 7QG, UK
Telephone number: +44 (0)20 7272 9619
Fax number: +44 (0)20 7272 5476
Email: nsc@nicaraguasc.org.uk
Website: www.nicaraguasc.org.uk

Established in 1978, NSC is a not-for-profit organisation.

Type: Short-term/intercultural.

Stated mission: 'NSC works to address economic disadvantage in Nicaragua by channelling material and moral support to partner organisations and communities and building solidarity with these organisations and communities. We also disseminate information and raise awareness in the UK and elsewhere of social and economic issues affecting Nicaragua.'

Countries: Latin America (Nicaragua)

Activities: Agriculture, community development, human rights, other.

Duration: 10 days to 3 weeks.

Age requirements: Minimum 18 years.

Disability access: Depends on placement; contact organisation for further details.

Language requirements: No. However, some language training is strongly recommended before visiting Nicaragua.

Educational/professional qualifications: No.

Other: No.

Application procedure: A mix of application forms, interviews, informal phone and face-to-face discussion, depending on type of work. No references required.

Costs: Yes. Contact the organisation for further details.

Benefits: Food and accommodation.

Work individually/in teams: In teams.

In-country support for volunteers	Pre-programme training	Post-programme debriefing	Contact with returned volunteers
Yes, available full-time while volunteers are in Nicaragua.	One- to two-day pre-departure training, covering topics including cultural orientation.	Day-long sessions involving evaluation and plans for the future.	Yes.

Orangutan Foundation

Address: 7 Kent Terrace, London, NW1 4RP, UK
Telephone number: +44 (0)20 7724 2912
Fax number: +44 (0)20 7706 2613
Email: info@orangutan.org.uk
Website: www.orangutan.org.uk

Established in 1991, the Orangutan Foundation is a not-for-profit organisation.

Type: Conservation/environment
Stated mission: 'The Orangutan Foundation actively conserves the orangutan and its rainforest habitat whilst conducting long-term research on the ecology of orangutans and other rainforest fauna and flora within their habitat. Foundation objectives are to support conservation work in Indonesia and Malaysia and to raise funds and awareness in the UK and overseas. In Indonesia, the Foundation actively protects Tanjung Puting National Park, cares for ex-captive, orphaned and injured orangutans and operates a rehabilitation programme that returns orangutans to a life in the wild.'
Countries: Asia (Indonesian Borneo)
Activities: Conservation/environment, construction.
Duration: Six weeks.
Age requirements: Minimum 18 years.
Disability access: No.
Language requirements: English or Indonesian.
Educational/professional qualifications: No.
Other requirements: Previous experience in the field is desirable but not necessary. Good health, team spirit, and a willingness to do manual work are necessary as well as a certain level of physical fitness.
Application procedure: Potential volunteers must submit an application form (obtainable from the Orangutan Foundation office) together with a CV and covering letter.
Costs: Yes. Programme cost of £550. Volunteers also cover travel costs.
Benefits: Accommodation, food and materials for the duration of the programme.
Work individually/in teams: Volunteers work in teams of up to 12 people.

In-country support for volunteers	Pre-programme training	Post-programme debriefing	Contact with returned volunteers
Yes, available full-time.	Pre-departure briefing day takes place in London.	No.	Yes.

Personal Overseas Development

Address: Linden Cottage, The Burgage, Prestbury, Cheltenham GL52 3DJ, UK
Telephone number: +44 (0)124 225 0901
Email: info@thepodsite.co.uk
Website: www.thepodsite.co.uk

Established in 2001, Personal Overseas Development is a for-profit organisation

Type: Short-term/intercultural, recruitment/placement, conservation/environment
Stated mission: 'PoD provides a link between small charities, other organisations in less developed countries and people in the UK & Ireland wishing to do something worthwhile abroad. Through every project that PoD is involved with, we aim to ensure benefits for the volunteers, our partners and importantly the local population. PoD takes great care in its selection of charities and local organisations to work with, in order to ensure a high quality of service to volunteers. We have two main groups of volunteer: people taking career breaks; and students leaving school or university. We are a small company that focuses on quality and safety rather than quantity.'
Countries: Africa (Tanzania), Asia (Nepal, Thailand), Latin America (Peru).
Activities: Children/young people, conservation/environment, construction, disability/special needs, education, other.
Duration: 1 week to 6 months
Age requirements: Minimum 18 years.
Disability access: No.
Language requirements: No, in general. Basic Spanish is required for placements in Peru.
Educational/professional qualifications: No.
Other requirements: No.
Application procedure: Applicants complete an application form which is then reviewed and followed by telephone interview. References are required.
Costs: Yes, starts from £250. Volunteers also cover travel costs.
Benefits: Depends on the package, but may include all accommodation, food, adventure activities, travel insurance, training and support. Visas are not included.
Work individually/in teams: Usually in small teams.

In-country support for volunteers	Pre-programme training	Post-programme debriefing	Contact with returned volunteers
Yes, available on a full-time basis.	Yes, two-day training event for some placements.	Usually carried out in-country at the end of a project.	Yes.

Project Mosaic Guatemala

Address: 3a Avenida Norte No. 3, Casa de Mito, Antigua, Guatemala
Telephone numbers: +502 7832 0955 (office); +502 5817 6660 (mobile)
Fax number: +502 7832 0955
Email: promigua@yahoo.com
Website: www.promosaico.org

Established in 1998, Project Mosaic Guatemala is a not-for-profit organisation.

Type: Placement/recruitment.
Stated mission: 'PMG is a non-profit, non-governmental resource center dedicated to linking international volunteers, as well as financial and material resources, to Guatemalan partner organisations in need of assistance. PMG believes that volunteerism, in its purest form, is inherently positive and beneficial. Volunteering is one of the most effective means of fostering communication and understanding between people of diverse backgrounds. Through first hand contact, we believe that, together, we can build a future that is more tolerant, just and compassionate. PMG is a non-profit, non-governmental, non-discriminatory organisation. PMG is not religiously or politically affiliated.'
Countries: Latin America (Guatemala)
Activities: Agriculture, children/young people, conservation/environment, disability/special needs, education, health/medical, women.
Duration: 1 week to 1 year.
Age requirements: Minimum 18 years.
Disability access: Depends on placement; contact organisation for further details.
Language requirements: Yes. Spanish is required for all projects, but level varies according to placement.
Educational/professional qualifications: Depends on placement; in general, qualifications are not required.
Application procedure: Applicants can go to the organisation's website and submit a form with their details, interests, background. They are then sent information about the projects, and any questions they may have are answered prior to arrival.
Costs: Yes, a donation is requested. Volunteers cover travel and living expenses.
Benefits: In-country orientation, assistance with finding a placement, support throughout project, workshops for volunteers, free emails and phone calls from office.
Work individually/in teams: Both.

In-country support for volunteers	Pre-programme training	Post-programme debriefing	Contact with returned volunteers
Yes, available full-time.	In-country orientation programme.		Yes.

Project Trust

Address: Hebridean Centre, Isle of Coll, Argyll PA78 6TE, Scotland
Telephone number: +44 (0)187 923 0444
Fax number: +44 (0)187 923 0357
Email: info@projecttrust.org.uk
Website: www.projecttrust.org.uk

Established in 1967, Project Trust is a not-for-profit organisation.

Type: Short-term/intercultural
Stated mission: '(1) To give young people the opportunity to learn about a wider community than that in which they have lived so far, in a country with a different culture to their own, and for a length of time which enables them to appreciate the complete cycle of the seasons; (2) to let them learn to use their imagination and skills by undertaking work which they may never have done before, to take up new interests and to utilise their initiative and resourcefulness to help others; (3) to return with an objective appreciation of both the community they lived in overseas and their home community, to use their newly learned skills to benefit others and to have a clearer picture of what they want to achieve in the future; and (4) to help others at home to understand the culture of countries outside their normal experience.'
Countries: Africa (Botswana, Lesotho, Malawi, Mauritania, Namibia, South Africa, Swaziland, Uganda), Asia (Cambodia, China, Hong Kong, India, Malaysia, Sri Lanka, Thailand, Vietnam), Latin America (Bolivia, Chile, Costa Rica, Dominican Republic, Guatemala, Guyana, Honduras, Peru).
Activities: Children/young people, community development, disability/special needs, education.
Duration: 11–12 months.
Age requirements: Minimum 17 years, maximum 19.5 years.
Disability access: Depends on placement; contact organisation for further details.
Language requirements: No. However, Spanish and French are useful for certain placements.
Educational/professional qualifications: No.
Other requirements: Volunteers should be completing their final year of secondary education.
Application procedure: Applicants complete an application form, which can be accessed through the website or sent by post. Two references are required, one personal and one school referee. All applicants must then attend a 5-day selection course on the Isle of Coll.
Costs: Yes. Volunteers are required to fundraise £4,190 for the 12-month programme.
Benefits: Flights, accommodation, food, residential selection and training courses, full medical insurance, in-country support and monthly pocket money.
Work individually/in teams: In teams.

In-country support for volunteers	Pre-programme training	Post-programme debriefing	Contact with returned volunteers
Yes, available on a part-time basis.	Week-long residential training course.	Two-day residential debriefing course.	Yes.

ProWorld

Address: 444 Fulwood Road, Sheffield S10 3GH, UK
Telephone number: +44 (0)870 750 7202
Fax number: + 44 (0)114 229 5614
Email: info@myproworld.org
Website: www.myproworld.org

Established in 1998, ProWorld is a for-profit organisation.

Type: Short-term/intercultural.
Stated mission: 'Our mission is to provide unique and challenging cross-cultural experiences by blending service, community development, and academic study. Hundreds of students and volunteers have joined our programs to perform service projects, internships, research and semester programmes throughout Peru, Belize and Mexico.'
Countries: Latin America (Belize, Mexico, Peru)
Activities: Business, children/young people, community development, conservation/environment, construction, education, health/medical, internships, women.
Duration: 3 weeks to 11 months.
Age requirements: Minimum 16 years.
Disability access: No.
Language requirements: No.
Educational/professional qualifications: No.
Other requirements: No.
Application procedure: Application form available on request from the organisation. References are not required.
Costs: Yes, costs start at £1,150. Volunteers also cover travel costs.
Benefits: Food, accommodation, on-site domestic travel, social/cultural activities, Spanish lessons in Peru.
Work individually/in teams: Both.

In-country support for volunteers	Pre-programme training	Post-programme debriefing	Contact with returned volunteers
Yes, available full-time.	On-site orientation is provided.	Debriefing and project evaluation take place at the end of placements.	Yes.

Quest Overseas

Address: North West Stables, Borde Hill Estate, Balcombe Road, Haywards Heath RH16 1XP, UK.
Telephone number: +44 (0)144 447 4744
Fax number: +44 (0)144 447 4799
Email: emailus@questoverseas.com
Website: www.questoverseas.com

Established in 1996, Quest Overseas is a for-profit organisation.

Type: Short-term/intercultural.
Stated mission: 'Quest Overseas specialises in professionally managed projects and expeditions in Africa and South America. Volunteers have the unique opportunity to join one of our long term Community or Conservation Projects working with some of the more fragile habitats, endangered species and threatened communities in the world. Quest Overseas have trips available for gap year travel, sabbaticals, divers and groups ... all designed to enable anyone to have the opportunity to experience these fascinating continents. The Quest Overseas experience is challenging, rewarding and fun.'
Countries: Africa (Botswana, Kenya, Mozambique, South Africa, Swaziland, Tanzania, Zambia), Latin America (Bolivia, Brazil, Chile, Ecuador, Peru)
Activities: Children/young people, community development, conservation/ environment, construction, other.
Duration: 4 weeks to 1 year.
Age requirements: Minimum 17 years; maximum approx. 60 years.
Language requirements: No. Language courses are sometimes part of the trip, depending on the country of placements.
Educational/professional qualifications: No, but some can be gained on our trips (e.g. PADI, Game Ranger Field Guide Certificate).
Other requirements: No.
Application procedure: Examine the options and select project/expedition. Complete and return the application form. A personal/phone interview is then arranged: if the client is successful, the organisation of the placement/expedition begins. Training weekends are held to prepare people for their project/expedition.
Costs: Yes. Prices comprise cost plus project donation and start from £1,310. Volunteers also cover travel costs and insurance.
Benefits: All activities, food, internal transport, accommodation, on-site project and expedition leaders, 24-hour UK support and comprehensive pre-departure training are included. Donations go direct to project sites. Groups are of similar-aged volunteers, i.e. gap students are not mixed with sabbatical travellers.
Work individually/in teams: Both.

In-country support for volunteers	Pre-departure training	Post-return debriefing	Contact with returned volunteers
Yes, available full-time.	Yes, training weekends are provided by Global Awareness.	Yes, takes place in-country at the end of projects and expeditions.	Yes.

RCDP-Nepal (Rural Community Development Program – Nepal)

Address: PO Box No. 8957, Ward No 14, Kathmandu, Nepal
Telephone number: +977 1 427 8305
Fax number: +977 1 428 2994
Email: rcdpn@mail.com.np
Website: www.rcdpnepal.com

Established in 1996, RCDP-Nepal is a not-for-profit organisation.

Type: Short-term/intercultural.
Stated mission: 'RCDP-Nepal was established in 1999 with the basic aim of empowering local communities to implement and organise community development, education and conservation projects. Since its establishment, it has been running its volunteers' programme in Nepal for volunteer promotion and cultural exchanges. RCDP-Nepal offers year-round volunteer programmes in the areas of teaching, orphanage, conservation and health. Our focus thus far has been primarily on community development and conservation projects. RCDP-Nepal is a non-profit organisation and receives no government support or major corporate backing. This is why it depends on the generosity of volunteers and contributors to promote its programme in different parts.'
Countries: Asia (India, Nepal, Tibet, Sri Lanka)
Activities: Children/young people, community development, conservation/environment, construction, education, health/medical, internships.
Duration: 2 weeks to 3 months.
Age requirements: Minimum 18 years.
Disability access: Depends on placement; contact organisation for further details.
Language requirements: English.
Educational/professional qualifications: No. Most projects do not require any experience except for health-related programmes, for which (due to the risks involved) medically qualified volunteers are required.
Other requirements: Flexibility, self-motivation, openness to a new culture, willingness to learn.
Application procedure: Application form is available on the organisation's website. No further references are required.
Costs: Yes. Costs start from $725 for a two-week programme. Volunteers also cover travel costs.
Benefits: Depending on the type of programme selected, benefits can include food and accommodation with the host family, two-way in-country transportation, sightseeing trips and other activities.
Work individually/in teams: In teams.

In-country support for volunteers	Pre-programme training	Post-programme debriefing	Contact with returned volunteers
Yes, available full-time.	Language training and programme briefings provided.	Yes.	Yes.

RedR-IHE

Address: 1 Great George Street, London SW1P 3AA, UK
Telephone number: +44 (0)20 7233 3116
Fax number: +44 (0)20 7222 0564
Email: recruitment@redr.org
Website: www. redr.org; www.redr.org/london/recruitment/index.htm

Established in 1979, RedR-IHE is a not-for-profit organisation.

Type: Recruitment/placement.
Stated mission: 'Our vision is: A world in which human suffering is alleviated, basic needs are met and rights are respected. Our mission: We improve humanitarian practice by training, providing and supporting competent and committed people to humanitarian programmes worldwide.'
Countries: Africa, Asia, and Europe (various)
Activities: Administration/management, agriculture, business, capacity building, children/young people, community development, conservation/environment, construction, disability/special needs, education, health/medical, human rights, technical support, women, other.
Duration: From several days to 3 years.
Age requirements: No.
Disability access: Depends on placement.
Language requirements: Depends on placement; most programmes will have language requirements. There is a high demand for French speakers who are familiar with working with English NGOs.
Educational/professional qualifications: Yes. Most roles require some kind of degree or professional affiliation; RedR-IHE rarely deals with entry-level positions.
Other requirements: Depends on placement; each agency has individual selection criteria, such as whether someone fits in with their organisation's ethos.
Application procedure: Candidates should sign up to http://onlinejobs.redr.org after reading the guidance notes on how to sign up and how to use the database (http://www.redr.org/london/recruitment/recruitInfo.htm). They then create one record, which can be updated by logging on periodically. Candidates can attach more than one individual job application to their online record once completed. This online jobs record will be their RedR-IHE CV. Candidates reviewed to be suitable for the position's shortlist will be contacted before information is given to the agency, so the candidate will have more information on the agency. Agencies then let RedR-IHE know who they are interested in interviewing; candidates should not apply directly to agencies if RedR-IHE is already representing their application.
Costs: No.

Benefits: Information, increased chances of getting a position.
Work individually/in teams: Both; depends on placement.

In-country support for volunteers	Pre-departure training	Post-return debriefing	Contact with returned volunteers
N/A	Yes, provides a wide range of training courses, including the 'Essentials of Humanitarian Practice' course.	Yes, see website for further information.	Resources permitting.

Right To Play

Address: 65 Queen Street West, Suite 1900, Box 64, Toronto, ON M5H 2M5, Canada
Telephone number: +1 416 498 1922
Fax number: +1 416 498 1942
Email: recruitment@righttoplay.com
Website: www.righttoplay.com

Established in 2001, Right To Play is a not-for-profit organisation.

Type: Long-term development.
Stated mission: 'Right To Play is a humanitarian organisation using sport and play programmes to encourage the healthy physical, social and emotional development of the world's most disadvantaged children. Right To Play is committed to improving the lives of these children and to strengthening their communities by translating the best values of sport into opportunities to promote development, health and peace. Right To Play is built on the belief that sport has the power to help create healthier children and safer communities. Right To Play engages and trains international and local volunteers who work with communities to implement our two programmes, SportWorks and SportHealth.'
Countries: Africa (Benin, Chad, Ethiopia, Ghana, Liberia, Mali, Mozambique, Rwanda, Sierra Leone, Sudan, Tanzania, Uganda, Zambia), Asia (Azerbaijan, Indonesia, Jordan, Lebanon, Pakistan, Palestinian Territories, Sri Lanka, Thailand, UAE).
Activities: Administration/management, capacity building, children/young people, community development, disability/special needs, education, health/medical, other.
Duration: 12-month or 2-year contracts.
Age requirements: 23–50 years.
Disability access: Yes, contact organisation for further details.
Language requirements: English, with some locations requiring one of the following: Portuguese, French, Russian/Azeri.
Educational/professional qualifications: Yes, in at least one of the following areas: Adult education/training of trainers; capacity building; child development and rights; communication and media; community health/public health; HIV/AIDS health promotion; project management; sports or leisure management. Volunteers must have an appreciation of sport and play and their role in the development process.
Other requirements: Normally single volunteers; will accept couples (including same-sex) if both are able to volunteer with RTP.
Application procedure: See application information on website (www.righttoplay.com/opportunities.asp); three references required at interview stage.
Costs: No.
Benefits: Travel, insurance, airfares, $8,000 per year honorarium.
Work individually or in teams: In teams.

In-country support for volunteers	Pre-programme training	Post-programme debriefing	Contact with returned volunteers
Depends on location.	Yes, two-week programme facilitated in Toronto.	Currently being developed.	Yes.

Rokpa UK Overseas Projects

Address: Kagyu Samye Ling, Eskdalemuir, Langholm DG13 0QL, Scotland
Telephone number: +44 (0)138 737 3232
Fax number: +44 (0)138 737 3223
Email: Diana108@btopenworld.com; charity@rokpauk.org
Website: www.rokpauk.org

Established in 1980, Rokpa UK is a not-for-profit organisation.

Type: Long-term development.
Stated mission: 'Rokpa is a non-profit making organisation that aims to help and support people in need and promote self-sufficiency, irrespective of religious, national, or cultural background. Rokpa's name is taken from the Tibetan word meaning "to help" or "to serve". In Tibetan areas, Rokpa supports children and young people from the poorest nomadic or farming backgrounds in over 70 schools – primary schools, middle schools, colleges and universities. Students are taught in their own language, receive a standard education and learn cultural subjects.'
Countries: Asia (Tibetan regions of China)
Activities: Capacity building, children/young people, education.
Duration: 6–9 months.
Age requirements: Minimum 25 years (unless exceptional experience).
Disability access: Depends if there are support needs.
Language requirements: We advise volunteers to learn some Tibetan before and during their placement.
Educational/professional qualifications: Minimum qualification is CTEFLA or equivalent course that includes supervised teaching practice.
Other requirements: No.
Application procedure: Send CV/resumé and brief letter of interest; interview by arrangement; references are taken up following interview.
Costs: Yes, volunteers cover travel costs and some living expenses.
Benefits: Room, board, fuel, information.
Work individually/in teams: All volunteers have to be prepared to work individually although there are occasional opportunities for pairing.

In-country support for volunteers	Pre-programme training	Post-programme debriefing	Contact with returned volunteers
No. Email contact with other volunteers and UK base is provided.	One-day introduction to the project (once or twice a year); handbook of information and background reading.	Yes; content varies to suit individual needs.	Yes, as a matter of course.

SCORE (Sports Coaches' OutReach)

Address: PO Box 4989, Cape Town 8000, South Africa
Telephone number: +27 21 418 3140
Fax number: +27 21 418 1549
Email: info@score.org.za
Website: www.score.org.za

Established in 1991, SCORE is a not-for-profit organisation.

Type: Long-term development.
Stated mission: 'SCORE places international volunteers as facilitators and trainers in underprivileged, mainly rural communities to implement and monitor sport & development programs. Volunteers provide coaching and skills training to increase activities and sports participation, to give children a chance to play and to build effective, sustainable local clubs and sports organising structures. SCORE programs use sports & recreation as a means to empower individuals and build stronger communities – to impart life and leadership skills, promote principles of equity, deliver social & educational messages especially to the youth, promote community involvement, develop local role models and bring people from different backgrounds together.'
Countries: Africa (Namibia, South Africa, Zambia).
Activities: Administration/management, capacity building, children/young people, community development, disability/special needs, education, other.
Duration: 6 months to 1 year +.
Age requirements: Minimum 20 years.
Disability access: Yes.
Language requirements: Fluent English.
Educational/professional qualifications: Yes. Third-level qualification in sport, sport management, recreation, physical education, sport science or teaching preferred. Previous involvement in sport, especially sports organisation and coaching/training are highly valued. A background in development, anthropology, or sociology is valued.
Other requirements: Flexibility, initiative, enthusiasm, and interest in learning about another culture.
Application procedure: Submit an application form with essays and a CV; this is followed by an interview. Three references are required.
Costs: Yes. Fee of €2,500. Volunteers also cover travel, visa and health insurance costs.
Benefits: Host family accommodation, work-related travel; volunteer support, monthly telephone calls and in-service training, sports equipment and training and activity resources.
Work individually/in teams: Both.

In-country support for volunteers	Pre-project training	Post-project debriefing	Contact with returned volunteers
Yes, available full-time.	Two-week in-country induction.	End of service debriefing is provided.	Yes.

SMILE Society

Address: Udayrajpur, Madhyamgram, No. 9 Railgate, Kolkata 700129, WB, India
Telephone numbers: +91 933 973 1462; 983 068 6828
Fax number: +91 33 253 76621
Email: info@smilengo.org
Website: www.smilengo.org

Established in 2003, SMILE Society is a not-for-profit organisation.

Type: Short-term/intercultural.
Stated mission: 'SMILE is a registered NGO and member of CCIVS (UNESCO). Our mission is to provide volunteers with a customised programme that will enable them to make an important contribution to the poor and needy kids of India. In the past 3 years we have placed many volunteers around various parts of India within different projects. Our foremost goal is to "Bring a Smile to Every Child". Our flexible approach means that you will be given a placement to suit your needs and time scale. Our unique placements could become the trip of a lifetime.'
Countries: Asia (India).
Activities: Administration/management, children/young people, community development, construction, education, health/medical, internships, other.
Duration: 2–48 weeks.
Age requirements: 18–86 years; children who are accompanied by parents/ guardians are also welcome.
Disability access: No.
Language requirements: English.
Educational/professional qualifications: Not required, but certain skills such as teaching, first aid, medicine, cooking, crafts, etc. are welcomed.
Other requirements: Clean criminal background, particularly in relation to children.
Application procedure: Apply online. Police clearance certificates are welcomed; if this is not possible, detailed references will be required.
Costs: Yes. Programme fee of US$ 250 for two-week placements; for placements of 4 to 48 weeks, the cost is $100 per week. The cost for internships of 2–12 weeks is $125 per week.
Benefits: Costs include three Indian meals a day, shared accommodation (2–4 people in a room), airport pick-up, in-country orientation, internal travel to work projects, appropriate training where necessary, clean safe drinking water, use of internet and TV with English-language channels.
Work individually/in teams: Mainly in teams; most teams also have a co-ordinator working with them.

In-country support for volunteers	Pre-programme training	Post-programme debriefing	Contact with returned volunteers
Yes.	Contact and information provided to volunteer pre-arrival; one-day in-country induction on arrival.	No.	Yes, subject to volunteers' consent.

SPW (Student Partnership Worldwide)

Address: 2nd Floor, Faith House, 7 Tufton Street, London SW1P 3QB, UK
Telephone number: +44 (0) 20 7222 0138
Fax number: +44 (0) 20 7233 0008
Email: info@spw.org
Website: www.spw.org

Established in 1985, SPW is a not-for-profit organisation.

Type: Long-term development.
Stated mission: 'SPW puts young people at the forefront of positive change and development.'
Countries: Africa (South Africa, Tanzania, Uganda, Zambia), Asia (India, Nepal).
Activities: Capacity building, children/young people, community development, conservation/environment, education, health/medical, human rights, women.
Duration: 6–11 months, depending on programme.
Age requirements: Minimum 18 years, maximum 28 years.
Disability access: Depends on placement; contact organisation for further information.
Language requirements: No. Volunteers receive relevant language training.
Educational/professional qualifications: Yes; volunteers must have completed secondary education.
Other requirements: No.
Application procedure: Download an application form from website: www.spw.org
Applicants attend a selection day in London and an interview.
Costs: Yes; £3,600.
Benefits: Pre-departure and in-country training, accommodation, basic living allowance, logistical costs are covered.
Work individually/in teams: Depends on programme; in partnership with a national volunteer in pairs or small groups.

In-country support for volunteers	Pre-departure training	Post-return debriefing	Contact with returned volunteers
Yes, available full-time.	Yes, pre-departure weekend briefing, support and guidance from London office.	Yes, debriefing takes place in-country and post-return.	Yes, Opportunities to stay involved with SPW on return.

Teaching and Projects Abroad

Address: Aldsworth Parade, Goring, Sussex BN12 4TX, UK
Telephone numbers: +44 (0)190 370 8300; (freephone from Ireland) 1800 300 163
Fax number: +44 (0)190 350 1026
Email: info@teaching-abroad.co.uk
Website: www.teaching-abroad.co.uk

Established in 1992, Teaching and Projects Abroad is a for-profit organisation.

Type: Short-term/intercultural.
Stated mission: 'Want a better future – brighter prospects? So do thousands in the third world! With Teaching and Projects Abroad you can enjoy adventurous foreign travel with a chance to do a worthwhile job. You can teach conversational English (no TEFL required) or gain experience in medicine, veterinary science, conservation, journalism or business. Placements are available throughout the year and last from one month upwards. Volunteers receive substantial home and overseas support and are not isolated.'
Countries: Africa (Ethiopia, Ghana, Morocco, Senegal, South Africa, Swaziland), Asia (Cambodia, China, India, Mongolia, Nepal, Sri Lanka, Thailand), Europe (Moldova, Romania), Latin America (Argentina, Bolivia, Chile, Costa Rica, Mexico, Peru).

Activities: Business, community development, conservation/environment, education, health/medicine, other.
Duration: 1 month to 1 year.
Age requirements: Minimum 17 years, maximum 70 years.
Disability access: Depends on placement; contact organisation for further details.
Language requirements: English.
Educational/professional qualifications: No.
Other requirements: No.
Application procedure: Volunteers can apply online or through application form in brochure. References are required.
Costs: Yes. Programme costs start from €1,245. Volunteers also cover travel costs.
Benefits: Food, accommodation, insurance, backup.
Work individually/in teams: In teams.

In-country support for volunteers	Pre-programme training	Post-programme debriefing	Contact with returned volunteers
Yes, available on a full-time basis.	Project details and information are sent to volunteers before they start.	Debriefing form sent to volunteers on their return.	Yes.

Today It's Me AIDS Foundation

Address: PO Box, Jinja, Uganda
Telephone number: +256 782 762793
Email: mujuzchrist@yahoo.co.uk

Established in 2004, Today It's Me AIDS Foundation is a not-for-profit organisation.

Type: Long-term development.

Stated mission: 'Today It's Me AIDS Foundation is an indigenous independent non-profit, non-governmental organization concerned with the improvement of lives of destitute and vulnerable people infected and affected with HIV/AIDS epidemic. HIV/AIDS continues to have a far greater impact on Africa than any other continent and Uganda is no exception. Many people living with HIV/AIDS in Uganda have no access to proper medication for treating the opportunistic infections and its impact in Uganda has been greatly felt by almost every close friend and close family members. Therefore, it was upon this background that the annual general meeting of Today It's Me AIDS Foundation 2006, adopted and ratified a modified mission statement: to respond to the increasing death rate of people with HIV/AIDS and above all, carry out an awareness and education about HIV/AIDS in educational institutions, religious institutions and communities.'

Countries: Africa (Uganda)

Activities: Capacity building, children/young people, community development, education, health/medical, women.

Duration: From one week to one year.

Age requirements: No.

Disability access: No.

Language requirements: English is required.

Educational/professional qualifications: No.

Other requirements: No.

Application procedure: Contact the organisation to provide personal details and CV, and ask for further information about applying.

Costs: Yes, programme costs start from $400. Volunteers also cover their travel costs.

Benefits: Accommodation and food.

Work individually/in teams: Both.

In-country support for volunteers	Pre-programme training	Post-programme debriefing	Contact with returned volunteers
Yes.	No.	Not available yet.	Yes.

Comhlámh

Transform (part of Tearfund)

Address: 100 Church Road, Teddington, Middlesex TW11 8QE, UK
Telephone number: +44 (0)20 8943 7777
Fax number: +44 (0)20 8943 3594
Email: transform@tearfund.org
Website: www.tearfund.org/transform

Established in 1968, Tearfund is a not-for-profit organisation.

Type: Short-term/intercultural.
Stated mission: 'Transform is Tearfund's short-term mission programme for Christian volunteers with teams [working for] 2, 4, and 6 weeks and 4 months. Each year more than 30 Transform teams work in 20 countries, including the UK, alongside Tearfund partner churches and organisations. Some teams focus on practical tasks such as building, painting and decorating. Many work with children, or give spiritual support to the vulnerable. Transform provides the training, orientation, safety and health information and support for teams before they go, while they are away and when they return.'
Countries: Africa (Kenya, Malawi, Rwanda, Tanzania, Zambia) Asia (Bangladesh, India, Thailand), Europe (Russia), Latin America (Bolivia, Brazil, Mexico, Nicaragua, Peru)
Activities: Children/young people, community development, construction, disability/special needs, education.
Duration: 2 weeks to 4 months.
Age requirements: Minimum 18 years; no upper age limit.
Disability access: Depends on placement; contact organisation for further details.
Language requirements: No. However, some experience of other languages is an advantage for some destinations (for example, Latin America, francophone Africa)
Educational/professional qualifications: No.
Other requirements: Volunteers need to be committed evangelical Christians, involved in a church or Christian fellowship, and currently living in the UK or Ireland.
Application procedure: Applicants complete and return an application form (available from website) which includes references from two people, one church-related, and one personal or work-related. They send in a deposit and two passport-sized photos of themselves. Once the application is received, an interview will be arranged, and if selected, the applicant attends an orientation with other team members, and is helped through the preparation process, which includes reading materials and applying for health clearance and visas.
Costs: Yes. Depends on placement and begins with £50 deposit submitted with application form.

Benefits: Flights, food and accommodation while abroad; visas, travel to and from destination in country, orientation, medical kits, logistical arrangements and a place at a reunion organised in UK after return.

Work individually/in teams: In teams.

In-country support for volunteers	Pre-programme training	Post-programme debriefing	Contact with returned volunteers
Yes, available on a full-time basis.	Two-day training event covering issues including health, safety and security; cultural issues; spiritual preparation, and meeting previous team members.	Medical debriefing; and each volunteer is asked to submit a report and complete a feedback form. Annual reunion weekend for all participants.	Yes.

Travellers Worldwide

Address: 7 Mulberry Close, Ferring, West Sussex BN12 5HY, UK
Telephone number: +44 (0)190 350 2595
Fax number: +44 (0)190 350 0364
Email: info@travellersworldwide.com
Website: www.travellersworldwide.com

Established in 1994, Travellers Worldwide is a for-profit organisation.

Type: Short-term/intercultural.

Stated mission: 'Travellers was established 12 years ago to provide the opportunity for people from all over the world to be able to experience what it is like to live and work in a foreign country with a different culture. Travellers concentrates on providing teaching and conservation placements in developing countries where help is most needed. Most importantly, from Argentina to Sri Lanka, underprivileged children, communities and animals have benefited enormously from work carried out by Travellers' volunteers.'

Countries: Africa (Ghana, Kenya, Malawi, South Africa, Zambia, Zimbabwe), Asia (Brunei, China, India, Malaysia, Sri Lanka, Thailand), Europe (Russia), Latin America (Argentina, Bolivia, Brazil, Cuba, Guatemala, Peru).

Activities: Conservation/environment, education, internships, other.

Duration: 1 week to 1 year.

Age requirements: Minimum 17 years.

Disability access: Depends on placement; contact organisation for further information.

Language requirements: No.

Educational/professional qualifications: No.

Other requirements: Enthusiasm; volunteers will be interviewed over the telephone to ensure they are suitable.

Application procedure: An application form is available from the organisation's website. References are required.

Costs: Yes. A deposit of £190 is required on application, and prices start from £695. Volunteers also cover travel costs.

Benefits: In general, food, accommodation, being met at the airport, and support and assistance throughout the placement.

Work individually/in teams: Both.

In-country support for volunteers	Pre-programme training	Post-programme debriefing	Contact with returned volunteers
Yes, available on a full-time basis.	Information on placement is provided; day-long workshop available for teaching programme participants. Weekend certificated TEFL courses available.	Provided for volunteers on their return.	Yes.

UBECI (Unión de Beneficios en Educación y Colaboración Internacional)

Address: Huacho E2-56 y José Peralta, Ecuador.
Telephone numbers: +593 2311 0113; 9614 2987
Email: ubeci@hotmail.com
Website: www.ubeci.org

Established in 1999, UBECI is a not-for-profit organisation.

Type: Short-term/intercultural.
Stated mission: 'We are an Ecuadorian non-profit organisation which works in the favor of impoverished people in Quito/Ecuador. UBECI wants to take part in the process of a social change that complies with the demands of our country. Through our work experience in social projects in the past we have realised that especially the children of our society need help. By working together with children and their families we want to give them the opportunity to escape poverty and reinvent a better future for themselves. Besides our own projects, UBECI collaborates with other organisations which work with immigrants, indigenous people and children who are mentally or physically handicapped. We support these organisations by helping them to get into contact with qualified volunteers. Moreover, our experience in founding an organisation and in drafting and developing projects allows us to assist smaller and lesser-known social organisations to expand. We help them to get in contact and work with volunteers.'
Countries: Latin America (Ecuador)
Activities: Children/young people, community development, disability/special needs, education, health/medical, other.
Duration: 4 weeks to 2 years
Age requirements: Minimum 18 years.
Disability access: No.
Language requirements: English, basic Spanish.
Educational/professional qualifications: No.
Other requirements: Volunteers need open minds and a willingness to share, help and work in a group.
Application procedure: Send a CV and answer a questionnaire; the volunteer programme organised by UBECI will depend on volunteer's answers, availability and knowledge of Spanish.
Costs: Yes. Registration fee of $80; price of 4-week programme starts from $555. Volunteers also cover travel costs.
Benefits: Programme costs cover accommodation, food, airport transfers, support and assistance, Spanish classes.
Work individually/in teams: Both.

In-country support for volunteers	Pre-programme training	Post-programme debriefing	Contact with returned volunteers
Yes, available full-time.	Contact and information provided to volunteer pre-arrival.	Yes, evaluation takes place at the start, middle and end of placements.	

United Nations Volunteers

Address: Postfach 260 111, D-53153 Bonn, Germany
Telephone number: +49 228 815 2000
Fax number: +49 228 815 2001
Website: http://www.unv.org/

Established by the UN General Assembly in 1970, UN Volunteers is a not-for-profit organization with approximately 8,000 volunteers in 140 countries worldwide.

Type: Long-term development, relief/emergency; and on-line virtual volunteering opportunities.

Stated mission: 'The United Nations Volunteers is the UN organization that supports sustainable human development globally through the promotion of volunteerism, including the mobilization of volunteers. It serves the causes of peace and development through enhancing opportunities for participation by all peoples. It is universal, inclusive and embraces volunteer action in all its diversity. It values free will, commitment, engagement and solidarity, which are the foundations of volunteerism.'

Countries: Africa, Asia, Europe, Latin America (various).

Activities: Administration/management, agriculture, business, capacity building, children/young people, community development, conservation/environment, construction, disability/special needs, education, health/medical, human rights, technical support, women, other. Agriculture, health and education feature prominently, as do human rights promotion, information and communication technology, community development, vocational training, industry and population.

Duration: Generally between one and two years; shorter placements of three to twelve months may also be available for emergency related activities

Age requirements: Minimum of 25 years.

Disability access: Depends on placement.

Language requirements: Depends on placement.

Educational/professional qualifications: Yes. UNV volunteers should have a university degree or a higher technical diploma and several years of relevant work experience.

Other requirements: Strong commitment to the values and principles of volunteerism; ability to work in a multi-cultural environment; ability to adjust to difficult living conditions; strong interpersonal and organizational skills; prior volunteering and/or working experience in a developing country.

Application: Complete and submit a questionnaire online. Applicants will receive an initial response within one week. If included in the roster of candidates, applications remain active for a maximum of two years or until the organization receives information that candidates are no longer available for a UNV assignment. Irish Aid funds intern and volunteer placements with UNV and also acts on behalf of the agency in Ireland, facilitating recruitment and placements.

Costs: No.

Benefits: Travel costs on appointment and at the end of assignment; settling-in grant, volunteer living allowance; life, health and permanent disability insurances, resettlement allowance upon satisfactory completion of the assignment.

VEEP Nepal (Volunteer for Environment and Education Programme, Nepal)

Address: GPO Box. 8975 EPC–5054, New Baneshwor -10, Kathmandu, Nepal
Telephone number: +977 1 449 7282
Email: info@veepnepal.org.np
Website: www.veepnepal.org.np

Established in 2002, VEEP Nepal is a not-for-profit organisation.

Type: Short-term/intercultural.
Stated mission: 'VEEP Nepal is a non-profit organisation dedicated to promoting volunteerism, providing community service, encouraging collaboration, and improving cultural awareness in various parts of Nepal. VEEP Nepal is a non-religious and non- political organisation, who works in rural and suburban parts of Nepal. This the only volunteer organisation run by volunteers from different fields. We are dedicated to providing people with meaningful volunteer experiences and providing opportunities to explore Nepal with different perspectives. [Our] aim is to provide quality volunteer service to people interested in coming to Nepal as volunteers, and better volunteer work for the Nepali community. We play a vital role in establishing relations between the international and Nepali community.'
Countries: Asia (Nepal).
Activities: Children/young people, conservation/environment, construction, education, health/medical, internships, other.
Duration: 2 weeks to 5 months.
Age requirements: Minimum 18 years.
Disability access: Not at present.
Language requirements: English.
Educational/professional qualifications: No.
Other requirements: No.
Application procedure: Details are available from the organisation; references are required, if possible.
Costs: Yes. From £300 for a two-week programme to £750 for a five-month programme. Volunteers must also cover their travel and visa costs.
Benefits: In-country transport, accommodation, meals, language and cultural information classes, training and staff support.
Work individually/in teams: Both, depending on placement.

In-country support for volunteers	Pre-programme training	Post-programme debriefing	Contact with returned volunteers
Yes, available part-time.	In-country training, including language and culture classes.	No.	Yes.

Visions in Action

Address: 2710 Ontario Road NW, Washington DC 20009, USA
Telephone number: +1 202 625 7402
Fax number: +1 202 625 2353
Email: visions@visionsinaction.org
Website: www.visionsinaction.org

Founded in 1989, Visions in Action is a not-for-profit organisation.

Type: Short-term/intercultural.
Stated mission: 'Grassroots Development: A low cost, grassroots approach is taken in all that we do, adopting a standard of living similar to those we are trying to assist. Volunteerism: We give of ourselves and make sacrifices for the betterment of others, expecting nothing in return. Community: Our volunteers work as a community, living together and supporting one another during the experience. Self-reliance: Participants and members of the community work together to attain self-reliance. Social Justice: Our efforts are directed at achieving social and economic justice for those in the developing world.'
Countries: Africa (South Africa, Tanzania, Uganda), Latin America (Mexico)
Activities: Agriculture, business, children/young people, community development, conservation/environment, health/medical, women, other.
Duration: 6 months to 1 year. Summer programmes of 4–6 weeks are also available.
Age requirements: Minimum 18 years for short-term programmes and 20 for long-term programmes.
Disability access: No.
Language requirements: No. However, basic Spanish is required for the Mexico programme.
Educational/professional qualifications: Yes, college degree or equivalent experience.
Other requirements: A demonstrated commitment to international development.
Application procedure: Applicants complete and application form and submit the required documentation and fees. An interview is scheduled, and once accepted, the applicant receives an acceptance packet that includes information on NGO placement and visa application.
Costs: Yes. Programme costs start from $2,800 for a 6-week summer camp. Volunteers also cover travel costs.
Benefits: Orientation, accommodation, food and health insurance.
Work individually/in teams: Both.

In-country support for volunteers	Pre-project training	Post-project debriefing	Contact with returned volunteers
Yes, provided by part-time in-country co-ordinators.	Four-week orientation in the country prior to placement with an NGO.	Provides 'Welcome Back' packs for returning volunteers.	Yes.

Volunteer Africa

Address: PO Box 24, Bakewell, Derbyshire DE45 1YP, UK
Email: moya@volunteerafrica.org
Website: www.volunteerafrica.org

Established in 2001, Volunteer Africa is a not-for-profit organisation

Type: Short-term/intercultural.
Stated mission: 'Volunteer Africa is an international "not for profit" organisation run by a team of volunteers spread around the world. Volunteer Africa has been established to give people the opportunity to work on community initiated projects in developing countries. In return for hosting these international volunteers the host organisation receives donations from the volunteers. Volunteer Africa works with four partner NGOs on three volunteer programmes in Tanzania. Volunteers can participate for between 4 and 12 weeks. Most volunteers head off on a safari or travel further in Africa on completing the project.'
Countries: Africa (Tanzania)
Activities: Community development, construction.
Duration: 4–12 weeks
Age requirements: Minimum 18 years.
Disability access: Depends on placement; contact office for further information.
Language requirements: No. Language training provided in-country.
Educational/professional qualifications: No.
Other requirements: Ability to live and work in a small team and to live in basic conditions.
Application procedure: Applicants first submit an online application at the Volunteer Africa website. Then they have an interview with a returned volunteer in Ireland. References, medical and police checks are required before departure.
Costs: Yes, amount depends on duration of participation. Volunteers also cover own travel costs.
Benefits: Food, accommodation, in-country travel and language training are included in the programme fee.
Work individually/in teams: Teams.

In-country support for volunteers	Pre-programme training	Post-programme debriefing	Contact with returned volunteers
Yes, available on a full-time basis.	Volunteers are provided with a travel manual for pre-departure training; in-country language training provided.	Feedback is requested in an annual evaluation form.	Yes.

Volunteer Petén

Address: Parque Ecológico Nueva Juventud, San Andres, Petén, Guatemala
Telephone number: +011 502 5711 0040
Email: volunteerpeten@hotmail.com
Website: www.volunteerpeten.com

Established in 2002, Volunteer Petén is a not-for-profit organisation.

Type: Conservation/environment
Stated mission: 'Volunteer Petén's mission is to 1) protect and manage ecological reserves San Andres, Petén, Guatemala; 2) provide educational classes, both environmental and traditional, to local schools; 3) assist and develop small community projects; and 4) provide quality volunteer experiences for international travellers and students.'
Countries: Latin America (Guatemala)
Activities: Conservation/environment, construction, education.
Duration: 1–3 months.
Age requirements: No.
Disability access: No.
Language requirements: No.
Educational/professional qualifications: No.
Other requirements: No.
Application procedure: Send request via email to volunteerpeten@hotmail.com stating possible start and end dates. Once the organisation can assure a space for a volunteer, half the volunteeer's financial contribution must be paid as soon as possible to confirm placement.
Costs: Yes; $350 for 1 month, $650 for 2 months, and $950 for 3 months. Volunteers also cover travel costs.
Benefits: Food, accommodation, airport pick-up, transport to project site, internet, all activities and materials for projects.
Work individually/in teams: In teams.

In-country support for volunteers	Pre-programme training	Post-programme debriefing	Contact with returned volunteers
Yes, on a full-time basis.	No.	No.	Yes.

Volunteers for Africa

Address: PO Box 2044-00100, GPO, Nairobi, Kenya
Telephone numbers: +254 (0)20 273 6733; (0)722 503639
Email: volunteersafrica5@yahoo.com
Website: www.volunteerforafrica.org

Established in 2001, Volunteers for Africa is a not-for-profit organisation.

Type: Conservation/environment and short-term/intercultural.
Stated mission: 'To network people, organisations and resources in Eastern Africa for sustainable development in natural resources conservation and social development through voluntarism.
Aims:

- To mobilise and disburse resources from local and international sources for grassroots community development, to recruit volunteers locally and internationally and place them in community based development projects and organisations in Eastern Africa.
- To link and network community based organisations with other groups worldwide for resource mobilisation, information sharing, and accessing development assistance in the area of Environment.
- To empower community organisations' leaders and members, women and youth through targeted training such as on partnership development and management, and effective organisational management tools, resources mobilisation.
- To engage in and with community based natural resources management including integrated water resource management programmes in Eastern Africa, for the benefit of the entire populace, and for the sake of future environmental trends.'

Countries: Africa (Kenya, Sudan, Tanzania, Uganda)
Activities: Capacity building, community development, conservation/environment, construction, education, health/medical, technical support, other.
Duration: From 2 weeks to 3 months.
Age requirements: Minimum 18 years, maximum 50 years.
Disability access: Yes, contact the organisation for further information.
Language requirements: Yes, contact the organisation for further information.
Educational/professional qualifications: Depends on placement.
Other requirements: Appropriate motivations, realistic expectations, willingness to learn from others, willingness to share with others, cultural sensitivity (respect for others, good conduct), good communication (interpersonal communication, language proficiency), observing health and safety considerations, adaptability, flexibility, dependability and reliability, patience and tolerance, positive attitude, relevant skills, etc.
Application procedure: Contact the organisation with a copy of CV.

Costs: Yes, a suggested donation of €600 per month.
Benefits: Pre-arrival information, in-country orientation, assistance with finding accommodation, ongoing support throughout the placement.
Work individually/in teams: Both, but team work is preferable.

In-country support for volunteers	Pre-programme training	Post-programme debriefing	Contact with returned volunteers
Yes, available full time.	Yes, includes in-country orientation and contact pre-arrival.	Yes, including a farewell ceremony and group discussion on placements.	Yes.

Wakuluzu: Friends of the Colobus Trust

Address: PO Box 5380, Diani, Kenya 80401
Telephone number: +254 40 320 3519
Fax number: +254 40 320 3519
Email: volunteers@colobustrust.org and info@colobustrust.org
Website: www.colobustrust.org

Established in 1997, Wakuluzu is a not-for-profit organisation.

Type: Conservation/environment.
Stated mission: 'To promote, in close co-operation with other organisations and local communities, the conservation, preservation and protection of primates, in particular, the Angolan black and white colobus monkey (*Colobus angolensis palliatus*) and its associated coastal forest habitat in Kenya.'
Countries: Africa (Kenya).
Activities: Business, conservation/environment, education, other.
Duration: 3 months.
Age requirements: Minimum 22 years.
Disability access: No.
Language requirements: No.
Educational/professional qualifications: Yes. Volunteers should generally have a third-level degree.
Other requirements: No.
Application procedure: Information about the application procedure is available on the website or by emailing volunteers@colobustrust.org.
Costs: Yes, €400 per month, plus approximately €15 a week for food. Volunteers also cover travel costs.
Benefits: Accommodation, food and laundry.
Work individually/in teams: Both.

In-country support for volunteers	Pre-programme training	Post-programme debriefing	Contact with returned volunteers
Yes, available full-time.	No.	No.	Yes.

WorkingAbroad Projects

Address: WorkingAbroad, PO Box 454, Flat 1, Brighton BN1 3ZS, East Sussex, UK; or 7, Rue d'Autan, 11290 Montreal d'Aude, France.
Telephone number: +33 4 6826 41 79
Fax number: +33 4 6826 4179
Email: info@workingabroad.com
Website: www.workingabroad.com

Established in 2002, WorkingAbroad Projects is a not-for-profit organisation.

Type: Short-term/intercultural.
Stated mission: 'WorkingAbroad Projects is a not-for-profit company, established in order to provide small scale organisations with need-based support from volunteers. The aim is also to create projects that are independent, small, effective and that work directly hands on with social, cultural, and environmental issues. The volunteer projects should benefit both the community and the volunteers, emphasising the benefit of working and learning at the same time, and the importance of celebrating the arts and culture, either locally or internationally. The advantage of small scale involvement is that volunteers can generate a person to person relation where both cultural backgrounds can be positively exchanged.'
Countries: Latin America (Costa Rica, Netherlands Antilles)
Activities: Community development, conservation/environment, construction, education.
Duration: 2–3 months.
Age requirements: Minimum 18 years.
Disability access: Depends on placement; contact organisation for further details.
Language requirements: No.
Educational/professional qualifications: No.
Other requirements: No.
Application procedure: Application form available from organisation. Two references are required before starting a programme.
Costs: Yes, from £550, depending on programme. Volunteers also cover travel costs.
Benefits: Food, accommodation, internal transport and project materials.
Work individually/in teams: Both.

In-country support for volunteers	Pre-programme training	Post-programme debriefing	Contact with returned volunteers
Yes, available on a full-time basis.	No.	No.	Yes.

World Service Enquiry

Address: Room 237, Bon Marché Centre, 241 Ferndale Road, London SW9 8BJ, UK
Telephone number: +44 (0)870 770 3274
Fax number: +44 (0)870 770 7991
Email: wse@cabroad.org.uk
Website: www.wse.org.uk

Established in 1973, World Service Enquiry is a not-for-profit organisation.

Type: Recruitment/placement.
Stated mission: World Service Enquiry (WSE) gives advice and information about working and volunteering in overseas development. Services include a free telephone/email advice line, published guides to volunteering and working in development, personal career and CV advice, job lists and an email coaching service. It is part of the charity Christians Abroad but has been set up specifically to give advice free of bias to people regardless of faith.
Countries: Africa, Asia, Europe, Latin America (various).
Activities: Administration/management, agriculture, business, capacity building, children/young people, community development, conservation/environment, construction, disability/special needs, education, health/medical, human rights, technical support, women, other.
Duration: N/A.
Age requirements: N/A.
Disability access: No.
Language requirements: Some resources will be available in French and Spanish during 2007.
Educational/professional qualifications: N/A.
Other requirements: N/A.
Application procedure: N/A.
Costs: Yes, fees are charged for some services and publications.
Benefits: Advice to help you make the right decision and information on how to proceed.
Work individually/in teams: N/A..

WWISA – Willing Workers in South Africa

Address: P O Box 2413, Plettenberg Bay, 6600, South Africa
Telephone numbers: +27 44 534 8958 (office); 44 534 8148
Fax number: +27 44 534 8958
Email: info@wwisa.co.za
Website: www.wwisa.co.za

Established in 2001, WWISA is a not-for-profit organisation.

Type: Short-term/intercultural.
Stated mission: 'WWISA is a community-focused organisation that aims to harness the energies of the international volunteer movement to support the development of independent and sustainable projects that respond to the identified needs of disadvantaged communities, assisting them in the enhancement of existing skills and the acquisition of new expertise to sustain and further such projects, thereby promoting the development of fully fledged, well-informed, productive citizens in democratic South Africa.'
Countries: Africa (South Africa).
Activities: Children/young people, community development, conservation/ environment, education.
Duration: 3 weeks to 12 months.
Age requirements: Minimum 18 years.
Disability access: Depends on placement; check with organisation.
Language requirements: English. For some projects, knowledge of Flemish or Dutch is advantageous but not essential.
Educational/professional qualifications: Depends on project. Further information is available from the organisation.
Other requirements: No.
Application procedure: Application is made via email on info@wwisa.co.za with a general background summary and followed by a more detailed CV (with references as required) when allocations are made to the recipient host organisation.
Costs: Yes. Depends on placement; average cost is £675 per month. Volunteers also cover travel costs.
Benefits: Accommodation and meals; transport to and from HQ to projects; a pool vehicle is also available to the volunteers for selected after-hours use.
Work individually/in teams: Both.

In-country support for volunteers	Pre-departure training	Post-return debriefing	Contact with returned volunteers
Yes, available on a full-time basis.	Yes, three-day orientation/ induction programme is provided.	Volunteers submit a project report on completion of placement.	Yes, actively encouraged.

CHAPTER 8

INDEXES OF VOLUNTEER PLACEMENT ORGANISATIONS

There are three indexes to help you find specific organisations, according to:

1 the types of activities they offer;
2 the continents where they organise placements; and
3 whether they require that volunteers have educational or professional qualifications, whether there are costs associated with the placement, and the duration of the placements available.

Index 1: Organisations' volunteer activities

The key for the activities arranged by the organisations is as follows:

Ad: Administration/management
Ag: Agriculture
Bus: Business
CB: Capacity building
CD: Community development
CE: Conservation/environment
Con: Construction
CYP: Children/young people
DSN: Disability/special needs
Ed: Education
HM: Health/medical
HR: Human rights
In: Internships
TS: Technical support
Wo: Women
O: Other

An 'x' marked under the heading indicates that the organisation in question arranges these types of activities for volunteers.

ORGANISATION	Ad	Ag	Bus	CB	CYP	CD	CE	Con	DSN	Ed	HM	HR	In	TS	Wo	O
2Way Development	x	x	x		x	x				x		x	x	x		x
Abandoned Street Kids of Brazil		x			x					x						
African Conservation Experience							x									
African Conservation Trust						x	x									
Africatrust Networks					x	x		x	x				x			
AidCamps International							x									
AIESEC	x		x	x	x	x				x	x		x			
Amizade					x	x		x		x	x					
ARCAS						x		x					x			
Ard El Insan	x			x	x	x				x	x				x	x
Asociación ANAI		x					x						x			
Assin Endwa							x	x					x			
Associação Iko Poran	x		x	x	x	x				x	x					x
Associazione Oikos				x	x	x	x			x						
Azafady			x			x				x	x					
Balkan Sunflowers					x	x	x						x			x
Bangladesh Work Camps		x			x	x	x	x	x	x						x
Billy Riordan Memorial Trust	x							x		x	x					
Bruce Peru				x				x		x	x					x
Camara				x						x			x			
Casa Guatemala	x	x	x		x			x		x	x					x
Chernobyl Children's Project	x				x	x	x	x		x			x			x
Christians Abroad										x	x					x
CIS										x						
Columban Lay Missionaries		x			x	x	x	x	x	x	x				x	x
Coral Cay Conservation							x									

ORGANISATION	Ad	Ag	Bus	CB	CYP	CD	CE	Con	DSN	Ed	HM	HR	In	TS	Wo	O
Cross-Cultural Solutions					x	x		x	x	x			x		x	x
Development in Action	x		x			x		x	x						x	
Ecologia Youth Trust					x		x	x		x						
Ecuador Volunteer					x	x	x			x	x					
EIL Intercultural Learning						x	x			x	x	x				x
Friends of Africa					x			x		x	x					
Friends of Londiani						x		x		x	x					x
Frontier							x			x						
Fundación Jatun Sacha		x			x	x				x			x			
GAP Activity Projects					x	x	x		x	x	x					
GAP Sports						x	x			x	x					x
Geekcorps	x		x	x						x				x		x
Genesis Volunteer Program					x					x						
Global Citizens Network		x			x	x		x							x	x
Global Service Corps		x								x	x					
Global Volunteer Network					x	x	x			x	x					x
GOAL	x			x	x			x		x	x			x		x
Gram Vikas		x		x		x		x		x			x	x		x
Greenforce					x											
Habitat for Humanity							x									
Health Action Overseas	x			x		x			x	x				x		
Health and Development Networks													x			
Himalayan Light Foundation			x			x	x	x		x			x	x	x	
Hope Foundation	x				x	x				x	x				x	
hopeXchange					x			x	x	x	x			x		
INFO Nepal					x					x	x					

ORGANISATION	Ad	Ag	Bus	CB	CYP	CD	CE	Con	DSN	Ed	HM	HR	In	TS	Wo	O
Interims for Development			x	x						x			x	x		
International Relief Friendship Foundation		x			x	x		x								x
International Service Ireland	x			x	x	x			x	x	x	x		x	x	x
Iracambi	x		x		x	x	x						x	x		x
i-to-i			x		x	x	x	x		x	x					x
Jubilee Ventures					x		x			x	x		x			
Kings World Trust					x					x	x					
Léargas					x	x	x		x	x						x
Link Community Development					x					x						
Mafanikio Community Based Organisation					x	x	x			x						
Medair	x			x			x			x						x
Médecins Sans Frontières (MSF)	x			x			x			x	x		x			x
Medical Missionaries of Mary	x	x	x	x	x	x				x	x				x	x
Niall Mellon Township Trust							x									
Nicaragua Solidarity Campaign		x				x					x					x
Orangutan Foundation						x	x									
Personal Overseas Development					x		x	x	x	x						
Progressio	x	x	x	x		x				x	x		x			
Project Mosaic Guatemala		x			x		x			x	x					x
Project Trust					x	x			x	x						
ProWorld		x			x	x	x	x		x	x		x		x	
Quest Overseas					x	x	x	x								x
Raleigh Ireland					x	x	x									x
RCDP Nepal					x	x	x	x		x			x	x		
RedR-IHE	x	x	x	x	x	x	x	x	x	x	x	x	x	x	x	x

ORGANISATION	Ad	Ag	Bus	CB	CYP	CD	CE	Con	DSN	Ed	HM	HR	In	TS	Wo	O
Right to Play	x			x	x	x			x	x	x					x
Rokpa UK			x	x						x						
SCORE	x			x	x	x			x	x						x
SERVE					x	x		x	x	x	x				x	x
Skillshare		x	x	x		x			x	x						x
Slí Eile					x	x			x							x
SMILE Society	x				x	x		x	x	x			x			x
SPW			x	x	x	x			x	x	x				x	
Suas					x	x			x							x
Teaching and Projects Abroad		x			x	x			x	x						x
Tekera Resource Centre		x				x			x	x						
To Russia With Love					x				x							x
Today It's Me AIDS Foundation		x		x	x				x	x				x		
Transform					x	x		x	x	x						
Travellers Worldwide						x			x				x			x
UBECI				x	x			x	x	x						x
UCD Volunteers Overseas						x	x		x	x						
United Nations Volunteers	x	x	x	x	x	x	x	x	x	x	x	x		x	x	x
USIT				x	x	x			x	x						
VEEP Nepal				x		x	x		x	x			x			x
Viatores Christi	x		x	x					x	x			x			
Vincentian Lay Missionaries				x					x							x
Visions in Action		x	x	x	x	x				x					x	x
Volunteer Africa					x		x									
Volunteer Missionary Movement	x	x	x	x		x			x	x			x			
Volunteers for Africa				x	x	x	x		x	x			x			x
Volunteer Petén						x	x			x						
VSI	x			x		x	x	x	x							x
VSO	x	x	x	x	x	x	x		x	x	x	x	x	x	x	x
Wakuluzu			x				x			x						x

ORGANISATION	Ad	Ag	Bus	CB	CYP	CD	CE	Con	DSN	Ed	HM	HR	In	TS	Wo	O
WorkingAbroad Projects						x	x	x		x						
World Service Enquiry	x	x	x	x	x	x	x	x	x	x	x	x	x		x	x
WWISA						x	x	x			x					

Index 2 Continents where organisations offer placements

For this index, continents are divided into Africa, Asia (including the Middle East), Europe (including Eastern Europe and Russia), and Latin America (including Central America and the Caribbean). If an organisation has placements in one of these continents, this will be marked with an 'x'.

	Africa	Asia	Europe	Latin America
2Way Development	x	x		x
Abandoned Street Kids of Brazil				x
African Conservation Experience	x			
African Conservation Trust	x			
Africatrust Networks	x			
AidCamps International	x	x		
AIESEC	x	x	x	x
Amizade	x			x
ARCAS				x
Ard El Insan		x		
Asociación ANAI				x
Assin Endwa	x			
Associação Iko Poran				x
Associazione Oikos	x	x		x
Azafady	x			
Balkan Sunflowers			x	
Bangladesh Work Camps		x		
Billy Riordan Memorial Trust	x			
Bruce Peru				x
Camara	x			
Casa Guatemala				x
Chernobyl Children's Project			x	
Christians Abroad	x	x		x
CIS				x
Columban Lay Missionaries		x		x
Coral Cay Conservation		x		x
Cross-Cultural Solutions	x	x	x	x
Development in Action		x		
Ecologia Youth Trust			x	
Ecuador Volunteer				x
EIL Intercultural Learning	x	x		x
Friends of Africa	x			
Friends of Londiani	x			
Frontier	x	x		x
Fundación Jatun Sacha				x

	Africa	Asia	Europe	Latin America
GAP Activity Projects	x	x	x	x
GAP Sports	x			x
Geekcorps	x	x	x	x
Genesis Volunteer Program				x
Global Citizens Network	x	x		x
Global Service Corps	x	x		
Global Volunteer Network	x	x	x	x
GOAL	x	x		x
Gram Vikas		x		
Greenforce	x	x		x
Habitat for Humanity	x	x		x
Health Action Overseas		x	x	
Health and Development Networks	x	x		
Himalayan Light Foundation		x		
Hope Foundation		x		
hopeXchange	x	x	x	
INFO Nepal		x		
Interims for Development	x			
International Relief Friendship Foundation	x	x	x	
International Service Ireland	x	x		x
Iracambi				x
i-to-i	x	x		x
Jubilee Ventures	x			
Kings World Trust		x		
Léargas	x	x	x	
Link Community Development	x			
Mafanikio Community Based Organisation	x			
Medair	x	x		
Médecins Sans Frontières (MSF)	x	x	x	x
Medical Missionaries of Mary	x			x
Niall Mellon Township Trust	x			
Nicaragua Solidarity Campaign				x
Orangutan Foundation		x		
Personal Overseas Development	x	x		x
Progressio	x	x		x
Project Mosaic Guatemala				x
Project Trust	x	x		x
ProWorld				x

	Africa	Asia	Europe	Latin America
Quest Overseas	x			x
Raleigh Ireland	x	x		x
RCDP Nepal		x		
RedR-IHE	x	x	x	
Right to Play	x	x		
Rokpa UK		x		
SCORE	x			
SERVE	x	x		x
Skillshare	x	x		
Slí Eile	x			x
SMILE Society		x		
SPW	x	x		
Suas	x	x		
Teaching and Projects Abroad	x	x	x	x
Tekera Resource Centre	x			
To Russia With Love			x	
Today It's Me AIDS Foundation	x			
Transform	x	x	x	x
Travellers Worldwide	x	x	x	x
UBECI				x
UCD Volunteers Overseas		x		x
United Nations Volunteers	x	x	x	x
USIT	x	x		x
VEEP Nepal		x		
Viatores Christi	x	x		x
Vincentian Lay Missionaries	x			
Visions in Action	x			x
Volunteer Africa	x			
Volunteer Missionary Movement	x	x		x
Volunteer Petén				x
Volunteers for Africa	x			
VSI	x	x	x	x
VSO	x	x		x
Wakuluzu	x			
WorkingAbroad Projects				x
World Service Enquiry	x	x	x	x
WWISA	x			

Index 3 Educational/professional qualifications; costs; duration of placements

This index sets out whether volunteers are required to have professional or educational qualifications: an 'x' means that they are required, while 'D' means that this depends on the particular placement on offer. 'Costs' refers to whether or not there are any costs (including travel) associated with the volunteer placements offered by the organisations. Finally, there are six different placement lengths: 0–4 weeks, 1–2 months, 3–6 months, 7–12 months, and 1 year +. Again, an 'x' is used to indicate the lengths of placements available.

	Ed/prof quals	Costs	0–4 wks	1–2 mths	3–6 mths	7–12 mths	1 yr +
2Way Development	x	x			x	x	x
Abandoned Street Kids of Brazil		x		x	x	x	x
African Conservation Experience		x	x	x	x		
African Conservation Trust		x	x	x	x		
Africatrust Networks		x			x		
AidCamps International		x	x				
AIESEC	x	x		x	x	x	x
Amizade		x	x	x	x		
ARCAS		x	x	x	x	x	x
Ard El Insan	x		x	x	x	x	x
Asociación ANAI	D	x	x	x	x	x	x
Assin Endwa	D	x	x	x	x		
Associação Iko Poran		x	x	x	x		
Associazione Oikos		x	x	x	x	x	x
Azafady		x	x	x			
Balkan Sunflowers		x			x	x	x
Bangladesh Work Camps		x	x	x	x	x	
Billy Riordan Memorial Trust	D	x			x	x	x
Bruce Peru	D	x		x	x	x	x
Camara		x	x				
Casa Guatemala	D	x			x	x	x
Chernobyl Children's Project	D	x	x	x			
Christians Abroad	D	x		x	x	x	x
CIS		x		x			
Columban Lay Missionaries	x						x
Coral Cay Conservation		x	x	x	x	x	
Cross-Cultural Solutions		x	x	x	x		

	Ed/prof quals	Costs	0–4 wks	1–2 mths	3–6 mths	7–12 mths	1 yr +
Development in Action	D	x		x	x		
Ecologia Youth Trust		x		x	x	x	
Ecuador Volunteer	D	x	x	x	x	x	
EIL Intercultural Learning		x		x	x	x	
Friends of Africa	D	x		x			x
Friends of Londiani		x	x	x			
Frontier		x	x	x			
Fundación Jatun Sacha		x	x	x	x	x	
GAP Activity Projects	D	x			x		
GAP Sports	D	x		x	x	x	
Geekcorps	x			x	x		
Genesis Volunteer Program		x	x	x	x		
Global Citizens Network		x	x				
Global Service Corps		x	x	x	x		
Global Volunteer Network	D	x	x	x	x		
GOAL	x						x
Gram Vikas	x	x			x	x	x
Greenforce		x		x	x		
Habitat for Humanity		x	x				
Health Action Overseas	x		x	x	x	x	
Health and Development Networks	D	x			x	x	
Himalayan Light Foundation		x	x	x	x		
Hope Foundation	x	x			x	x	x
hopeXchange		x		x	x		
INFO Nepal		x	x	x	x	x	
Interims for Development	x		x	x	x	x	
International Relief Friendship Foundation		x	x	x	x	x	
International Service Ireland	x						x
Iracambi		x		x	x		
i-to-i		x	x	x	x	x	
Jubilee Ventures	D	x	x	x	x		
Kings World Trust	D	x		x	x		
Léargas			x	x	x	x	
Link Community Development	x	x		x			
Mafanikio Community Based Organisation		x		x	x	x	
Medair	x						x

	Ed/prof quals	Costs	0–4 wks	1–2 mths	3–6 mths	7–12 mths	1 yr +
Médecins Sans Frontières (MSF)	x				x	x	
Medical Missionaries of Mary	x						x
Niall Mellon Township Trust		x	x				
Nicaragua Solidarity Campaign		x	x				
Orangutan Foundation		x		x			
Personal Overseas Development		x	x	x	x		
Progressio	x						x
Project Mosaic Guatemala	D	x	x	x	x	x	
Project Trust		x				x	
ProWorld		x	x	x	x	x	
Quest Overseas		x	x	x	x	x	
Raleigh Ireland		x	x	x	x		
RCDP Nepal	D	x	x	x	x		
RedR-IHE	x		x	x	x	x	x
Right to Play	x						x
Rokpa UK	x	x			x	x	x
SCORE	x	x			x	x	x
SERVE		x		x	x		
Skillshare	x						x
Slí Eile		x	x				
SMILE Society	D	x	x	x	x		
SPW	x	x			x	x	
Suas		x			x	x	
Teaching and Projects Abroad		x		x	x	x	
Tekera Resource Centre	x				x	x	x
To Russia With Love		x			x		
Today It's Me AIDS Foundation		x	x	x	x	x	
Transform		x	x	x	x		
Travellers Worldwide		x	x	x	x	x	
UBECI		x	x	x	x	x	x
UCD Volunteers Overseas		x	x				
United Nations Volunteers	x		x	x			x
USIT		x		x	x	x	x

	Ed/prof quals	Costs	0–4 wks	1–2 mths	3–6 mths	7–12 mths	1 yr +
VEEP Nepal		x	x	x	x		
Viatores Christi	D						x
Vincentian Lay Missionaries (VLM)	x	x		x	x		
Visions in Action	x	x		x	x	x	
Volunteer Africa		x	x	x	x		
Volunteer Petén		x	x	x	x		
Volunteer Missionary Movement (VMM)	x						x
Volunteers for Africa	D	x	x	x	x		
VSI		x	x	x	x	x	
VSO	x			x	x	x	x
Wakuluzu	x	x			x		
WorkingAbroad Projects		x		x	x		
World Service Enquiry		x					
WWISA	D	x	x	x	x	x	

APPENDIX

Comhlámh's Code of Good Practice for Sending Organisations and Volunteer Charter

Comhlámh has developed a Code of Practice and a Volunteer Charter in order to encourage best practice in the overseas volunteering sector and to support volunteers in a longer-term commitment to development. These resources were developed through close consultations with sending organisations, returned volunteers and host organisations. If you are planning to volunteer with an Irish-based sending organisation, ask them whether they have signed up to the Code. Organisations that are signatories of the Code will be able to show you the eleven principles that they have agreed to work towards putting in place. The organisation may also ask you to sign a copy of the Volunteer Charter, which includes seven principles that you'll agree to uphold before, during and after your placement.

A summary of both resources is set out below: if you would like to learn more about them, please go to www.volunteeringoptions.org/index.php/plain/volunteer_charter, or contact Comhlámh's office.

All the organisations that have signed up to the Code of Practice and that support the Volunteer Charter are listed in the directory of Irish-based organisations. This information is given under the headings 'Code of Practice' and 'Volunteer Charter'.

Code of Practice for Sending Organisations

The Code sets out standards for organisations involved in facilitating international volunteer placements in developing countries. It reflects a number of core values, including partnership, quality, security, sustainability and solidarity. An increasing number of organisations based in Ireland are signing up to the Code, and committing to work towards implementing the eleven principles it sets out. These principles are that sending organisations agree to:

- have volunteer programmes based on realistic aims and objectives, with appropriate and useful volunteer roles;
- provide sufficient resources and support to run volunteer programmes in an efficient and sustainable manner;
- provide marketing and imagery consistent with good practice, and clear expressions of organisational aims, ethos and values;
- provide potential volunteers with free, fair and unbiased information on their organisation and volunteer placements;
- use fair, consistent and transparent recruitment procedures;

- assist and provide for the varying support needs of volunteers;
- ensure that volunteers participate in appropriate preparation, training and induction;
- ensure the protection, safety and well-being of volunteers and those they work with, as far as possible;
- provide recognition for volunteers;
- provide ongoing monitoring and evaluations;
- provide debriefing for returned volunteers.

Volunteer Charter

The Charter provides a guide for people who are going to volunteer overseas. It sets out seven principles that aim to encourage responsible, responsive volunteering. Each of the principles has a list of questions to help volunteers make sure that they have thought about the issues raised, and that they know why they are important. By agreeing to sign the Charter, you will demonstrate your support for the principles it sets out.

According to the Charter, volunteers should agree to:

- Inform themselves about all relevant issues relating to their placement. For example, have you spent time considering your motivations for wanting to volunteer overseas? Have you thought about the issues that will inform the context in which your placement will take place?
- Familiarise themselves thoroughly with their role description before departure. This includes reading and signing the role description provided by your sending organisation, asking the organisation any questions you have about the role, and taking part in all training and induction that is provided.
- Respect local customs and adopt the role of learners and guests: Have you considered how you can make sure that you'll be sensitive to the local culture? Have you agreed to try to learn some of the local language, and to respect and work to uphold the aims of your host project?
- Act always in a professional manner and be flexible and adaptable while in their placement. For example, have you agreed to stick to the role description that you were given, and to fulfil the minimum working hours that were agreed at the start of your placement?
- Take due care with their personal safety and physical and mental health. As a volunteer, you are encouraged to consider issues such as ensuring that you have the relevant health and travel insurance you need, and that you have all the vaccinations you require.
- Channel the experiences and knowledge gained while overseas into Irish society: For example, do you commit to being available to correspond with other potential volunteers about your time overseas? Do you agree to examine and consider your options for staying involved in global development issues on your return home?
- Accept and sign a Code of Conduct embodying these principles.